T0298700

NEGOTIATING THE TRANSPORT SYSTEM

For my parents

Negotiating the Transport System
User Contexts, Experiences and Needs

FIONA RAJÉ
Northumbria University, UK

Routledge
Taylor & Francis Group

LONDON AND NEW YORK

First published 2007 by Ashgate Publishing

Published 2016 by Routledge
2 Park Square, Milton Park, Abingdon, Oxon OX14 4RN
711 Third Avenue, New York, NY 10017, USA

Routledge is an imprint of the Taylor & Francis Group, an informa business

British Library Cataloguing in Publication Data
Rajé, Fiona, 1966-
    Negotiating the transport system : user contexts,
    experiences and needs. - (Transport and society)
    1. Transportation - Social aspects - Great Britain
    2. Transportation and state - Great Britain 3. Social
    isolation - Great Britain
    I. Title
    388'.0941

Library of Congress Cataloging-in-Publication Data
Rajé, Fiona, 1966-
    Negotiating the transport system : user contexts, experiences, and needs / by Fiona
Rajé.
        p. cm. -- (Transport and society)
    Includes bibliographical references and index.
    ISBN-13: 978-0-7546-4992-2
    1. Transportation--Social aspects--Great Britain. 2. Marginality, Social--Great
Britain. I. Title.

    HE243.R33 2007
    388.0941--dc22
                                                                        2006031460

ISBN 13: 978-0-7546-4992-2 (hbk)

Contents

List of Figures		*vii*
List of Tables		*ix*
List of Plates		*xi*
Acknowledgements		*xiii*

1   Negotiating the Transport System: An Introduction   1

Introduction: The emergent field of transport and social inclusion   1
Objective of the research and definition of social categories   3
State of the art   8
Research approach and existing gaps in the literature   14
Conclusion and outline structure   17

2   Transport and Social Inclusion: The Literature and Policy Background   19

Introduction: a changing policy environment   19
Key legislation and policy   19
Transport and traffic schemes: the social dimension   23
Transport and social inclusion/exclusion   37
Conclusion   49

3   Research Approach and Methodology   53

Introduction: methods, techniques and options   53
Research questions   54
Using case studies   58
Conducting the research: techniques and considerations   66
Advantages and disadvantages of qualitative work   76
Conclusion: using empirical investigation to develop new understandings   77

4   Transport and Social Inclusion: The Urban Experience   79

Introduction: locating the urban case study   79
Life in Barton: some empirical insights   87
Empirical research findings: key impacts of transport identified   91
Identifying dynamics and projecting forward: the baseline scenario, policy changes and transport interventions   116
Conclusion: urban concerns, urban solutions   124

5   Transport and Social Inclusion: The Rural Experience   125

         Introduction: locating the rural case study   125
         Life in Charlbury: some empirical insights   132
         Empirical research findings: key impacts of transport identified   133
         Identifying dynamics and projecting forward: the baseline
           scenario, policy changes and transport interventions   154
         Conclusion: rural stories, rural lessons   160

**6   Revealed Perspectives: Common Themes and Disparate
         Discourses**   161

         Introduction: transport and social inclusion through an alternative
         lens   161
         Q methodology: a response to the need for more perceptive insights   161
         Detailed research design: the Q methodology study   162
         New insights: themes, discourses and perspectives   172
         Discourse A   175
         Discourse B   178
         Discourse C   180
         Discourse D   182
         The value of Q   186
         Conclusion: reflecting on the Q study findings   189

**7   Contemporary Transport Issues and Contexts: Theoretical,
         Methodological and Policy and Planning Implications**   191

         Introduction: key findings, contexts and implications   191
         Theoretical implications of the research   192
         Methodological implications of the research   198
         Policy and planning implications of the research   201
         Future research and policy recommendations: eliminating
           transport based exclusion   205
         Conclusion: creating transport transparencies   206

Appendix 1: Interview Guide   *211*
Appendix 2: Principal participants in study   *215*
Consolidated Bibliography   *217*
Index   *233*

List of Figures

Figure 1.1   Diagrammatic map of Oxfordshire showing case study sites   16
Figure 2.1   Example of Potential Social Transportation Framework   36
Figure 4.1   Diagrammatic map showing Barton Estate   80
Figure 4.2   Thematic map displaying the IMD 2004 results for the
              city of Oxford   83
Figure 4.3   Proposed roundabout layout   118
Figure 5.1   Map showing location of proposed home zone, railway
              station and main routes in Charlbury   126
Figure 5.2   Plan showing proposed preliminary design of Home Zone   155

List of Tables

Table 1.1	Examples of types of impacts of transport on different social groups	6
Table 2.1	UK Transport Policy Evolution: A selective timeline	21
Table 2.2	Trips per person per year by purpose (2003-2004)	27
Table 2.3	Definitions and explanations of the term 'social exclusion'	39
Table 3.1	Main research questions	54
Table 3.2	Case studies	59
Table 3.3	Primary data sources and methods of informant interaction	59
Table 4.1	Age profile of Barton and Sandhills ward (2001)	80
Table 4.2	Ethnic profile of Barton and Sandhills ward	81
Table 4.3	Car ownership in Barton and Sandhills	84
Table 5.1	Age profile of Charlbury and Finstock ward (2001)	127
Table 5.2	Ethnic profile of Charlbury and Finstock ward	128
Table 5.3	Car ownership – Charlbury and Finstock	129
Table 5.4	Summary of Consultation Responses provided in report to Committee, Oxfordshire County Council – Charlbury Home Zone Stakeholder Consultation Responses	158
Table 6.1	P Set structure	165
Table 6.2	Quasi-normal distribution	165
Table 6.3	Participant profile	167
Table 6.4	Unrotated factor matrix	169
Table 6.5	Illustration of iteration towards maximized number of participants with significant loadings	170
Table 6.6	Factor matrix	171
Table 6.7	Statements and scores on four extracted discourses	172

List of Plates

Plate 4.1   View from North Way, Barton, towards the north   90
Plate 4.2   Gated development adjacent to local authority housing,
             North Way   99
Plate 4.3   Making a feature of consultation in the affected
             community, Cowley Road, Oxford   122
Plate 5.1   Spill-over parking on railway station access road   137
Plate 5.2   Parking restrictions on the east side of Church Lane   138
Plate 5.3   Parking restrictions on the west side of Church Lane   138

Acknowledgements

This book is based on my D.Phil. research carried out at the Transport Studies Unit, University of Oxford between 2002 and 2006.

I am very grateful to my supervisor, Professor John Preston, now of the University of Southampton, for support and advice during the research. I would also like to thank the Economic and Social Research Council, Department for Transport and the Office of the Deputy Prime Minister for financing my studentship. A special thank you to Professor Margaret Grieco of the Transport Research Institute and Department of Sociology and Psychology, Napier University and the Institute for African Development, Cornell University for advice, support and many discussions of the social issues around travel and transport. To the people of Barton and Charlbury, who took the time to share their experiences with me and without whom I would not have been able to write this book, a very big thank you. Finally, thanks to my colleagues at Newcastle Business School for allowing me the flexibility, so soon after I joined the School, to bring this book to completion.

Chapter 1

Negotiating the Transport System:
An Introduction

Introduction: The emergent field of transport and social inclusion

Transport is an important factor in people's lives. It is a facilitator of travel, enabling access to people, goods and services (Davis, 1998; Acheson, 1998) and is, thus, a fundamental need in an increasingly mobile, modern society.

Although every citizen is entitled to a basic level of mobility, travel decision-making can be more complex for members of marginalized groups than it is for mainstream society (Oxfordshire County Council, 2000; McCray et al., 2003). In researching the relationship between transport and social exclusion, it becomes readily apparent that there are complexities around journeying at every stage of the process (see, for example, Clifton, 2003; Grayling, 2002; Joseph Rowntree Foundation, 2001). It is equally clear that these complexities are sometimes hidden from transport professionals because transport planning developed traditionally out of engineering and economics where concerns about value for money and accommodation of traffic (Banister, 2002; 2005) may have taken greater importance than social impacts. This means that useful insights into people's lived experience of transport[1] may have been lost or hidden from the planning and policy-making practitioner.

In this volume, the nature of the complexities associated with travel are explored. A range of experiences is investigated from those of people located towards the excluded extreme of a social inclusion/exclusion continuum to those who are nearer to the fully-included pole.

By examining the impacts of transport on individuals at different points on a scale of social inclusion/exclusion, the research described in this book sought to reveal the nuanced and textured ways in which transport is embedded in people's lives and lifestyles. In so doing, the volume aims to expand the literature on social dimensions of transport and traffic schemes which has historically been neglected.

---

1 For example, Kenyon (2002:1) provides one of these often-hidden insights in the following quote which describes the complex impact of the lack of transport on a person's life: "If people can't travel, they have reduced access to the goods, opportunities, services and social networks that are necessary to participate in modern society. Lack of adequate transport meant that the lives of the people we interviewed were made more complicated, more tiring, more expensive, and more lonely than they would have been if transport had been readily available."

Indeed, the social exclusion literature has largely ignored the complexity of travel behaviour. Clifton (2003:3) reports that:

> The study of the role that transportation plays in the well being of low-income populations is not new. However, the overwhelming research emphasis has been on the relationship between transportation and access to employment opportunities for low-wage workers. Much less attention has been placed upon the full array of activity and travel needs of this population segment and their ensuing travel decisions and behaviours.

One source of complexity, for example, is the interaction between and interdependence of different social networks and social circles that may take place when an individual needs to make a trip[2].

In situating the approach of this book, it is also important to state that, as Latham (2003:1993) writes in the following quote, this research took the viewpoint that the 'small and everyday' can be complex and interesting:

> Over the last couple of decades we have seen something of a revolution in ways we frame what it is that geography is concerned with. We have seen that it is as much about discourses as about 'actual' events; that things that seem small and everyday can be as interesting and complex as phenomenon that appear much larger and more general...

Efforts to understand the more mundane and normal dimensions of daily life may be seen as an unnecessary examination of minutiae but it is these familiar, day-to-day, yet often complex, issues that need to be understood if policy and planning is to take a closer account of how people conduct their lives with a view to more socially-relevant policy-making and scheme design.

So to summarize, this volume looks at transport in its most basic role as a means of access to the activities, goods and services an individual feels that they need to participate in or partake of. Accessibility does not equate solely with mobility (Cloke, 1984; Farrington and Farrington, 2005) since "access deficiencies" or "poverty of access" are "also a result of a wide range of factors including people's time budgets, household commitments, physical capabilities and attitudes to participation" (Farrington and Farrington, 2005:3).

It is also important to note in this introduction the definition of "social exclusion" which has been adopted for this book. Social exclusion is a highly contested term (Shucksmith, 2000; Hills et al., 2001), despite the creation of bodies such as the Social Exclusion Unit of the Office of the Deputy Prime Minister (http://www.socialexclusionunit.gov.uk/) and the ESRC's Centre for Analysis of Social Exclusion (http://sticerd.lse.ac.uk/case/), based at the London School of Economics. Following the review of literature which is described in greater detail in Chapter 2, for the purposes of this work, social exclusion has been defined as a process which causes

---

2   For example, an elderly woman may rely on her daughter to take her to the doctor, the daughter may have to make arrangements with her son's friend's mother to pick up her son from school in order to allow her to be able to take her mother to the surgery, the other mother may then need to negotiate with her husband to use the family car for the school trip – all participants in this scenario having to organize and negotiate around time, space, activity and personal network issues to allow travel to take place.

individuals or groups not to participate in the normal activities of the society in which they are residents and has spatial manifestations.

In the following section, the research's aims are set out and the social categories examined are outlined. Then, an overview of current understanding of transport and social inclusion/exclusion is given. This is followed by a brief introduction to the research approach and case studies and, in the final section, an outline of the book's structure is provided.

Objective of the research and definition of social categories

Research aims

When this research began in 2002, the Government had recently published a ten year plan for transport. At the inception stage then, the overall aim of the research was to assess the potential for the Government's 10 Year Plan for Transport (DETR, 2000a) to deliver for everyone reliable, safe and integrated transport which respects the environment. However, as the research progressed, it started to become evident in policy circles that some of the Plan's targets had been somewhat optimistic. As a result of this movement in the policy arena, and a change of Transport Secretary[3], a new white paper "The Future of Transport" looking ahead to 2030 was published by the Department for Transport (DfT) in July 2004.

Given the apparent transience of the ten year plan and shift in policy emphasis, the overall aim of the research was subsequently revised to give the study a more directed and localized focus: To assess the potential for transport interventions and investments to deliver for everyone reliable, safe and integrated transport which respects the environment. The specific objectives were:

1. To investigate the ways in which transport impacts on people's lives.
2. To determine how different social groups make transport choices.
3. To determine the likely impacts of transport interventions and related measures on these different social groups.
4. To investigate the geographical dimensions of transport choices and impacts.
5. To assess, for two different areas (1 urban, 1 rural), the extent to which particular interventions will promote social inclusion.

It was envisaged that this research would produce an improved understanding of the extent to which transport investments can promote social inclusion. The interaction between social inclusion and transport has not been closely charted in Britain to date. Despite this, there is growing recognition amongst the academic

---

3   Alistair Darling replaced Stephen Byers as Secretary of State for Transport in May 2002, amidst allegations that Mr Byers had lied to Parliament over an internal feud in the transport department press office - all of which he denied - and an MPs' report published the previous weekend which branded his 10-year transport plan "incomprehensible". (http://news.bbc.co.uk/1/hi/uk_politics/2014220.stm). Stephen Byers had been given responsibility for transport one year earlier, replacing John Prescott.

and planning communities that there is a relationship between transport and social exclusion. Oxfordshire County Council, for example, alludes to this interaction in its Local Transport Plan when it states that:

> Transport's main purpose is to enable people to visit other people, or gain access to goods and services. Transport difficulties can be a major barrier to people wishing to gain access to employment, education, health care services, and leisure facilities, or even to shops so that people can get access to a balanced diet. Transport also provides important access to social support networks through links with family and friends. Put more simply, access to transport can dictate people's ability to take part in 'normal' day to day activities. (Oxfordshire County Council, 2000:33)

The Social Exclusion Unit[4] (2003:2) recognizes that "over the past 50 years, the need to travel has become greater and more complex". Social inclusion/exclusion has emerged in transport-related discourse in the past few years, although the visibility of the term coupled with transport has been seen to operate more strongly at the level of rhetoric rather than in the commissioning of substantial research into the relationship between social inclusion/exclusion and transport (Grieco et al., 2000). Kintrea and Atkinson (2001), writing about neighbourhoods and social exclusion, state that social exclusion has not been of great concern in UK transport policy and suggest that the White Paper on Transport concentrated mainly on themes such as congestion, car use and the environmental impact of transport, rather than the social aspects of transport provision.

Despite the apparent absence of a transport policy framework for social inclusion/exclusion, there has been some movement towards a greater understanding of the social aspects of transport in the research sphere. The way in which social inclusion/exclusion has been entering the discourse includes inputs such as a recent report by the Social Exclusion Unit (2003) which highlights the contribution that transport can make to social exclusionary processes.

Typology of exclusion

Social groups can be defined as:

> ...consisting of a number of people who share certain aspects, interact with one another, accept rights and obligations as members of the group and share a common identity...a group in sociology exhibits cohesiveness to a larger degree. Aspects that members in the group may share include interests, values, ethnic/linguistic background and kinship. (http://www.wordiq.com/ accessed 220703)

---

4   The Social Exclusion Unit was set up by the Prime Minister in 1997. It was initially part of the Cabinet Office and moved over to the Office of the Deputy Prime Minister (ODPM) in May 2002. The unit reports that it is "working to create prosperous, inclusive and sustainable communities for the 21st century - places where people want to live that promote opportunity and a better quality of life for all...The work of the Social Exclusion Unit includes specific projects to tackle specific issues and wide-ranging programmes to assess past policy and identify future trends." (http://www.socialexclusion.gov.uk/page.asp?id=10 accessed 261004)

There are many means for classifying different social groups using indicators such as gender, ethnicity, age, residential location, disability, educational attainment and income. Members of a particular social group are seen to be more likely to share similar life experiences (Evans, 1997:374) which then shape their attitudes. Each individual is a member of more than one social group and the significance, and consequent impact, of membership of one's various social groups varies according to the circumstances and conditions in which one finds oneself. Payne describes this succinctly in the following extract (in Payne, ed., 2000:4):

> In any one situation, a particular social division may assume greater importance, but people do not exist in a social world where only class, or only gender, or only ethnicity matters. It is not that there is a single category which is distinctive. All of us have multiple-membership in a number of such groups, so that depending on one's standpoint, people may be different in one context, but similar in another. Personal links with people in one category may sometimes be at odds with one's differences from them owing to membership of some category on another social division.

Smith (in Cloke et al., 1999) asserts that an individual's membership of a particular social group has a direct impact on his/her life chances. For example, certain social groups are more vulnerable to the social exclusionary aspects of transport as this quotation from a summary of issues discussed at a conference on Transportation, Environmental Justice and Social Equity (Anonymous, 1994) sets out:

> Marginalized people and their communities bear the brunt of society's ills, grapple with the costliest of society's tradeoffs, and have the least amount of society's resources to deal with them. Transportation's role in these dimensions of inequity is ubiquitous. The availability of transportation services in a community often determines its economic and social viability. In particular, low-income individuals, people of color, aged and disabled people experience increasing difficulty in gaining access to work, tapping into social and commercial services, and interacting with others. The physical placement of jobs and services also has serious public health, environmental and other impacts.

Acheson (1998), in a report on health inequalities, also draws attention to the vulnerability of some citizens to the effects of a lack of access to transport. He suggests that these effects are disproportionately experienced by women, children, disabled people, people from minority ethnic groups, older people and people with low socioeconomic status, especially those living in remote rural areas. Acheson (1998) also highlights the social impacts of high traffic volumes, suggesting that they are associated with lower levels of non-traffic street level activity and walking and result in feelings of insecurity, especially amongst families with children and older people (Klaeboe, 1992). He goes on to suggest that this can result in a community with limited potential for building or maintaining social networks (Gillies, 1997).

As Acheson indicates, it has been identified that women (see, for example, Hamilton et al., 1999; Grieco et al., 1989), the young (see, for example, Storey and Brannen, 2000; McWhannell and Braunholtz, 2002), the elderly (see, for example, MORI, 2001; WS Atkins, 2000; Rosenbloom, 1988), non-car-owners (see, for example, TRaC, 2000; Social Exclusion Unit, 2003), ethnic minorities (see, for example, Beuret et al., 2000; Rajé et al., 2004a), the disabled (see, for example,

DPTAC, 2002; Henderson and Henderson, 1999) and those on low incomes (see, for example, Hine and Mitchell, 2003; Grieco et al., 1989) or unemployed (Cartmel and Furlong, 2000; Social Exclusion Unit, 2003) may be particularly vulnerable to adverse transport impacts. In addition, rural dwelling can mean that people are more reliant on transport to access services that are located at a distance (Gray, 2001; Countryside Agency, 2004) and are, therefore, more vulnerable to adverse impacts if there is a lack of appropriate transport provision. For people living in urban areas, there are other transport-related difficulties: congestion and associated pollution and accidents are some of the main unfavourable impacts of transport for city-dwellers. While Chapter 2 concentrates on the detailed findings of the literature review on transport-related social exclusion, Table 1.1 provides a brief insight into some examples of the impacts of transport on different social groups identified in the literature.

Table 1.1   Examples of types of impacts of transport on different social groups

Social Group	Example of type of transport impact described in the literature
Women	"…women's use of public transport is underpinned by their need to juggle a number of obligations into their day. Much of this activity is local: a part time job, the food shopping, taking a relative to the doctor, ferrying the children to and from school. Where finances are restricted and the family has only one car, the man usually has first call on its use. Regular, reliable and affordable public transport is crucial to managing the range of tasks that have to be fitted into the day." (Hamilton et al., 1999 @ www.dft.gov.uk/stellent/groups/dft_mobility/documents/page/dft_mobility_506789-01.hcsp#P23_609 accessed 070904)
Young people	"Research to date suggests that children and young people experience: physical inaccessibility; lack of affordability; lack of personal security; negative perceptions of personal security; lack of safety" (London Health Commission, no date @ http://www.londonshealth.gov.uk/transprt.htm accessed 070904)
Elderly	"Transport provides an essential link to friends, family and the wider community - a vital lifeline to maintaining independence. Research has shown that a lack of mobility can prevent older people from participating in social activities and lead to low morale, depression and loneliness. It can also impact upon others, such as carers, social services and health agencies." (WS Atkins, 2000 @ http://www.dft.gov.uk/stellent/groups/dft_mobility/documents/page/dft_mobility_506793-02.hcsp#P25_2092 accessed 070904)

Non-car owners	"Social exclusion in rural areas is not just confined to people on low incomes. Those who are too young, too old or have permanent or temporary medical conditions which prevent them driving will not have full access to a car even if they live in car-owning households. Car ownership and use is high in rural areas – 40% of rural households have two or more cars and three-quarters of all journeys are by car but for the 16% of households without a car, the lack of mobility can cause real hardship." (Countryside Agency, Social Exclusion and Transport @ http://www.countryside.gov.uk/EssentialServices/Transport/socialExclusionAndTransport/index.asp accessed 070904)
People from ethnic minorities	"The research carried out for this project shows that some minority ethnic groups are under represented on public transport and that others experience considerable problems." (Social Research Associates, Public transport needs of minority ethnic and faith communities guidance pack @ http://www.dft.gov.uk/stellent/groups/dft_mobility/documents/page/dft_mobility_025601-01.hcsp#P18_551 accessed 070904)
Disabled	"Transport issues are important to disabled peoples lives - being the single most prominent concern at the local level. Pavement and road maintenance generate the most dissatisfaction, along with access for disabled people to transport vehicles and the frequency of public transport…Disabled people travel a third less often than the general public." (DPTAC, 2002 @ http://www.dptac.gov.uk/research/apt/01.htm accessed 140904)
Low income earners	"Although poor transport provision is not always a primary preoccupation of many low-income groups, it often acts as a barrier to their economic and social inclusion." (Lucas et al., 2001 @ http://www.jrf.org.uk/knowledge/findings/housing/721.asp accessed 140904)
Unemployed	"Around 30% of the responses from the unemployed quoted insufficient transport provision as a reason for declining employment." (CfIT, 2002a @ http://www.cfit.gov.uk/reports/psbi/cfit/a1.htm accessed 140904)
Rural dwellers	"Life for young people in the countryside is characterized by a lack of public services and facilities close at hand. As a consequence, issues of travel and transport loom large in young people's lives." Storey and Brannen, 2000

This book concentrates on the impacts of transport on the elderly and young adults in Barton in Oxford and on people with access to a car and those without access to a car in Charlbury in West Oxfordshire. Within each case study, consideration is also given to the variation in potential impacts of planned transport interventions on other social groups such as those defined by income and gender. In order to address this aspect of the work, secondary data from research carried out in Bristol and Nottingham on gender, ethnicity and lifecycle issues is used as an enhancer and comparator. Primary data collected for this research on an accident reduction and environmental improvement scheme on the ethnically-diverse Cowley Road in

Oxford are also used for this purpose. Chapter 3 provides a more detailed description of the methodology adopted for this research.

State of the art

Significance of problem

Our societies cannot function without transport (Smyth et al., 2001). However, while transport is essential for a modern society and economic competitiveness (CBI, 2005; Royal Academy of Engineering, 2005), increased mobility is not without attendant unfavourable aspects. In a recent report on traffic trends, the Department for Transport (DfT, 2003a) states that road traffic in Great Britain has grown by 73 per cent since 1980. The DfT ascribes this growth to a number of factors including increasing car ownership and falling car occupancy levels. In parallel, however, bus patronage has declined (outside London) and rail travel has increased. According to the report, "growth in motorized transport has resulted in a 39 per cent increase in greenhouse gas emissions from transport, which now accounts for 26 per cent of UK emissions" (DfT, 2003a). Despite the reduction in local air pollution with the advent of catalytic converters and cleaner fuels, energy consumption by transport (all modes) has increased continuously since 1981, rising by 62 per cent. The South East has one of the highest levels of greenhouse gas emissions from private vehicles (Foley et al., 2005): 3.2 tonnes of CO_2 from private vehicles per household compared with a UK average of 2.6 tonnes in 2004.

The DfT reports further that the number of trips made and distance travelled have been found to increase with income. In addition, between 1996 and 2002, "the South East had the highest proportion of households with two cars and the lowest proportion of households with no car compared to other English regions" (Foley et al., 2005:6). Adults in households with two cars travel on average nearly four times further than those in households without a car. Men travel, on average, forty per cent further than women. According to Foley et al. (2005:6), between 1992-94 and 2003, "trip distances in the South East have been higher than the average for Great Britain. In 2003, the average trip distance in the South East was 7.5 miles compared to the average for Great Britain of 6.9 miles (about 9 per cent higher)". Car access has increased in all income groups since 1985/86, most notably in the lowest income group, where the proportion of households with access to a car increased from 26 to 38 per cent. However, with reference to access to key services, over a quarter of people without access to a car are reported to find it difficult to get to hospital (Social Exclusion Unit, 2003).

Against this backdrop of rising traffic levels, growing car ownership, increasing energy consumption, falling bus patronage and difficulties accessing key services, greater mobility can be seen to both damage and enhance quality of life (Root, 1998). The Social Exclusion Unit (2003) states that the last fifty years have seen an increased and more complex need to travel as society became organized around the car and average distances to work, learning, hospitals and shops increased. Kenyon et al. (2002) suggest that the assumption of car ownership in the UK has resulted in both a culture and a landscape in which mobility is expected and necessary to participate in society. Docherty (2001) describes the way in which widespread car ownership and use has transformed society by providing increased flexibility and individual choice of when and where to travel:

> As access to cars increased, people began to travel further between their homes, workplaces and places of consumption. The urban decentralization and deconcentration of the post-war era has also made these patterns more complex, as trunk radial flows of movement to and from major urban centres have been supplemented by a web of circumferential and tangential trips. (Docherty, 2001:321)

Adams (2001:4-5; 2005:5-8) reminds us of the unfavourable social and cultural consequences of increasing car dependence and subsequent hypermobility[5] when he states that the hypermobile society will be, among other characteristics, "more dispersed", "more polarized", "more dangerous for those not in cars", "more hostile to children", "less culturally varied", "more anonymous and less convivial", "less democratic", and "more crime ridden". Drawing on Putnam's "Bowling Alone" (Putnam, 2000) which documents the rise and decline of civic engagement in American life over a century of increasing physical and electronic mobility, Adams (2005) posits a causative link between a step change in US society from hypo- to hyper- mobility and a decline in civic participation. He points out that Putnam associates the deterioration in civic engagement to television but highlights that Putnam also cited geographic sprawl as a factor in the social decline.

While carrying out empirical research on the psycho-social benefits people seem to derive from their cars, Hiscock et al. (2002) found that although they had anticipated that interviewees would be very positive about the extra comfort and privacy that cars can provide, respondents were ambivalent about comfort which was not always seen as a high priority. In addition, being sociable and happy to mix with other people were more highly valued by some people. Hiscock et al.'s findings suggest that there is a latent desire even among some car users to take advantage of

---

5   "Hypermobility" is a term used by Adams (for example in Adams 2001& 2005) to describe what he perceives as too great a dependence on vehicular mobility which has resulted in increases in the numbers and use of cars and growth in air travel: "Mobility is liberating and empowering but it is possible to have too much of a good thing" (Adams, 2005:2). He is particularly concerned about the social impacts of hypermobility in his 2005 book section where he sets out his viewpoint by contrasting the social effects of hypermobility to hypomobility, suggesting that there will be undesirable consequences for society if current mobility trends are allowed to continue unabated: "As we spread ourselves ever wider, we must spread ourselves thinner. If we spend more time interacting with people at a distance, we must spend less time with those closer to home, and if we have contact with more people, we must devote less time and attention to each one. In small-scale pedestrian societies, hypomobile societies, everyone knows everyone. In hypermobile societies old-fashioned geographical communities are replaced by aspatial communities of interest – we spend more of our time, physically, in the midst of strangers. The advantages of mobility are heavily advertized; the disadvantages of hypermobility receive much less attention. Many of the unwelcome characteristics of the hypermobile society can readily be imagined by extrapolating existing trends". (Adams, 2005:2-3)

the sociability that public transport can bestow and car travel can impede. In this way, public transport is seen as a tool for facilitating networking. The important message of this insight for this work is that the autonomy and isolation that car dependence conveys may not be desirable for all individuals but has become a necessity because of an inability to access services or facilities through public transport.

In order to have the opportunity to participate in society, individuals must be able to access key services with relative ease. The decline of local service provision associated with movement of facilities such as grocery shops to out of town locations (as a result of land-use planning policies in the 1980s and early 1990s), necessitating increased travel (see, for example, Hay, 2005; Royal Academy of Engineering, 2005), has resulted in certain groups finding participation in the normal activities of their society difficult. In addition, nearly one in three households do not have access to a car (Social Exclusion Unit, 2003) and viable public transport alternatives may not be available. The Social Exclusion Unit states that, "Some people, in both urban and rural areas, cannot reliably get to key places in a reasonable time". It can be inferred then, that as Root (1998) indicates transport is capable of creating huge social change: in the case of the coupling of rising car ownership with attendant policy permitting flight of local services, this change has not always been positive for some, more vulnerable, social groups. In the following chapters, this book explores the extent to which transport can create positive social change at a local and individual[6] level. In so doing, however, the research also investigates the degree to which transport can be a contributor to the processes of social exclusion of some individuals and groups.

Policy background

In July 2000, the Government published Transport 2010: The 10 Year Plan (DETR, 2000a). The Plan "encompasses and integrates the contribution of all land-based modes" (CfIT, 2002b). It sought to build on the integrated transport White Paper, A New Deal for Transport: Better for Everyone (DETR, 1998a) and the Transport Bill 2000, which together put 'in place new policies, new structures, and new powers'(DETR, 2000a:5), through a strategy

---

6   Developing understandings of individual transport needs is important if solutions are to be responsive to the mix of concerns, needs and aspirations of a heterogeneous society. Bentley and Wilsdon (2003:22) highlight the importance of individual understandings and personalisation in the public sphere:

Personalisation…requires services to be actively shaped in response to individual profiles. This does not mean separate, isolated programmes; many of the activities involved in being healthy or learning effectively are collaborative and intensively social. But it does mean that provider organisations must be capable of adapting and reconfiguring what they offer to ensure that it fits the profile of individual needs. This in turn requires structures of governance, resourcing and accountability that reward improved outcomes and support the flexibility required to offer personalisation on a mass scale.

Thus, personalized approaches are particularly relevant for a study such as this which seeks to contribute to a transport and social inclusion discourse that is centred on the user and emphasizes the need for a more adaptive policy-making and planning environment.

...to tackle congestion and pollution by improving all types of transport – rail and road, public and private – in ways that increase choice. It is a strategy for investment in the future to create prosperity and a better environment.

According to the House of Commons Transport, Local Government and the Regions Committee (2002), the main focus of the Plan was on large scale infrastructure projects with brief references being made to policies on walking, cycling, car dependence, travel behaviour, land use and transport pricing. May et al. (2002) indicate that the Plan "was broadly welcomed as a commitment to tackle the country's acknowledged transport problems". However, May et al. state that two years later there was widespread criticism of the Government "both for what it left out of the Plan and for failure to deliver on what was included in it".

Examining UK transport policy from 1997-2001, Glaister (2002:177) contends that neither "integration" nor "social inclusion" was improved. Glaister states instead that:

> The 10 Year Plan says that, among other objectives, it will 'enhance access and opportunity in rural areas' and 'reduce social exclusion'. Yet it is far from clear by what mechanisms it will achieve these two objectives and it is most unlikely to do much to help the poor and the socially excluded...

The view that social inclusion has been largely ignored in the 10 Year Plan is also expressed by Docherty (2001:325):

> The plan has surprisingly little to say on these fundamental issues of social geography, despite the priority attached to social inclusion and urban regeneration in other areas of government policy.

In a report which sought to gauge local authorities' progress in delivering transport improvements at the local level, and to determine perceived and actual barriers to delivery of 10-Year Transport Plan objectives, the Commission for Integrated Transport[7] (CfIT, 2003) stated that half of all local authorities (LAs) were behind schedule in delivering Local Transport Plans (LTPs) while 82% of authorities thought that traffic congestion will be worse in 10 years. CfIT also pointed to other difficulties such as a lack of joined up thinking indicated by the closure of local hospitals with large new facilities located on the edge of town; a strong belief that transport was not considered enough when planning major sites (including employment, retail and leisure, hospitals and healthcare, schools, colleges and social services) and concerns

---

7   The Commission for Integrated Transport (CfIT) is an independent body advising the Government on integrated transport policy. CfIT takes a broad view of integrated transport policy and its interface with wider Government objectives for economic prosperity, environmental protection, health and social inclusion. It was established in the 1998 Integrated Transport White Paper 'to provide independent advice to Government on the implementation of integrated transport policy, to monitor developments across transport, environment, health and other sectors and to review progress towards meeting our objectives'. (http://www.cfit.gov.uk/#role accessed 070705)

that overspent priority budgets for education and social services would draw from the transport budget.

Despite the apparent difficulties expressed above, the CfIT report goes on to state that "the actions and attitudes of local authorities confirm a clear commitment to delivering local transport improvements and to the LTP (Local Transport Plan) process". However, there was apparent doubt about any specific commitment to delivering the 10 Year Plan with the report stating that "there is significant risk in our view that the effectiveness of what many local authorities deliver will not match their own and the Government's expectations". According to CfIT (CfIT, 2003:8.11), there was evidence that the 10 Year Plan was perceived as:

> ...underpinned by ambiguity in national transport policy. The Integrated Transport White Paper was seen to provide a clear commitment to integrated transport policy, whereas the 10 Year Plan does not.

CfIT perceived that there was a possibility that, should the local authorities continue to interpret Government policy as ambiguous, then "the tactical response will be for LTPs (Local Transport Plans) and the delivery of local transport to lose focus on 'soft' policies and move towards infrastructure schemes". Against this background of an ostensible gap between the integrated transport White Paper and 10 Year Plan policies, there were concerns about the potential for local authorities to make real and positive changes for local residents through transport.

In its progress report on the 10 Year Plan, the Department for Transport (DfT, 2002a) stated that the Plan "is an over-arching investment strategy, not a detailed blueprint". The report highlighted evidence of progress made, listing a number of milestones which reflected achievements that were heavily weighted towards infrastructure investments. It thus appeared to indicate that CfIT's aforementioned concern about the lack of focus on "soft" policies may have been justified. This had implications for the Plan's objective of reducing social exclusion and delivering a transport system to meet people's needs and match the aspirations of individuals, families, communities and businesses (DETR, 2000a).

Given the apparent anomalies between the transport needs of society and some of the 10 Year Plan's contents, the emergence of a shift in the policy arena seemed inevitable. As the current research progressed, it became apparent that certain targets within the 10 year plan would not be met and, with a new Secretary of State for Transport in post, there was a discernible movement away from some of the goals of the Plan. This culminated in the publication in July 2004 of a new white paper for transport "The Future of Transport" (DfT, 2004a) which looks further ahead to 2030. As a result of the movement in the policy arena, this research's aim was revised to have a more local focus as outlined in Section 1.2.

With a new, more local focus to the study, local transport planning policy gained greater importance as a context for the research. Local Transport Plans (LTPs) replaced the Transport Policies and Programme (TPP) system of bidding for capital resources in 2000. The LTP system is built round 5-year integrated transport strategies which are devised at local level in partnership with the community (DETR, 2000a). Revised draft guidance on LTPs was published for consultation in July 2004. A more in-depth examination of the policy background to this work is presented in Chapter 2.

Emergence of a discourse on transport and social inclusion

In order to provide a basis for the ensuing investigation of transport from a social context, it is useful to begin with an insight into the development of a transport and social inclusion literature. While Chapter 2 provides a more detailed description of this literature, the purpose here is to provide an introduction to the context for the research.

In recent years, there has been increasing recognition that (poor) transport can contribute to exclusionary mechanisms. Grayling (2002) states that "(p)oor transport can restrict access to jobs, education, shops and services, social and cultural life". There is empirical evidence to highlight the social inequalities that exist in the transport sector (see, for example, Beuret et al., 2000, Lucas et al., 2001, Rajé et al., 2003a). However, despite this background, there is still a lack of precise mapping of the links between transport and social inclusion/exclusion. It should be noted that it is not only with respect to transport that the research and policy debates have appeared to largely neglect social inclusion/exclusion, for example, urban social marginalization has tended not to address trends in a range of essential services such as food retailing, energy, telephony and financial services (Speak and Graham, 2000).

Despite the absence of a transport policy framework for social inclusion/exclusion in the past, there has been some movement towards a greater understanding of the social aspects of transport in the research sphere. This is discussed in more detail in the literature review section in Chapter 2. However, it is also apparent that there has been a policy evolution towards a position that recognizes the importance of transport in the social inclusion arena. In February 2003, the Social Exclusion Unit in the Office of the Deputy Prime Minister published a report on transport and social exclusion (Social Exclusion Unit, 2003) which was the culmination of almost two years' work, carried out at the request of the Prime Minister to explore, and make recommendations to overcome, the problems experienced by people facing social exclusion in reaching work and key services in England.

Taking one example from the literature of the challenges faced by people needing to access facilities and services, Boardman's (1998) contention that, "in rural areas, the debate needs to be wide enough to incorporate land use planning and recognize that one way to make essential facilities more accessible is to make them more widely available", is also relevant in the urban setting. For example, on the large post-war estate of Clifton south west of the city of Nottingham, residents described the need to travel off the estate to buy good, inexpensive food (Rajé et al., 2002):

> "I end up going to the expensive shops (on the estate) because I can't get to the supermarket."

> "Yeah, I have to stick in Clifton to go shopping, not that I want to."

"You can't get to Asda (by public transport) and that's nearby in West Bridgford."

(Quotations from 3 participants at focus groups held in 2002 and reported on in Rajé et al., 2003a)

Other research has examined the interface between transport and social inclusion to varying degrees. Projects have included a gender audit of public transport (Hamilton et al., 1999), an examination of ethnic minority needs in relation to public transport (Beuret et al., 2000), a study of social exclusion and the provision and availability of public transport (TRaC, 2000) and an investigation of the role of transport in the lives of economically and socially disadvantaged groups and communities (Lucas et al., 2001).

It appears, then, that while the policy and research environments have become more concerned about transport and social inclusion, there is also a need for studies to examine the operational impacts of transport on individuals, such as how people plan shopping trips if available bus services do not take them to the nearest supermarket or how they go to a hospital appointment when parking at the hospital is extremely difficult, bus services are poor or they do not have access to a car. This type of study could also usefully look at the implications of the empirical research findings for the development of policy that can make a real difference to particular social groups' experience not only of transport but their wider ability to participate in their society.

Research approach and existing gaps in the literature

Introduction

Transport impacts on the individual, the community, the environment and the economy. In the past, traditional measurement of potential impacts of transport schemes tended to focus on the costs and benefits of various scenarios in order to determine a net present (economic) value of a chosen scheme rather than exploring impacts of competing schemes on the individual. In other words, the social costs were not given any real weight in transport policy appraisal. There have been recent advances in the assessment of transport proposals through development of tools such as Integrated Policy Appraisal (DEFRA, 2002a). Yet there is still a need to understand that individual members of society experience different levels of impacts and these often depend on their social grouping. According to the Social Exclusion Unit (2003),

> (p)roblems with transport provision and the location of services can reinforce social exclusion. They prevent people from accessing key local services and activities such as jobs, learning, healthcare, food shopping or leisure. Problems can vary by type of area (for example urban or rural) and for different groups of people, such as disabled people, older people or families with children.

This book seeks to contribute to the literature on transport-related social exclusion by providing empirical insights into the ways in which transport impacts on people's lives. While the research approach is described in detail in Chapter 3, an overview of the methodology is given here to provide a context for the ensuing volume.

Outline of methodology

The methodology is based on two substantive case studies: an urban periphery enclave – Barton, Oxford and a rural area – Charlbury, West Oxfordshire. The findings of these two cases are complemented by other data sources:

- primary data collected from other residents of Oxfordshire through interviews and focus groups, in particular from the multi-ethnic community around the Cowley Road in East Oxford, and
- secondary data from two projects recently completed by the researcher on a) transport, social exclusion and different social groups in Bristol and Nottingham, and b) access to healthcare in Oxfordshire.

This section outlines the empirical framework and gives an overview of the methodology that has been adopted. The rationale for choosing the two case studies, as well as a more detailed description of the research approach and why it was adopted are given in Chapter 3.

For each of the case studies, particular transport interventions are examined. In Barton, a proposed junction improvement scheme is looked at to ascertain how it may impact on the social groups of interest in this area. The Charlbury case study investigates the impacts of a proposed home zone in one of the residential areas of the town. Both case studies also examine participants' wider views on transport issues to investigate how transport impacts on their lives.

The empirical research adopts a multi-methods approach using focus group, interview and web-based material obtained from both this study and previous work. The findings of this qualitative research are discussed for each case study respectively in Chapter 4 (urban) and Chapter 5 (rural). In addition, a Q Methodology study (Chapter 6) provides an exploratory, alternative investigation of participant opinion.

The case studies

Both case studies are in Oxfordshire (Figure 1.1). The County is centrally located in England with the city of Oxford lying 55 miles from London and 68 miles from Birmingham by road. The M40 runs through the east of the county and there are mainline rail links from Oxford and some of the market towns and villages. Oxfordshire has strong economic links with both London and the Midlands. It is a predominantly rural county with the lowest population density in the South East (Oxfordshire County Council, 2005a).

The South East is a leading economic growth region (Foley et al., 2005) and is one of the most prosperous regions in Europe. However, there is a need to strike a balance between the goal of maintaining the South East's economic success, while also "enhancing its environment and improving the wellbeing and quality of life of

Figure 1.1   Diagrammatic map of Oxfordshire showing case study sites

all its citizens" (Foley, 2004:5). This concern about economic success and quality of life requires reconciliation between the demands of both of these issues within the context of all citizens of the area, both the socially excluded and included. Selection of the two case studies from Oxfordshire allows for such an investigation of a microcosm of experience of transport from rural and urban South Eastern perspectives.

Although Oxfordshire is part of the buoyant economy of the South East of England, parts of its population are vulnerable and socially excluded (Oxfordshire County Council, 2004; Foley, 2004) or have the potential for becoming socially excluded. Fifteen areas (Super Output Areas or SOAs) of Oxfordshire are in the most deprived 20% in England, according to the Index of Multiple Deprivation 2004. The existence of these "pockets of deprivation" (Oxfordshire County Council, 2004) means people in these areas may experience a number of disadvantages. As Oxfordshire County Council recognizes, it is important that public services

> …reach the groups or individuals in society who experience the most disadvantage…not just those who are most visible, or who can shout the loudest. This is particularly important in an area where there is a great deal of affluence, which masks the differences between how people in the County are faring. (Oxfordshire County Council, 2004:13)

Indeed, the County Council's Corporate Governance Scrutiny Committee has expressed concern about the Council's lack of progress around issues of social inclusion (Oxfordshire County Council, 2004). This book investigates one aspect of public service - transport - in the County in relation to this theme.

Conclusion and outline structure

This chapter introduced the book's aims and objectives and outlined the methodology that was adopted. It also described relevant findings from the literature reviewed in brief and introduced the two case study sites.

In Chapter 2, the changing nature of the transport and social inclusion policy environment is described. This chapter also describes the wider social context in which transport decisions and transport planning take place and provides an assessment of evidence from the literature on the social aspects of transport.

Chapter 3 provides a detailed description of the methodology used. It describes the need for an evolving methodology to meet the study's objectives, the methods used and an innovative and exploratory approach in transport research which uses Q methodology to provide insights into opinions of the population of participants.

Chapter 4 concentrates on the relationship between transport and social inclusion in the urban context, while Chapter 5 examines the rural perspective on this relationship.

In Chapter 6, the ways in which participants perceive that transport impacts on their lives are explored. This analysis uses Q methodology to investigate the appropriateness of approaching transport and social inclusion/exclusion from a category perspective as other researchers have done, or whether there are benefits in looking across a wider spectrum of study to obtain commonalities and differences in experiences that may transcend traditional social groupings.

Finally, Chapter 7 contextualizes the research findings and suggests ways in which they may bring new understandings to the field of transport and social exclusion.

Chapter 2

Transport and Social Inclusion: The Literature and Policy Background

Introduction: a changing policy environment

The previous chapter defined the scope of the research and introduced the key concepts which will be explored in this and subsequent chapters. This chapter provides a policy context and assessment of the literature to set the stage for the discussion of the methodology adopted in the next chapter and the case study findings described in subsequent chapters.

The chapter begins with an outline of the key legislation and policy documents which have shaped transport policy in recent years and the emergence of social exclusion in transport discourses. The chapter then focuses on the wider social context in which transport decisions and transport planning take place. This discussion explores the definition of the term 'social exclusion' in the context of this research and refers to the many ways in which transport-related social exclusion is manifest in society.

Key legislation and policy

In this section, we look briefly at the main policy documents that have informed local transport policy and, in particular, trace the emergence of social exclusion in UK transport policy.

The Royal Academy of Engineering (2005:38) has characterized UK transport policy as short-sighted and prone to inconsistency over time, despite the need for transport to have "a commonly agreed core strategy that can be planned and implemented consistently over several decades". The CBI (2005) also indicates that there is a need to overcome past under-investment in transport to enable business to compete and the transport system to serve customers efficiently.

Looking at this imperative in transport policy making to better meet customer or social needs, a brief review indicates the changes in transport policy focus over the past 50 years and highlights the appearance of social exclusion in transport policy discourse in the late 1990s. In the 1960s, concerns began to be raised about the detrimental effects of increasing traffic volumes. According to Docherty (2001:322), the Buchanan Report (Ministry of Transport, 1963) "envisaged how the physical structure of British towns and cities would need to adapt to accommodate unrestricted use of the car". Docherty states further that "...its core message was that congestion was the inevitable outcome of the failure to match increased supply of roadspace to the voracious appetite for car travel" (Docherty, 2001:332). During the 1980s, road building was still being seen as a solution to rising traffic volumes and resultant congestion. The policy environment's coupling of roads to economic benefit is implied in the title of the 1989 Government White Paper "Roads to Prosperity".

However, within a few years, several concerns would come together to impact on the direction of UK transport policy. This cluster of events (Docherty, 2001) included the 1992 Rio Earth Summit, the publication in 1994 of the Royal Commission on Environmental Pollution's report 'Transport and the Environment' and the 1997 publication of the Road Traffic Reduction Act in response to pressure group campaigns. Of particular importance to this study was the advent of an overt concern about transport's role in social exclusion[1]. The modern concept of social exclusion had evolved in France from the 1960s onwards (Bonsall and Kelly, 2005) but it only appeared to become a central concern of UK government towards the end of the 1990s.

Thus, with a change of government from Conservative to Labour and despite transport receiving a low priority in Labour's 1997 election manifesto where it was "buried at the back of the brochure along with sport, the arts and voluntary services" (Tempest, 2002), the concept of social exclusion began to feature in transport policy discourse. Table 2.1 lists the documents which have helped shape recent transport policy and traces the re-focusing of policy-making emphasis from road building towards concerns about impacts of traffic and transport-related social exclusion. For this research, the publication of the 1998 Transport White Paper was particularly relevant. The White Paper has been described as:

> ... ambitious in the scope and breadth of its policies – bringing in social inclusion, environmental impact and sustainability, transport safety and more citizen participation. It was, frankly, short on the 'how' on the traditionally difficult issues, such as congestion and the growth of road traffic. But it expected a much wider range of policy options to be considered than would have been the case 10 or 15 years previously – congestion charging; workplace-parking charges; alternative modes, including light rail; radical measures for bus priority; significant traffic restraint; the encouragement of green travel plans; serious encouragement for cycling and so on. (Quarmby, 2002:55)

In terms of this study, the following documents are particularly important: the 10 Year Plan for Transport, the 2000 Government White Paper and the 2004 White Paper. In addition, the Transport Act 2000 gave local authorities a statutory requirement to produce Local Transport Plans (LTPs). As indicated in Chapter 1, LTPs were introduced as a response to the previous system of Transport Policies and Programmes (TPPs) which were considered to no longer be delivering efficiently (DETR, 2000b). It is within the context of the policies contained in the 10 Year Plan for Transport and the strategy set out in the 2000 White Paper that the Local Transport Plan guidance (DETR, 2000b) was built. Revised draft guidance on LTPs was published in 2004 for the second round of LTPs, covering the years 2006-07

---

1   The definition of social exclusion which was adopted for this work is discussed later in this chapter.

to 2010-2011. This guidance takes account of the Government's "overall transport strategy" (DfT, 2004b:9) and replaces the previous guidance issued in March 2000.

Table 2.1   UK Transport Policy Evolution: A selective timeline[2]

Date	Problem recognition	Policy report/ instrument	Policy outcome
1989	Need to provide increased road capacity to meet forecast traffic levels.	**UK Government White Paper** Roads to Prosperity	Envisaged an £18bn road-building programme to meet levels of traffic predicted to increase by between 83 and 142 per cent by 2025
1994	Recognition of negative effects of vehicle use	**Royal Commission on Environmental Pollution** Transport and the Environment	Recommended that transport policy should be based on the identification and pursuit of the best practicable environmental option.
1994	Doubts about 'predict and provide' that had been prevailing policy response to rising travel demand and car traffic	**Standing Advisory Committee on Trunk Road Assessment (SACTRA)** Trunk Roads and the Generation of Traffic	Recognized that new roads could generate some extra traffic and that any benefits from road-building were often very short term
1994	Recognized interaction between land use and transport	**UK Government Planning and Policy Guidance Note 13 (PPG13) for Transport**	Provided guidance on ways in which development could be located for access to variety of modes of transport
1997	Need to reduce traffic on local routes	**Road Traffic Reduction Act**	Local authorities required to take steps to reduce traffic in local areas

---

2   The timeline is selective in that it concentrates on the documents that show how the dominance of road-building was replaced by a concern about the impacts of traffic and, in 1998, the emergence of the term 'social exclusion' in relation to Government transport policy.

1998	Concerns about how to manage travel demand and traffic	**UK Government White Paper** A New Deal for Transport: Better for Everyone	Set out policy framework in which need to reduce society's dependence on the car was central. Highlighted government concern about social inclusion, environmental impact and sustainability, transport safety and the need for more citizen participation.
2000	Need for investment in alternative modes to lessen car dependence	**UK Government 10 Year Plan for Transport** Transport 2010: The Ten Year Plan	Set out plans for large-scale investment and wide-ranging targets for lessening car dependence in order to 'deliver for everyone reliable, safe and integrated transport which respects the environment'
2000	Need for regulatory backing for 10 year plan policies	**Transport Act 2000** Regulatory Impact Assessment	Established regulatory framework and context for 10 year plan to tackle congestion and pollution by improving all types of transport
2001	Increased recognition of the interaction between land use and transport	**UK Government Planning and Policy Guidance Note 13 (PPG13) for Transport revised**	Provided guidance on ways in which car dependence could be reduced as schemes were being planned
2002	Need to report on progress towards 10 year plan objectives	**UK Government 10 Year Plan Review** Delivering Better Transport: A progress report	Sought to underline that 10 year plan was 'an over-arching investment strategy, not a detailed blueprint'. Progress appeared to be dominated by infrastructure investment.
2004	Recognition that certain targets within the 10 year plan would not be met	**UK Government White Paper** The Future of Transport	Set out longer term goals for transport looking towards 2030

Sources: DfT website www.dft.gov.uk; *Ledbury (2004)*

Local transport plans were seen as a way of putting in place a structural change in the way policy was developed and to deliver a step change in transport investment. In this light, Local Transport Plans were regarded as the essential building blocks of an integrated transport policy (DETR, 2000b). The guidance document (DETR,

2000b:10) stated that local transport plans would deliver by harnessing local opinion:

> One of the keys to a plan's success will be the extent to which it meets the local vision of where a community wants to be in the future and how transport will contribute. Local people know the problems that their communities face better than anyone. By working with a wide range of partners, authorities can produce the strategies to tackle the problems causing local people and businesses most concern, and produce a LTP that commands widespread support.

The guidance document (DETR, 2000b:11) went on to suggest that a key element in the success of local transport plans would be public involvement in both transport planning and delivery:

> To be effective, authorities cannot work in isolation. The involvement and support of interest groups, businesses, neighbouring authorities, and local people is essential at all stages of transport planning and delivery…Lack of access to safe, affordable transport can contribute to social exclusion. Local transport plans must tackle these issues. So it is important that public consultation reaches out to groups such as older people, women, disabled people and people from ethnic minorities who may face particular problems.

Within the LTP guidance issued in 2004 is a recognition of transport's role in social inclusion and the significant impact 'that local transport can play in reducing social exclusion' (DfT, 2004b: 33). The guidance (DfT, 2004b:33) states that:

> Different people have different transport needs so local authorities should consider how their policies address the transport requirements of different groups, including disabled people, women, older people, younger people, carers, people from ethnic communities and people on lower incomes. Improving access to jobs and services is the key means of helping to meet these requirements through transport planning, but authorities should also take opportunities to ensure local transport policies across the board contribute towards social inclusion objectives.

Given this policy context, the remainder of this chapter looks at the wider social context in which transport planning and policy making operate and the issues around transport and social exclusion raised in the literature.

Transport and traffic schemes: the social dimension

Introduction

Following the overview of UK transport policy within the context of the advent of policy concern about social exclusion given in the preceding section, this literature review section involves an assessment of empirical and policy evidence concerning transport and social exclusion. The review of literature begins with a discussion of recent social trends in the UK and the implications of these trends for people's travel and transport needs. The review then concentrates on the theme of transport and social exclusion as it moves towards a definition of the term 'social exclusion' which best meets the needs of this research.

Placing transport in a wider social context

Social trends and transport implications: an overview   During the late 20th Century and the early years of the new millennium, there have been major changes in UK society. A recent Government report on social trends (ONS, 2005) looks back over the 35 years since the report was first published and summarizes these changes as:

> The UK has an ageing population, and growth in the minority ethnic population has resulted in a more diverse society. Household income has risen over the past 35 years, although income inequality has widened. Life expectancy has also increased but so have the number of years that we can expect to live in poor health or with a disability. Technology has transformed many of our lives and our dependence on the car is greater than ever. (Social Trends 35 @ http://www.statistics.gov.uk/socialtrends35/ accessed 150106)

In the following sections, we concentrate on these and other social changes which have greatest potential for changing our transport and travel needs.

New household forms   There has been a decline in the average size of household in the UK, from 2.91 persons in 1971 to 2.31 in 2002 (ONS, 2005). At the same time, the types of households that people live in are more diverse. Between 1971 and 1998, the overall proportion of one person households almost doubled from 17 per cent to 31 per cent and the proportion of households consisting of one person aged 16 to 59 tripled from 5 per cent to 15 per cent (ONS, 2005). Although the population has been increasing, the number of households has increased at a much faster rate due to the trend towards smaller household sizes. The population grew by 6 per cent between 1971 and 2003, while the number of households increased by 32 per cent (ONS, 2005). Thus, there are more one person households, lone parent families and smaller family sizes than there were 35 years ago.

In terms of social exclusion, single people have twice the risk of living in poverty compared to couples without children and single pensioners have a higher risk than pensioners who are part of a couple (Bradshaw et al., 2004). In addition, these new, smaller household forms indicate that society has become more atomistic and suggest that there may be a higher degree of autonomy with regard to individual transport decision-making than there may have been in the past.

An ageing population: transport implications   Turning to the relationship between transport and ageing, the European Conference of Ministers of Transport (ECMT, 2000) states that the number of older people in developed countries represents a growing percentage of the total population and forecasts that generations of older people to come will be more mobile. The report makes special mention of older female drivers and suggests that women are driving much more than in the past, although their trips are normally shorter and they travel less annual kilometres than men. These findings indicate the importance of considering effects of policy changes on this section of the population and the need to look beyond forecast traffic figures to ascertain the nature of their composition and implications for different types of individuals.

As a corollary, in its policy statement on mobility and transport for senior citizens, Help the Aged (2001) states that although older people travel if they are able to but, for all too many, there are barriers to getting out and about. While 91% of single pensioners and 53% of pensioner couples do not own a car, 58% of men and 16% of women aged 60 to 69 drive their own vehicles. It follows then that policies that influence car use will have both direct effects on a relatively large number of drivers in their 60s and indirect effects on non-car owners who may rely on others for lifts.

Phillipson et al. (in McRae, 1999:244), reporting on research on older people in three urban areas, make a link between owning or having use of a car and being "generally better placed to cope with changes to their personal networks". These authors go on to state that:

> This illustrates some of the ways in which social networks vary in their capacity to handle what Fischer (1982) refers to as the freight of distance. For some groups, notably our predominantly working-class older people in Bethnal Green, managing the distance between close kin can pose great problems especially when one is reliant on public transport...

Brook Lyndhurst (2003:42) also highlight the importance to older people of transport for sustaining social connections but, at the same time, indicate that the nature of transport provided can detrimentally affect the nature of social contact made or activity that can be pursued:

> Lack, or loss, of personal transport is often identified as a key barrier to maintaining existing social relationships. State provided or subsidized transport may only be available to venues or activities that older people would not otherwise choose to patronize.

Other work by this researcher (Rajé et al., 2003a) underlines the importance of transport in providing social connectivity for older people. They may express frustration with their tendency to miss out or suffer in terms of sociability because of transport. For example, an elderly woman living in the inner city of Bristol described how much she wished she could travel from her high-rise apartment block to her daughter's suburban home by bus so that she could sit in the garden on summer days. However, with no bus service available between these two points, unaffordability of taxis on her pension income and the daughter's unavailability to provide a lift because she works full-time, the woman reported that she would sit looking out of her window feeling lonely instead.

Sometimes publicly-funded services may be available to the elderly but not to attend the activities they would prefer to do, such as going to a garden centre. Instead, the transport takes them to places such as organized lunch clubs where they may be expected to mix with people with whom they have little in common (Personal interview, 86 year old woman). Likewise, visits to friends and relatives in hospital may be made difficult or impossible for many people by lack of public transport especially at weekends and in the evenings. This can result in the trip being foregone, the use of tedious and tiring bus routings, the expense of taxi fares or dependence on others for lifts: all stressful and inadequate solutions at a time when the health of the friend or relative may already be causing distress.

Against this background, the important role of transport as a facilitator of social contact is underlined by the Pedestrians' Association (2001) who report that low levels of social contact may be linked to increased mortality from all causes. With a growing elderly population who are dependent on mobility to maintain social contact, it is essential that efforts are made to understand older people's varied transport needs and build sensitivity to the contexts of their daily lives into policy making and planning. Without such focus, the needs of the elderly will not be met and their vulnerability to transport-related social exclusion will continue.

Women's wider participation in the labour market   In 2001, McDowell (2001:449) stated that "(o)ne of the most noticeable features of the last decade is that the rise in women's labour market participation rates has continued" and this trend appears to be continuing. While the male working age employment rate of 79 per cent in Spring 2004 was much the same as it had been in Spring 1984, the female rate rose gradually over the period from 59 per cent to 70 per cent (ONS, 2005). Over the same period, the gap between economic activity rates for men and women more than halved (from 22 percentage points in 1984 to 10 percentage points in 2004). In spring 2004, it was estimated that around 4 in 5 part-time employees were women (ONS, 2005). The recent Social Trends report (ONS, 2005) indicates that the presence of a dependent child in the household has a major effect on the economic activity of women of working age. For both lone mothers and those with a partner, employment rates are lowest when they have a child under five. Lone mothers with a pre-school child aged under five are less likely to be working than those who have a partner (33 per cent compared with 58 per cent in Spring 2004). This differential decreases as the child gets older. These findings indicate that women with children may be most vulnerable to income-based social exclusion.

Although the gap between economic rates of men and women may have halved, the UK 2000 Time Use Survey found that there were substantial differences between men and women in the amount of time they spent on various activities:

> Women still do the majority of the household chores: on average women spent 4 hours 3 minutes a day on housework and childcare compared with 2 hours 17 minutes for men. Men, on the other hand, worked or studied 1 hour 35 minutes a day more than women. Men also spent more time than women on leisure activities (5 hours 17 minutes compared with 4 hours 52 minutes). Men and women spent a similar amount of time sleeping, travelling, and on personal care. (ONS, 2005: ch 13)

In addition, when trip purposes of both males and females are compared, differences between the responsibilities of each gender are revealed. Taking DfT statistics for 2003-2004 (DfT, 2005 @ http://www.dft.gov.uk/stellent/groups/dft_foi/documents/divisionhomepage/610891.hcsp accessed 040106), compared with males, a higher proportion of trips by females were for shopping or escorting people to education and fewer for commuting and business (Table 2.2).

Table 2.2   Trips per person per year by purpose (2003-2004)

	Commuting & business	Education	Escort education	Shopping	Other	All purposes
Males	221	71	29	172	488	980
Females	144	65	70	213	505	997

Source: DfT, 2005 @ http://www.dft.gov.uk/stellent/groups/dft_foi/documents/ divisionhomepage/610891.hcsp

Thus, although women's participation in the labour market has increased, in comparison to men, they "continue to be responsible for the majority of domestic labour and childcare" (McDowell et al., 2005:447) and for providing caring functions in the travel environment. Sarmiento (1996:37) draws out the linkage between household composition and travel with particular reference to women:

> Transportation measures do not affect the population uniformly because each individual faces a different set of constraints. Some constraints are a function of income and other economic factors…Other constraints are a function of household composition, the male/ female division of labor in the household, and the individual roles in the household. These have received relatively little attention until recently.

> Travel is part of a larger structure of household activities (Giuliano, 1992). We take trips to go grocery shopping, to go to the bank, to take clothes to the dry cleaner, and to do many other errands…The circumstances of other household members affect one's travel choices. Children have to be shuttled to and from the school or day care. A sick family member has to be taken to the doctor. Some household activities need to be performed together with other household members. These impose additional constraints in scheduling individual activities including travel. Gender is an issue to the extent that the division of labor in the household differs between men and women.

Sarmiento (1996) draws attention to other work which illustrates the effects of gendered household responsibilities on travel such as Rosenbloom and Burns (1989) which found significant differences in the travel patterns of men and women, particularly among those who are married with children, and the findings of Wachs (1988) and Hanson and Johnston (1985) which indicated that women's travel choices reflect the need to juggle work and household responsibilities. Recent research by Kim (2005) into gendered travel patterns in Portland, Oregon concurs:

> The results showed that, in addition to women's lower accessibility in absolute terms, women's temporal autonomy was strictly entrapped at only a particular time of day (in the late afternoon, specifically) regardless of employment status. Furthermore, the study has examined gender differences in determinants of accessibility and in travel/location/ activity contexts where people participate in discretionary activities. Women's lower levels of accessibility than men were largely due to additional constraints: household responsibilities. Compared to men, the level of availability of urban opportunities near home was found to be crucial in determining accessibility. In addition, people tend to enjoy the space-time autonomy in the work-to-home travel situation, and so the workplace and home are the most central locations of accessibility, as an origin and a destination. The

importance of other locations is relatively higher for women than for men. Women have more household work, and so need to be at home more. Therefore, women's need to be attached to home renders their accessibility more sensitive to the availability of local urban opportunities. (Kim, 2005 @ http://www.ohiolink.edu/etd/send-pdf.cgi?osu1117637933 accessed 040106)

Donaghy et al. (2004) also recognize the constraining effects of social obligations on women's travel, suggesting that these effects can be seen in the differences between women's and men's travel patterns at the micro level. Women tend to trip-chain while men tend make single-purpose trips (Schintler, 2002). Women tend to be more constrained in their mobility by their obligations as primary care providers (Kwan, 2003). As more women drive, Donaghy et al. (2004) suggest that their accident rates are expected to increase proportionately, but injuries are expected to increase more than proportionately. This is not because women are less safe drivers than men, but because they are more vulnerable physically (Rosenbloom and Hakamin-Blomqvist, 2004).

It is also important to note that there is a danger that the challenges of meeting the travel and access needs of women may remain largely hidden from policy makers and planners if new methods of consultation with women are not found which give due regard to the ways in which they participate in their social networks. Abbott (in Payne, 2000:89), in a critique of the policies of the Social Exclusion Unit, states that:

> Policies (such as 'employment action zones', 'health action zones' and 'new deals for communities') designed to encourage community participation take no account of the ways in which men and women involve themselves in the community. While women tend to play a greater role, it is generally on an informal basis, helping neighbours and other members of the community. When men become involved in the community, it is normally in formal organisations. Agencies working with communities are more likely to work with organisations and therefore men are likely to be over-represented in consultation and empowerment exercises, thus marginalising women. Finally, these policies are likely to have little impact on the economic plight of older women as they are designed predominantly to help young people and those of working age.

Hirst (1996) suggests that the most significant determinant of access difficulties is lack of car ownership. Hamilton et al. (1999) state that women have different levels of access to cars than men which can help explain the differences in their travel behaviour. By extension, lack of access to a car can be seen to contribute to the isolation of women. Household responsibilities are another significant constraint on women's accessibility. The literature indicates that women and men experience accessibility differently. Although it is important to note that women's travel needs and problems are not homogeneous, there is a potential in the way in which gendered household car availability and social responsibilities tend to be structured for women to be more vulnerable to transport-related social exclusion.

Transport and ethnicity   It is important to highlight the basic difficulty, at the macro level, of defining the term "ethnicity" itself. This has implications for its use as a delimiter within the analysis of social impacts since its fundamental meaning is open to ambiguity. Mason (in Payne, 2000:93) states that there is no universal definition of ethnicity but that a "cultural distinctiveness" is the mark of an ethnic grouping. According to Mason, Smith (1986:192) defined an ethnic unit as "…a population whose members believe that in some sense they share common descent and a common cultural heritage or tradition, and who are so regarded by others".

The official UK statistics website "National Statistics" (www.statistics.gov.uk) provides Census 2001 data which indicate that 9% of the population of England were from ethnic minority groups.

According to the Social Exclusion Unit (2000), people from minority ethnic communities are more likely than others to live in deprived areas, be poor, unemployed, suffer ill-health and live in overcrowded and unpopular housing. Yet, there is still very little publicly-available research on how ethnicity influences transport choice and a paucity of data on the patterns of travel of the various ethnic minority communities in the UK. Research by Beuret et al. (2000) and Rajé et al. (2004a) has started to make a contribution to the investigation of ethnicity and transport and indicates that ethnicity is indeed an important factor in the experience of transport. For example, Rajé et al. (2004a:36) found that the advent of a multi-cultural society in Britain had not been accompanied by any refinement of the analysis of individual entitlement to movement:

> Yet…there are minorities present who practice the social seclusion of women. The number of women secluded in Britain has neither been investigated nor is it known. Whilst the research into transport and social exclusion in Bristol and Nottingham did not provide examples of absolute seclusion of women, references are made by respondents to the partial seclusion of Asian women. A Muslim woman in Bristol reports on her preference for using Muslim driven taxis whilst an Asian shopkeeper in Bristol reports on the chaperon practices surrounding his daughter's mobility even as a professional woman. A Somali man reports on shopping being undertaken for his family not by his wife, as we would find in mainstream British society, but by himself or others performing the service for him. Significantly, in the research Asian women showed a propensity to be car passengers…

It has also been recognized that there are differences in economic activity rates amongst different ethnic groups and between the two genders within these groups (The Prince's Trust, 2001).

The definitional difficulties described earlier may go some way to explaining the challenges faced in conducting research on ethnicity. Nevertheless, the literature review indicates that there is very little empirical evidence on ethnicity and transport. The literature that exists is primarily focused upon personal security, very often in the context of gender, with very little literature, other than the studies mentioned above, attuned to the accessibility and mobility issues necessary to the obtaining of mainstream services by the ethnic population.

The car: availability and impacts   The General Household Survey (ONS, 2000) reveals that car availability may impact on local sociability. A higher percentage of people in a household where there is no car available reported speaking to neighbours on a daily basis (34%) than those living in households with one (29%) or two cars (21%) (ONS, 2000). It is not clear from the available data why this would be the case, however, it is possible that members of non-car owning households have to rely on the people living around them for help in making trips and this may to some extent contribute to their increased contact with neighbours. It is equally likely that people without cars live in higher density housing, walk to local shops and are therefore more likely to meet and talk to neighbours in their local community on a daily basis.

However, access to a car can facilitate access to activities and services when public transport fails to provide the necessary links. For example, people with children may find leisure activities inaccessible without a car because public transport services do not operate to the destinations they would like to visit. With luxuries like holidays usually unfeasible, day-trips can be very important to mothers and their children (Middleton et al., 1997). Yet, Bostock (2001:16) suggests that low income mothers can find that carlessness compounds their feelings of social isolation and social exclusion:

> When living in neighbourhoods with few amenities for children or with poorly managed grass areas that are littered with glass, dog faeces and soiled needles, day-trips promote a sense of inclusion and connection with the outside world. However, lack of private transport excluded mothers and children in a particularly harsh way from day-trips to the park and other places suitable for children.

This is the experience of a young mother in Nottingham who reported that she would enjoy taking her children to an out-of-town theme park during the school holidays but she is unable to do so because she has not got access to a car, there are no bus or train services operating to the destination from her area and she cannot afford a taxi. Even a shopping trip may be difficult for low income earners with children who do not have access to a car. As the following quote indicates, juggling financial, mobility and accessibility constraints can be quite a challenge:

> "Spent all my money this week on transport. I like to walk but if I go shopping, I have to take the taxi back. I also take buses and they're OK but I seem to spend all my money getting places. If I have the kids, I take a taxi. Yesterday, I went shopping in town on the bus and then came home by bus. I get very tired at the moment but I still try to walk as much as possible." (Heavily-pregnant woman, participant in Nottingham research, Rajé et al., 2004a:61)

However, it should also be noted that the car can have adverse impacts which might exacerbate social exclusion. For example, Foley et al. (2005:29) state that "road traffic impinges on the quality of life of people, particularly in residential areas". For local people, one of the most tangible means by which traffic may impose itself on a community is through the occurrence of road traffic accidents. Analysis of the then Department of Transport, Local Government and the Region's data (Graham et al., 2002) suggests that the most deprived local authority districts have up to five times as many child pedestrian accidents per child as the least deprived. It has been suggested that these figures are compounded by the finding that more children live in deprived areas and, therefore, there may be eight times as many child pedestrian casualties in the most deprived tenth of wards compared to the least deprived tenth.

This inequality of accident distribution has been found to pertain to adult pedestrians also but to a lesser extent (Foley et al., 2005; Grayling et al., 2002). In addition, DfT (2001) indicates that Asian children in the UK are involved in up to twice as many pedestrian accidents as the national average and that the risk is greatest in families where parents or carers are unfamiliar with UK traffic conditions, particularly for those Asian families who are more likely to be recent arrivals from abroad. This study only looked at Asian children but suggests that children of other ethnic minority backgrounds may be similarly compromised. Clearly then for ethnic minority families who are often concentrated in inner city suburbs where traffic flows are heavy and consequent exposure to risk great, the car can become a major cause of social exclusion.

The Acheson report (1998) concluded that deprived communities suffer the worst traffic pollution. This is supported by two studies which have mapped social deprivation against air quality: research for the Department for the Environment, Food and Rural Affairs (DEFRA) has provided tentative evidence for a positive correlation (King and Stedman, 2000). Friends of the Earth (2001) also found a positive correlation between levels of deprivation and traffic in their study of Bradford.

Impact of new forms of technology on mobility   Castells (2001:2) argues that a new social structure largely based on networks was ushered in during the last quarter of the twentieth century as a result of the three independent processes he describes in the following quote coming together:

> …the needs of the economy for management flexibility and for the globalization of capital, production, and trade; the demands of society in which the values of individual freedom and open communication became paramount; and the extraordinary advances in computing and telecommunications made possible by the micro-electronics revolution.

Banister (2005:169) relates the late twentieth century economic transformation to a "transition from an industrial mode of production to an information mode where the fundamental inputs are knowledge-based".

The movement towards a more information communication technology (ICT) based society is reflected in the extent of technological change registered in surveys by the Office of National Statistics. The latest edition of its report on social trends (ONS, 2005) captures this change:

> We are living through a historic period of technological change, brought about by the development and the widening application of information and communications technology (ICT). ICT is already an integral part of our daily lives…(H)ousehold ownership of mobile phones in the United Kingdom more than quadrupled between 1996/97 and 2002/03 to 70 per cent. In 2002/03, 45 per cent of households (10.9 million) could access the Internet from home. This was more than four times the proportion in 1998/99. Ownership of other technological goods has also increased. (ONS, 2005 @ http://www.statistics.gov.uk/ downloads/theme_social/Social_Trends35/Social_Trends_35_Ch13.pdf accessed 040106)

The potential effects of technological change associated with ICT on transport are multifarious. Banister (2005) provides a holistic approach to structuring these effects by dividing impacts of ICT on transport into three 'types' – production, living and working.

While many of the impacts Banister describes are provided by the virtual mobility that ICT can bestow, in terms of the social aspects of transport which this book is particularly concerned with, new information communication technology has two important roles. It makes the recording of social patterns easier, thereby providing planners with better data and it can also be used by the public to interact with (and substitute for) transport services (Grieco, 2005 @ www.geocities.com/gender_and_transport/braunschweiglecture.htm?200520 accessed 201205).

One example of the harnessing of new information communication technology in transport is its application in demand responsive transport solutions. Demand responsive transport options have recently emerged as an important policy option in the context of policy concern with congestion and the constraining of car based mobility. New information technology can readily collect together information on persons with low mobility wishing to make similar journeys, provide a booking or intelligent reservation system which permits the pick up and drop off at home and organize this in a way which is cost effective at the community level (Grieco and Hine, 2002). The authors suggest that buses routing around the needs of low mobility passengers is an existing capability of the new information age.

In its study of European best practice in the delivery of integrated transport, the Commission for Integrated Transport (CfIT, 2001) states that demand responsive transport schemes are becoming more common in the UK but are still basic in comparison to services provide abroad. CfIT suggests that, by exploiting the potential of new information technology[3], demand responsive transport schemes could help optimize resources in the long term by lowering subsidy costs per passenger.

Social capital, social networks and transport   The preceding sections highlighted the role of transport as a facilitator of travel and of travel as a catalyst for social interaction. Accordingly, it is evident that transport plays a fundamental role in a life that is social. In this section of the literature review, we build on the concepts

---

3   Telematic developments create opportunities for 'smart' or 'intelligent' demand responsive transport schemes which can reduce the length of booking window required. There are several software solutions available. The goal of these applications is to never have empty vehicles in circulation and to use the vehicle best suited to transportation needs in order to satisfy customer demand. By pooling users together in the same vehicle, customized transportation moves more people, more quickly and at a lesser cost. Horn (2002) describes fleet scheduling and dispatch in the context of demand responsive passenger services. He states that 'Responsiveness to demand…requires effective communication between prospective travellers and a scheduling centre, and between the centre and the drivers of the various vehicles'. Schwartz (2000) has explored 'the role of demand responsive public transport as a tool for providing an equitable and cost effective transport service to supplement mass transit and reduce transport disadvantage'. These are all examples of the potential of new forms of information technology to transform the mobility and accessibility needs of those who are vulnerable to transport-related social exclusion.

introduced earlier in the chapter by setting this research in the context of the literature on social capital, social networks and transport.

According to Acheson (1998:55), "(t)he primary function of transport is in enabling access to people, goods and services. In so doing it also promotes health indirectly through the achievement and maintenance of social networks". It follows that within any discussion of the impacts of transport on individual lives, it is apt to give due recognition to the social aspects of transport and the ways in which social connections can influence transport demand and supply. Yet, Axhausen (2003) draws attention to the lack of a social structural dimension in transport planning discourse. Axhausen (2003:3) suggests further that

> (I)t is the spatial structure of the social networks which is crucial (to an understanding of leisure travel and its potential for further growth), as the flows of information, prestige, affirmation and resources in the social networks, to which a traveller belongs, will direct the direction and amount of travel.

This research seeks to explore whether social networks provide an individual with transport choices and solutions which cannot be obtained by other means because of factors such as financial exclusion from owning an automobile, geographical exclusion from services associated with the decline in local amenity provision and time-based exclusion resulting from poor public transport provision outside of peak hours and at weekends. As such, social capital and social networks are conceptual tools for "characterizing local community life" (Campbell and Gillies, 2001:330) and thereby facilitating an investigation of transport and social exclusion.

The relevance of social capital to a discussion of transport's impacts is succinctly underlined in the observation that "Ten minutes of commuting reduces social capital by 10%" (Putnam, 2000 @ http://www.bowlingalone.com/ accessed 240404): a statement which makes the link between personal mobility and declining social capital. Urry (2003) provides another perspective on social capital and travel, suggesting that it is travel that helps establish the strength of connections between individuals in a network who require intermittent face-to-face meetings to maintain trust. For Urry (2003:171), travel is seen as essential to social life and "is not optional".

However, while Urry may view travel as strengthening an individual's social connectedness, Campbell and Gillies (2001:336), reporting on qualitative research into people's experiences of local community life in a town in the south-east of England, found that a decline in common social identity, related to the need to travel away from local neighbourhoods, had caused a decline in positive social values in communities. In this case, travel could be a potential threat to social capital:

> They said (the decline in positive social virtues) was due to changing living conditions which undermined community contact: better transport, commuters working away from home, better shopping opportunities outside the area...meant that local people had fewer opportunities to get to know one other.

Fernandez (1993:365-366) also suggests that increased travel, which has resulted from improvements in transportation, has meant that people now have a wider geographic vista with social relations being "'liberated' from geography".

However, it can be argued that the 'liberation' of social relations may be an inaccurate account of the impacts that the opportunities for travel beyond the neighbourhood have afforded. Based on Campbell and Gillies' findings, local social networks appear to have deteriorated as a consequence of provision of facilities and work opportunities away from residential neighbourhoods and consequent need for travel away from local areas. This means that, as Urry (2003) suggests, transport and travel may facilitate the building of social bonds over wider geographic space but to the possible detriment of the construction of neighbourhood ties and networks. Indeed, this may produce a "vicious circle" effect with people feeling they have to travel further in order to participate in the "face-to-face" activities that Urry sees as enriching social lives because they have weaker and weaker local connections as they travel more. Participants in Campbell and Gillies' study perceived the need to travel away from the residential area as an obstacle to the development of 'robust neighbourhood networks'. The authors described this as "...the 'emptying out' of the community during the day as growing numbers of people worked increasingly far from home..."(Campbell and Gillies, 2001:337).

It is equally important to note that, while transport may allow the mobile to leave their neighbourhood for work, social and other purposes, the lack of access to transport of others renders them isolated and cut off from key services in neighbourhoods where facilities are unavailable. If Wellman's (1996:348) assertion that "Most intimate and other active ties are not with neighbors" (as a result of his view that "People get out of their neighbourhoods quite easily"), then the geographic isolation from services and facilities as a result of lack of transport can only be compounded by a social isolation from personal community relationships. This study investigates the importance of local ties and personal community networks to the impacts that transport has on individuals in different social groups.

At the same time, the research also explores the potential impacts of transport interventions. This examination facilitates a discussion of the "social difficulties" (Banister, 1980:1) caused by the "distributional effects as to who benefits and who loses from transport decisions" (Banister, 1980:4). At a basic level then, the study seeks to contribute to a greater understanding of the day to day social impacts of transport decisions. The Benevolent Society in Australia provides an instructive insight into the need for social capital to be operationalized in its area of work. This is equally relevant to the transport sphere:

> Much has been written about social capital in recent times and it usually refers to the norms of trust, reciprocity and citizen participation. But there hasn't been a great deal written about what it means to apply some of the theory of social capital to the day to day workings of organisations like ours - social capital in practice. (The Benevolent Society, 2000)

The quote above relates to the work of not-for-profit organizations in developing community engagement and social capital, yet the concept of taking the theory of social capital and applying it to day-to-day life is one that it is useful to borrow for the purposes of this work. This research is investigating the operational or practical impacts of social capital within the context of communities and the people who live in them. As in the research of the Australian Benevolent Society (from which the above quotation is taken) which recognized that "Social capital provides a much needed alternative framework for responding to people experiencing disadvantage and social marginalization" (Hampshire and Healy, 2000), this study strives to take the theory of social capital and operationalize it through the investigation of transport's role in people's lives.

This objective is directed towards a goal that Hampshire and Healy (2000) set out in their assertion that "research must move beyond the conceptualisation and measurement of social capital towards a practical understanding of the elements that promote and detract from social capital" (Hampshire and Healy, 2000 @ http://www. bensoc.asn.au/research/sc_practice.html accessed 240904). Thus, the concept of social capital theory is being used here as a basis for describing the daily experiences of, and developing more effective responses to, people experiencing disadvantage and social isolation related to transport.

Payne (in Payne, 2000:245) writes that "...social inequality is a condition of disproportionate access to 'resources' – that is, not just financial resources but any human or cultural resources". This statement highlights the importance of social resources to social equality: in other words, social capacity is necessary to achieve desired participation in society. Within the context of social capital, access to transport can give a flexibility to distance, allowing access to kinship networks where people live in different neighbourhoods, regions or countries and to services that are beyond the local area's boundaries. Thus, access to transport allows the conduct of social relationships and the procurement of goods and services over longer distances than that afforded by inadequate access to transport resources.

However, social capital's relationship with transport does not operate purely from the unilateral perspective which views transport as a facilitator of social interaction. Instead, social networks can also be usefully seen as facilitators of transport provision. This view is informed by a framework presented by Casas et al. (2003) at a STELLA[4] workshop held in Lisbon in 2004 (Figure 2.1).

Casas et al. (2003) suggest a "way of reframing social problems that reorients the perspective to one that may shift the policies, institutions, methods and evaluation tools away from transportation and place them in a more appropriate or comparative context".

Casas et al. suggest that a transportation perspective should not be replaced by a social needs perspective, but that the two can be evaluated side by side. Figure 2.1 illustrates the incorporation of social networks into the activity and transportation infrastructure inputs of transportation planning, research and policy.

Casas et al.'s argument is that, in the diagram shown in Figure 2.1:

---

4   Sustainable Transport in Europe and Links and Liaisons with America: Thematic Network project of the European Commission's 5th Framework Programme for Research and Development.

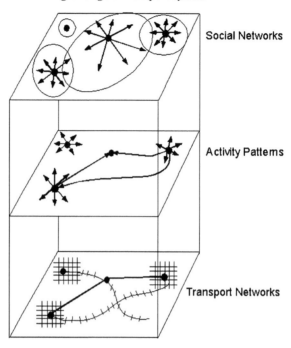

Social Networks

Activity Patterns

Transport Networks

Figure 2.1   Example of Potential Social Transportation Framework

...certain individuals within a region may be isolated (upper left corner of each plane) not due to lack of transportation infrastructure and connectivity, but due to lack of social networks that extend the physical space of one's home. Interventions in such cases may or may not be transportation based. From a transportation perspective, it may be that such isolated individuals may need transit riding education or a personal transit escort to utilize existing transportation resources. From a non-transportation intervention, local social service providers may need to do better jobs at reaching out to incorporate such isolated individuals. Once such outreach is successfully accomplished, then those individuals may make use of the transportation infrastructure.

It can be seen, then, that there is a relationship between social networks and transport or travel. Approaches to transport problems may be helpfully framed from a social perspective and, similarly, approaches to social problems may also be approached from a travel and transport viewpoint in order for individual social needs to be more adequately met. This highlights the importance of appropriate transport investment for an individual's ability to participate in society. This view is summarized in the following quote from the New Zealand Ministry of Economic Development "..."enough" and "appropriate" transport system investment can make an invaluable contribution to access, mobility and social connectedness" (Chapman et al., 2003:1).

Before we leave this overview of opinion on social capital's connections with transport, it is important to draw attention to the role of trust in the context of social connectedness and transport. Giddens is quoted in Skidmore and Harkin (2003:2) as perceiving trust as acting as "a protective cocoon which all normal individuals carry around with them as the means whereby they are able to get on with the affairs of day-to-day life". Skidmore and Harkin 2003:2 take this concept further suggesting that "(t)rust is a basic human need" which "knits us together, and makes social interaction and co-operation possible". This implies then that there must be a relationship between trust and transport.

Perhaps it would be best to see this operating on a number of levels. At a basic level, it is our trust in the availability of a good or provision of a service at a particular destination that motivates our need to travel and therefore use the transport system. On another level, it is our trust in others that enables us to form social connections with them that may subsequently require travel to maintain. From another perspective, a lack of trust in a transport service may affect whether we are willing to use it. Indeed, trust in another person such as a neighbour or friend may help us to travel e.g. the neighbour who looks after your child to allow you to be free to go food shopping on the bus or the colleague who lives two streets away who gives you a lift to work each day are both facilitating transport through a trust-based relationship. As a corollary, an absence of such relationships and a wariness with regard to trust can have implications for our ability to make trips.

Transport and social inclusion/exclusion

Introduction

Having reviewed some of the key trends in UK society and their implications for travel and transport above, this section concentrates on the search for a definition of social exclusion which captures the essence of the theme most effectively for the purposes of this research. The review starts by examining the literature on social inclusion/exclusion. It then looks at the literature on transport and social inclusion/ exclusion and the ways in which the literature suggests that transport-related exclusion can be manifest in society.

Social inclusion and exclusion

In recent years, the term "social exclusion" has come to occupy a central place in the discussion of social policy and inequality in Europe (Atkinson and Davoudi, 2000) and policy debates about inequality have tended to focus on social exclusion rather than on poverty (Shucksmith, 2000). Scourfield (no date) suggests that the notion of a "cycle of disadvantage" is key to understanding social exclusion. It appears that social exclusion is tied to disadvantage and injustice. However, in terms of defining social exclusion[5], a clear definition remains elusive. Kenyon et al. (2002:207) note that "social exclusion is endlessly redefined, yet the concept remains vague". Lyons

---

5   The word exclusion tends to be used because that has been the focus of the policy debate to date. Nevertheless, there are indications of a relatively recent shift in the emphasis from exclusion to inclusion, although much of the literature does not yet reflect this change. The tension between the two terms, social inclusion and exclusion, is evident in the discourse.

(2003:340) reports on three interpretations of the term from a recent workshop on travel chances and social exclusion held at the International Association of Travel Behaviour Research:

> There is an abundance of literature that attempts to capture, within a concise definition, the essence of what constitutes social exclusion. Three interpretations were offered in the workshop:
>
> 1. "experiencing public service failure"—this recognizes that while it is the individual or the community that suffers the consequence of or experiences social exclusion, it is the system or societal structure that has given rise to their circumstances.
>
> 2. "the discrepancy between what you can do and what you want to do"—this is a helpful interpretation which reflects the perspective of the individual concerned and suggests the beginnings of a means to measure in absolute and relative terms the extent of exclusion experienced.
>
> 3. "a spectrum of deprivation"—this interpretation aims to highlight that social exclusion is not something that has a binary state (i.e. an individual is excluded or is included) but rather that everyone in society sits on a multidimensional scale of exclusion or deprivation: social policy and benchmarking then determines the point on that scale beyond which the level of deprivation is considered unacceptable.

Lyons (2003) reminds us that the three interpretations are conceptual in nature and that planners and policy-makers will each seek a definition that is operational or "fit for purpose" that they are addressing. It would appear, then, that multiple definitions are acceptable as long as the objective for which the definition is made is clearly stated. In terms of this study, several explanations of the term have been found in the literature reviewed. For completeness, these are shown in Table 2.3. This is followed by a justification for the adoption of a working definition of social exclusion for this work.

It should be noted that this table does not purport to provide a definitive list of all available descriptions of the term but is indicative of the range of definitions in recent literature. It can be seen that although there is not one specific definition, it is possible to extract the salient concepts of the various authors' perspectives on social exclusion and conclude that it is a process which is understood to be multi-dimensional and prevents individuals or groups from participating in normal activities of their society. It is linked to inaccessibility of goods and services which contribute to a feeling of not belonging. It should also be pointed out that the literature recognizes that social exclusion is relative and identifies a link between exclusion and transport.

It should, however, be apparent that reducing social exclusion and promoting social inclusion are very similar, if not identical processes.

Table 2.3   Definitions and explanations of the term 'social exclusion'

Definition/Explanation	Source
Social exclusion is a process, which causes individuals or groups, who are geographically resident in a society, not to participate in the normal activities of citizens in that society.	Hine and Mitchell (2001)
Social exclusion is a shorthand term for what can happen when people or areas suffer from a combination of linked problems such as unemployment, poor skills, low incomes, poor housing, high crime, bad health and family breakdown.	Social Exclusion Unit (2001)
The condition of living in a society but not having the opportunity to participate in the normal activities of citizens in that society.	Sinclair (2001)
Exclusion springs from the desire to belong while not being able to.	McCluskey (1997)
Social exclusion is related to relative poverty where groups or individuals lack the resources to obtain type of diet, participate in the activities and have the living conditions and amenities which are customary, or at least widely acknowledged or approved, in the societies to which they belong.	TRaC (2000) after Townsend (1979)
A situation in which certain members of a society are, or become, separated from much that comprises the normal round of living and working in that society.	Philo (2000)
The outcome of processes and/or factors which bar access to participation in civil society	Eisenstadt and Witcher (1998)
A multi-dimensional process, in which various forms of exclusion are combined: participation in decision-making and political processes, access to employment and material resources, and integration into common cultural processes. When combined, they create acute forms of exclusion that find a spatial manifestation in particular neighbourhoods.	Madanipour et al. (1998)
Social exclusion is more influenced by accessibility of goods and services than by mobility per se.	CfIT (2001)
Social exclusion appears to have replaced 'poverty' and related concepts such as 'underclass'. However, these terms are not synonymous and 'social exclusion' has a markedly different provenance.	Pearce (2001)
The concept of social exclusion is understood as a multidimensional phenomenon, where exclusion is characterized conceptually as the process which prevents people from a full participation in the society i.e. from being socially integrated.	EU Business (2000)
Social exclusion is understood to denote a set of factors and processes that accentuate material and social deprivation.	Arthurson (2003)

Social exclusion has a broader and more comprehensive meaning than poverty. It can be a cause as well as a consequence of income poverty and material deprivation. It refers to the dynamic processes of being shut out, partially or fully, from any or all of several systems which influence the economic and social integration of people into their society. It points to 'system failures' rather than individual failings as causes of social exclusion. Interpreted in its widest sense, it constitutes a denial of full citizenship – the collection of rights and responsibilities that one acquires as a member of society.	Commins (2004)
The notion of 'social exclusion' has gained currency because it encapsulates the ideas that people are not just disadvantaged because of a lack of money, but may also be excluded from the day to day norm of living standards by fact of a physical disability, being isolated due to poor services, being discriminated against in the job market because of where they live and other factors.	Oxfordshire County Council, 2004

(Adapted from Rajé et al., 2004a:8)

For the purposes of this research, Hine and Mitchell (2001) and Sinclair (2001) appear to offer the most succinct and relevant explanations of social exclusion: linking activity participation to accessibility (which is linked to transport). Importantly, as some of the other definitions also recognize, they see social exclusion as a condition that affects an individual/group's ability to participate in the normal activities of other citizens. However, there is one key element that Hine and Mitchell's and Sinclair's definitions do not specifically include which is of importance to this research: there is no spatial dimension within their definitions. Madanipour et al. (1998) provide a definition of the term which stresses the importance of location in determining social exclusion (Hodgson and Turner, 2003), indicating that there is a spatial dimension, related to neighbourhoods, to social exclusion. Thus, following Madanipour et al. (1998), Hine and Mitchell (2001) and Sinclair (2001), the working definition adopted for this research is:

> Social exclusion is a process which causes individuals or groups not to participate in the normal activities of the society in which they are residents and has spatial manifestations.

Importantly, unlike some (including, to an extent, the Social Exclusion Unit), the book does not use social exclusion as a synonym for income-based deprivation. Instead, the book recognizes that transport is a rather blunt instrument to effect income re-distribution and hence if social exclusion was purely about income, the transport-related dimension would be modest.

Thus, the book's focus is on participation in civil society. In part, this is determined by access to work, education, healthcare, shops, leisure facilities, welfare, finance and housing, only some of which have a material transport dimension. It is also determined by personal contacts, based on familial, kinship and organisational ties. One of the alleged features of post-modern society is the reduced participation in civil organisations (Putnam, 2000). This decline in collectivism and emergence of more individualized, atomistic lifestyles, in part promoted by technological developments such as the automobile and the television, arguably increases the risks of social exclusion (Preston and Rajé, 2005).

In terms of transport, recognition that the relationship between spatial location and social exclusion is highly complex (Madanipour et al., 1998; Power and Wilson, 2000) is important as the spatial dimension introduces the concept of accessibility to the social exclusion discourse. Farrington and Farrington (2005:2) have underlined the significance and centrality of accessibility to debates about social exclusion when they state that:

> (G)reater social justice cannot be achieved without greater social inclusion, which requires that people have access to a range of services regarded as typical of their society; greater social inclusion requires greater accessibility which often (but emphatically not inevitably) implies mobility and transport use. This is not to say, of course, that social inclusion of itself achieves greater social justice, and particularly it is not to say that accessibility of itself achieves social inclusion.

A criticism of social exclusion is that it revives prejudicial notions of an underclass and the undeserving poor (Samers, 1998 cited in Preston et al., 2003). In response to this, more recently, emphasis has been placed on the concept of social inclusion. The Centre for Economic and Social Inclusion (2002) highlights that this is "understood as a process away from exclusion, it is a process for dealing with social exclusion and integrating individuals into society". Broadening its definition the Centre states that:

> Social inclusion is the process by which efforts are made to ensure that everyone, regardless of their experiences and circumstances, can achieve their potential in life. To achieve inclusion, income and employment are necessary but not sufficient. An inclusive society is also characterized by a striving for reduced inequality, a balance between individuals' rights and duties and increased social cohesion.

Oxfordshire County Council (2004:8) portrays the language around social exclusion and social inclusion as an important descriptor of the role and responsibility local government has towards members of the local community:

> The language of 'social inclusion' and 'social exclusion' has come from debates about how to best help people overcome disadvantages in their lives and allow them to live their life to the fullest. These terms are widely used by practitioners and all levels of government...The debate about the terms 'social inclusion' and 'social exclusion' is not just an 'academic' argument, but relates directly to what local government sees as its role and responsibility towards people who are in need of assistance, and to the community as a whole.

For Farrington and Farrington (2005), social inclusion is closely linked to social justice. The authors describe Hay's (Hay, 1995) discussion of equity, fairness and justice in geography as particularly useful since it identifies "'access across space' as a fundamental and pervasive issue in achieving social justice in the geographical context" (Farrington and Farrington, 2005:3). Thus, the authors conceptualize social inclusion and social justice in relation to accessibility.

Before leaving this section on social inclusion and exclusion to discuss these issues in the context of transport in greater detail, it is instructive to examine Shucksmith's conception of social inclusion and exclusion since it clearly describes the approach to these concepts that informs this work and highlights the importance of power in the social inclusion/exclusion discourse. Shucksmith (2000; also Philip and Shucksmith, 1999) asserts that viewing processes of social inclusion and exclusion as overlapping spheres of integration is a particularly fruitful approach:

> The different spheres relate to the different ways in which resources are allocated in society – through market processes (e.g. payment for work); through transfer payments and services provided by the state; through collective action organised via voluntary bodies; and through reciprocal, cultural and other non-market processes associated with networks of family and friends. One's sense of belonging in society depends on most or all of these systems. (Shucksmith, 2000:12)

Based on his perspective on social inclusion and exclusion, Shucksmith suggests that processes of social inclusion and exclusion should be "analysed in relation to the means by which resources and status are allocated in society, and especially in relation to the exercise of power" (Shucksmith, 2000:12).

Pursuing the theme of power in the context of social inclusion/exclusion briefly, in their paper on time-space networks of power in the city, Bridge and Watson (2002) describe the character of a deprived or affluent neighbourhood as "an outcome of the network relations to elsewhere that distanciate from there". They provide a useful example, which is particularly relevant to this research, of access to resources being an

> ...outcome of the net-work that has to be done to get them. These network relations may differentiate between men and women, or minority ethnic groups within a deprived neighbourhood in the conventional way or may crucially differentiate within these categories, thus breaking down distinct social divisions and opening up a space for the notion of difference. They also have an impact on how space and time are experienced in the city and the way that this relates to the experience of power. Deprivation may be experienced as disconnection from larger networks of flow; Thrift (1995) for example, points to the absence of banking facilities, cash machines and credit outlets in south central Los Angeles. Given this kind of network rupture the form that access to credit or cash takes will differentiate according to personal network characteristics. (Bridge and Watson, 2002:514)

The literature has established that the term social exclusion is highly contested and thus, by extension, the term social inclusion is also rather nebulous, though arguably more easily definable. By introducing the theme of power to the social inclusion/exclusion discourse, another contentious concept in social science (Law, 1991; Scott, 1994; Few, 2002) has been brought into the frame. While a detailed theoretical discussion of the concept is not possible, or indeed, appropriate here, it is perhaps more important to convey the key aspects of power that are relevant to the ensuing study. Few (2002:30) argues that power is not "firmly fixed in certain locations (be it people, institutions or places)". Expanding this notion, it is helpful to consider Foucault's view that power is not a commodity that can be appropriated but as something much more fluid and ubiquitous (Foucault, 1986 cited in Few, 2002:30). Thus, power is one of the principal textiles of a rich social tapestry:

> Power in this sense is 'embedded in the very fabric' of the social system and 'resides in every perception, judgement and act' of every individual (Hardy and Leiba-O'Sullivan, 1998:459-460). Sharp et al. (2000) also argue that there is a complex spatiality to the entanglements of domination and resistance. It is within material spaces that people, institutions and social structures become 'entangled' and generate relational power, some places becoming particular sites of contestation in the process. (Few, 2002:30)

The complex interactions and tensions between people, institutions, social structures and power relations are all relevant to the discussion of transport and social inclusion and exclusion. In order to emphasize how these interactions are manifest and the mechanisms through which power may be exercised, amongst different social groups, it is enlightening to borrow an example from an environment/development context. Schmink and Wood (1992 cited in Few, 2002:30) see social groups employing degrees of power drawn from multiple sources including wealth, force, access to state apparatus and idea systems. Similarly, transport system users are faced with varying levels of access to such sources of power and the extent to which an individual can manipulate his resources (i.e. his social power) will affect his flexibility in partaking of the transport options that may be available to him or over-coming barriers which may present themselves as he negotiates the complexities of the transport system. Hence, transport-related social inclusion may be closely linked to the relational social power of the potential system user[6].

Transport and social inclusion/exclusion

Turning specifically to transport, The World Bank (2001) describes transport provision as a part of a social safety net which can affect specific categories of disadvantaged groups characterized by issues such as income, gender and age. The Oxfordshire Local Transport Plan (Oxfordshire County Council, 2000:3) also draws attention to the vulnerability of certain social groups to transport-related social exclusion:

> Particular groups can be affected disproportionately by lack of access to transport services: women; ethnic groups; young people; older people; and people with sensory or mobility difficulties. These groups have the greatest travel problems and yet, together, they form a majority of the population.

---

6   For example, a higher income managerial worker may choose to move from the city to live in the countryside because his material wealth provides him with a source of power that enables him to transcend the paucity of public transport options in his chosen rural setting because he is able to own and operate a new car which bestows flexibility and dominance over time and space that other, less well-off residents of his village cannot avail themselves of.

The Plan adds that:

> These problems can take the form of three levels of exclusion: individual exclusion (e.g. a user of a wheelchair unable to gain access to the bus network); group exclusion (e.g. older people on low incomes being unable to afford access to a private car); and community exclusion (e.g. area isolation due to exclusion from the public transport network).

In their 2001 report, Hine and Mitchell (2001) point to the paucity of data on the link between transport and social exclusion. Their work in Scotland is one of the few empirical studies that have sought a better understanding of the role that transport plays in social exclusion in urban areas. Hine and Mitchell categorize groups who are more likely to experience transport disadvantage (and, as a consequence, transport related exclusion) into physical exclusion (health and age related), geographical exclusion (dependent on locality of residence and transport provision), exclusion from facilities (facilities located at distance from home making access difficult), economic exclusion (associated with high monetary or temporal costs of travel that prevent/limit access to facilities/jobs), fear and space based exclusion (where worry/ fear/terror influence how public spaces and public transport are used) and time-based exclusion (related to time taken to access facilities)[7].

Luxton (2002) identified five critical dimensions for social inclusion:

* Valuing individuals or groups with sensitivity to cultural, ethnic, gender or age differences.
* Allowing and enabling individuals to make life choices and, if desired, to make a contribution.
* The right and support to be involved in decisions affecting oneself, family and community.
* Reduction of social distances and provision of opportunities, if desired.
* Resources to participate fully in community and society.

Transport contributes to all of these dimensions. The valuing of individual groups in a framework of sensitivity has to do with public exposure to the presence of such groups and public exposure requires travel and transport to accomplish visibility. The ability to make life choices only makes sense in the context where life choices can be accessed and this too necessarily involves transport and travel. The right to be involved in decision-making requires presence at the decision table and this has clear physical and virtual access dimensions. The reduction of social distance involves interaction and interaction is accomplished by meeting in a range of social grounds

---

7   To this final dimension, the time that services are actually open should be added. An example of such time-based exclusion would be the branch General Practitioner's surgery that is open for two-hour period on two days a week on an inner city estate. At times when it is closed, residents have to travel away from their neighbourhood to the main practice. Time can, in this case, become exclusionary on two levels: 1) users may not know what time the local branch is open and have to make a trip there on foot (travel time) to see if it is, and 2) if it is not open, they have to decide whether they need to travel to the main practice (time arranging appointment, time travelling to and from surgery).

all of which involve transport and travel and, finally, having access to the resources to participate is predicated in previous interaction, negotiation and bargaining for resources, all of which are related to the extent to which mobility is either constrained or unconstrained (the immobile are in a very weak social bargaining position) (Rajé et al., 2004a:6-7). All these issues are important in the context of the examination of the needs of different social groups (defined by designations such as ethnicity, income level) that are described in this book.

In its 2003 report on transport and social exclusion (Social Exclusion Unit, 2003), the Social Exclusion Unit identified five key barriers to accessing services: the availability and physical accessibility of transport; the cost of transport; services and activities located in inaccessible places; safety and security and travel horizons. These outcomes of the Social Exclusion Unit's study of the links between social exclusion, transport and the location of services highlight the complex and negative role that transport can have in social exclusion.

Hine and Grieco (2002) elucidate further the complexity of examining social exclusion issues. The authors state that the socially excluded are not only clustered together in areas or zones where transport is particularly bad or particularly inappropriate but are also scattered as a consequence of life circumstance. They consider the importance of new information technologies accompanied by demand responsive transport (discussed earlier in this chapter) in accommodating the transport needs of scatters as well as clusters of the socially excluded. Conceived of in this context, demand responsive transport solutions can be seen to provide a practical application of transport as a facilitator of inclusion to meet the needs of those who are experiencing scattered social exclusion.

The importance of understanding everyday experience of transport

The literature review indicates that transport and, by extension accessibility, can have varied effects on different people and this underlines the importance of feeding everyday experience of the transport system into the policy making and planning process. Without understandings of what people expect of their transport system and how it affects the activities they are able to carry out, it is not possible to develop effective transport interventions and solutions to meet local needs. To some extent, this is an area that has been investigated in such studies as those carried out by TRaC (2000), Lucas et al. (2001) and the Social Exclusion Unit (2003). However, these studies mainly presuppose that transport is a problem for the people being studied and they do not seek to develop insights into how these research participants see transport's role in their lives. The apparent obfuscation of the importance of the lived experience of transport, in the context of the individual as a social being living within a community, may also be a function of the more traditional approaches to transport policy making that have been part of mainstream planning for many years. Van Exel (2003:2-3) writes that:

> Transport economists have had considerable influence on transport policy making in the last decades. Most of them hold strong beliefs in rational choice, survey analysis, modeling and forecasting. Basically, though a bit caricatural, transport economists and their models

assume travelers to be highly motivated and involved in searching for the optimal travel solution for each trip they want to make, based on complete and well-defined preferences over all aspects of travel. Travelers are supposed to have stable preferences between different points in time and space and between different socio-economic contexts, to have all travel alternatives at their disposal and to be able to use them, and to consider them all each time using all information concerning these alternatives. Finally, this high quality decision making process is supposedly undisturbed by repetition and, as a possible consequence, habituation. Transport models fed through large surveys and expectations about people's travel behavior are usually based on fairly aggregate price and substitution elasticities. Track records of these models are poor: predictions have often been inaccurate and thus the transport policies based on them have not been very effective in achieving their stated objectives.

For van Exel (2003), the development of greater understanding of attitudes, motivation and behaviour of transport system users is important if transport planning and policy making is to achieve the objectives of lessening the impacts of congestion by convincing people to change the decisions they make about travel. Development of such understandings requires a closer look at how people see transport as a component of daily life.

In recent years, transport planning has turned towards accessibility[8] measurement as a means of revealing the degree of ease with which particular services and locations may be accessed. However, rather than unveiling the difficulties that people experience in using the transport system to access key services and destinations, measures of accessibility have tended to focus on the aggregate rather than individual experience.

For example, Halden et al. (2000), in a study conducted in Scotland, describe four case studies each with three alternative methods of measuring accessibility for car available and car not available travel. Each case study addresses a particular policy issue - economic development and social inclusion, access to shopping and employment, identifying traffic reduction policies which achieve improved access to healthcare and access to higher education. The methods used include:

- simple spreadsheet modelling to calculate accessibility from readily available planning and transport data;
- the use of input data and zoning from a regional Integrated Transport Model to demonstrate how the characteristics of alternative locations can be defined in accessibility terms;
- the use of travel plans and data from a Council's geographical information systems to determine the accessibility of a new hospital for all groups in society and all modes;
- the use of accessibility analysis techniques even if no transport data are available, relying instead on population census data and estimating travel time by mode.

---

8   In its simplest form, accessibility can be defined as "the ability to reach desired goods, services, activities and destinations" http://www.vtpi.org/tdm/tdm84.htm accessed 040306).

All these methods rely on the use of available data and are therefore likely to be the most cost effective approaches to accessibility measurement. Their usefulness as indicators of real world experience is not, however, so clear. Despite the assertion that "A major strength of accessibility analysis is that it focuses on the people rather than transport modes" (Halden et al., 2000:Chapter 13), there is no evidence that any of these methods involve assessing accessibility from the perspective of the system user. There is no capacity within these techniques for exploring people's experience of accessibility by talking to members of the public. The danger of approaches that do not correctly convey real experience of accessibility is that the policy and planning arena is blind to the community's needs and devises solutions to problems that either do not exist or that are more detrimental to the impacted community than the prevailing, do nothing situation.

The hazards of not examining everyday lived experience in studies of deprived neighbourhoods has been highlighted by Williams and Windebank (2000) in their paper on community exchange which draws attention to the pitfalls of taking 'solutions that appear to have worked elsewhere' and 'parachuting' them 'into localities before any bottom-up analysis has been conducted of the problems confronting that area to assess whether the solution is appropriate'.

There is evidence from other studies to suggest that public experience of accessibility is not matched with professional perceptions of accessibility (Rajé and Grieco, 2004a). In qualitative research carried out in Bristol, the authors found that focus group members' accessibility to key services such as food shops, GP, hospital and work/college was poor. However, benchmarking of accessibility did not seem to reflect the participants' experience:

> ...for example, two of the inner city wards where this research was conducted in Bristol are in the 20 per cent least deprived with respect to access of English wards. The Bristol Indicators of Quality of Life Report states that the access deprivation indicator does not consider vulnerable groups such as the elderly, ill and disabled people and this could explain why it does not accurately represent some of the accessibility issues raised by the participants of this research. Nevertheless, this does not account for the findings related to access difficulties reported by women and ethnic minorities in these wards. (Rajé and Grieco, 2004a:10)

The gap between public and professional perceptions of accessibility needs to be addressed: there must be equity in respect of mobility and equity in respect of accessibility for public acceptance of transport policies (Rajé, 2003). In addition, there is a need to progress beyond discourse to practical effort towards service provision that is inclusive and does not aggravate the difficulties already being experienced by certain groups in society. Litman (2003) provides a reminder of the importance of multiple perspectives on accessibility to the evolution of equitable transport solutions:

> It is important to evaluate accessibility from various perspectives, including those of different modes (driving, transit, walking), and different geographic and demographic groups (children, commuters, parents, elders). A policy or project may improve accessibility for some people but degrade it for others. For example, increasing road and

parking capacity, and increasing vehicle traffic volumes and speeds, tends to increase mobility and access for automobile trips, but reduce access for nonmotorised trips...

Techniques that enable the development of an understanding of people's experiences of accessibility are required if schemes are to be designed that are responsive to the needs of members of all communities affected by transport decisions.

After the Social Exclusion Unit report on transport and social exclusion (Social Exclusion Unit, 2003) recommendation of the need for accessibility auditing, the Department for Transport began to emphasize the need for accessibility planning. The Department commissioned research to look into ways in which accessibility could be measured and issued draft guidance for local authorities on accessibility planning in Autumn 2004. However, some of the evidence of what the DfT viewed as good accessibility planning raises some concerns[9].

There needs to be an examination of individual lived experience of the transport system rather than the generation of numerous measures of the more aggregate, group based data that has been gathered thus far. By understanding the nuanced experiences of individuals, policy makers and planners will be better equipped to develop solutions that meet real needs. There appears to be an absence in much of the accessibility literature of the 'how': it seems that there is an emphasis on the exploration of the 'what' in the problem, albeit at a rather aggregate scale, but that this does not seem to lead to the development of effective solutions. Without creation of solutions that can be implemented, there is a danger that resources will continue to be used by academics and consultants to generate lengthy reports for the DfT but that, despite the investment in research, no actual change will filter through to the public.

It would appear, then, that although there have been increasing efforts to measure accessibility, the focus of this activity has been on the global or larger-scale measures rather than on the individual or personal experience. As a result, such approaches can mean that there is no resultant improvement in accessibility for some members of the public because their needs are simply not being identified. Without an understanding of individual barriers to access and experience of the transport system as it is used by the potentially affected public, it is impossible for transport researchers and planning and policy practitioners to tailor recommendations to meet these personalized needs.

While social exclusion has become one of the key concerns of transport policy in the United Kingdom, the inexorable rise of the social exclusion policy paradigm has not been matched by the development of more people-centred transport planning. One of the main developments to date has been the promotion by the Department for Transport of accessibility planning and the launch by MVA and Citilabs of the accompanying Accession software. Although this initiative is not totally without merit, the resulting analysis may be too aggregate, both spatially and socially. In addition, the focus may be too much on problems rather than solutions. The weakness

---

9   For example, the discussion of hospital access in Chapter 3 raises some of the concerns in relation to the DfT's designation of good practice as this example is described positively on the Department's accessibility website.

of such approaches is that transport-related social exclusion is not always a socially concentrated or spatially concentrated phenomenon (Preston and Rajé, 2005).

Conclusion

The literature review indicates that social exclusion is a nebulous term, perhaps akin to such themes as integration and sustainability which are also often seen in the transport literature and are equally difficult to conceptualize[10]. Perhaps social exclusion's (and latterly, social inclusion's) greatest attribute is that it has drawn attention to the social philosophy of travel and transport, an area that had been suffering from neglect during the period of dominance of engineering and economics as the main domains for transport study prior to the relatively recent introduction of social exclusion to the discourse. Indeed, the very imprecision of the term 'social exclusion' may have paradoxically served to highlight the importance of the social in transport since a less tenuous term may not have generated as much debate and academic attention.

The review of literature indicates that there is a paucity of nuanced understandings available about the lived experience of the UK transport system. It is important that policy makers recognize the imperative to understand the needs and experiences of the members of the communities they serve. For example, transport and equity has not been well investigated at the policy level in Britain. Indeed authors such as Metz (2002:134) have claimed that transport is 'a relatively egalitarian domain'. A level of rebuttal has been given (for example, Grieco (2002) and Hine (2002)) and findings of research carried out by the author in Bristol on road user charging and Nottingham on workplace parking levy (Rajé et al., 2003a; Rajé et al., 2004a), along with those of others, dispute Metz's view and highlight the social inequities that exist in the transport sector.

Broad-brush approaches appear to abound, while close local authority attention to meeting local need seems to be largely neglected. This may help explain why the review did not reveal a database of evidence on social inclusion and transport's symbiosis. Without such a database, viable solutions to individual problems will remain ad hoc, while policy-makers and intervention designers will not have data available to indicate what works where and for whom. Only by systematically and centrally gathering such evidence can barriers in the transport system be identified and effective solutions be formulated, tested and shared.

There is evidence to suggest that in the policy environment, due recognition is now being given to the role of transport as a force to lessen social exclusion, seen in the quote below in the context of neighbourhood renewal:

> Poor transport conditions often contribute to making areas deprived as it is often those people most at risk of social exclusion who have the greatest difficulty in accessing key services and facilities, such as work, education, healthcare and food shops. Guidance for

---

10   These terms are not easy to define and each writer appears to have their own view of how they should be best described. Nevertheless, the essence of each of these terms is important to current transport policy and academic thought.

local authorities on conducting accessibility planning is to be issued shortly by DfT and this will work alongside guidance for authorities on developing their Local Transport Plans (LTPs). In addition, DfT and other departments will ensure that accessibility planning is a priority for local transport authorities and other agencies.

Deprived communities can also suffer disproportionately from the effects of transport, such as pollution and pedestrian accidents. More specifically, evidence shows that members of lower social classes are generally more likely to become road accident casualties than their better-off peers and this is most prevalent in child pedestrians.

> (Secretary of State for Transport The Rt Hon Alistair Darling MP @ http:// www.neighbourhood.gov.uk/page.asp?id=699 accessed 040705)

The emphasis on neighbourhood renewal can, however, mean that the lived experience of people in areas that are not undergoing renewal schemes may be outside of the policy gaze. For example, people without access to a car living in relatively well-off rural communities may be experiencing transport-related exclusion which is hidden because their difficulties go un-noticed in neighbourhoods of mobile residents. The elderly may be particularly vulnerable to such effects. In addition, where public transport services do operate in such neighbourhoods, their quality, reliability and cost can also be an exclusionary factor for those on limited incomes or who are time constrained. Having a scheduled train service to an area is not going to enable an unemployed local resident to access work opportunities further afield if the service is often late, cancelled or too expensive.

The ODPM states that neighbourhood renewal can be facilitated through the LTP process (http://www.neighbourhood.gov.uk/odpm/odpm-transport.asp accessed 111004), implying that there is a relationship between transport and neighbourhood. However, there are some concerns about the ODPM's follow-up statement which suggests that any infrastructure improvement may be beneficial to a deprived neighbourhood, even when the change is not within the neighbourhood:

> It is also worth noting that improving transport infrastructure in a wider area will often benefit the most deprived residents, even if the location of the new infrastructure is not entirely within a deprived neighbourhood. For example, improvements to a bus corridor (e.g. bus priority; better information; better buses and bus shelters) may provide benefits for journeys to work, healthcare, education, food shopping etc.

This is one of the issues that this study investigates: whether a roundabout improvement at the main entry point to a neighbourhood will be beneficial to local residents and, if so, in what ways and for whom do local people perceive that it may be of benefit?

Literature on social exclusion and transport in the UK has focused on public transport, road user charging and the different groups which researchers view as likely to be suffering from transport-related exclusion. There has been little attention given to the micro-scale experiences in the transport environment, yet it is as individuals transact the business of their day-to-day lives that the real effect of the transport system on their access to services and activities comes into play. Policy that is focused on macro-scale or high level goals such as attaining several percentage point gains in modal share of non-car modes will not succeed unless it takes account of micro-scale barriers which prevent individual people making the mode choice changes which will contribute to the achievement of the strategic macro-scale objective. Solutions such as DRT have emerged to address local needs while achieving strategic goals of lessening car dependence and increasing accessibility for some vulnerable groups.

In summary, the literature suggests that transport is an important factor in people's lives and can act as a facilitator of social interaction. Equally, however, the literature also suggests that poor transport provision can be socially divisive and contribute to an even more atomistic society. It is within the context of these findings that the methodology described in the following chapter was developed to gain insights into transport 'from the ground up', at the micro-scale, in order to contribute to a dialogue of practical understandings of individual situations which can feed into macro-scale policy making.

Chapter 3 provides a detailed account of the methodology adopted including a description of the methods used, discussion of the need for an evolving methodology and reflection on the case study approach.

Chapter 3

Research Approach and Methodology

Introduction: methods, techniques and options

The previous chapter outlined the policy context of the study and the review of literature which helped identify gaps in current knowledge of transport-related social exclusion, extending the key concepts introduced in Chapter 1. This chapter describes the research approach which arose from a desire to fill some of the gaps in the literature identified in Chapter 2 and, in particular, the evolution of a methodology that would meet the outcomes set out in Chapter 1. An introduction to the methodology was provided in Chapter 1. This chapter aims to build on that introduction and to provide a rationale for the choice of methods.

The methodology set out to investigate actual user experience of the transport system within its wider social context. This objective was met through the use of qualitative research techniques, including semi-structured interviews, focus groups and analysis of web-based talk, which are complemented by an exploratory Q methodology study of people's views on transport, their social lives and neighbourhoods. This method was adopted as an experimental way of looking beyond what people state at interview to the way they structure their thoughts on the issues being researched. This technique was used to see whether there is merit in looking at individual perceptions and how they may vary between transport system users. In so doing, it was anticipated that, by gaining greater understanding of people's priorities and views, some contribution may be made towards scheme design and policy development that takes account of such subjectivity, or is, in other words, more finely-tuned to individual needs. The Q study provides an alternative method for unravelling qualitative viewpoints through the use of quantitative structuring of opinion. The technique has not been widely used in transport. No other studies have been found in which it has been applied to transport and social inclusion/exclusion discourse.

The chapter starts by identifying the research questions arising from the apparent gaps in current understandings of transport-related social exclusion revealed in Chapter 2. It then moves on to a detailed discussion of the methodology adopted for this research. This includes a discussion of why other approaches would not have been suitable, consideration of the advantages and disadvantages of qualitative research and the use of case studies.

Research questions

Chapter 2 described the review of literature which was carried out to identify gaps in current knowledge about transport-related social exclusion. Arising from the review, the main research questions were drawn up. The process of generating the research questions involved initially brainstorming around the central theme of developing an understanding of how transport affects access to services and activities. This resulted in a broad range of questions which was then narrowed down, using filters such as what, why, how, who, when, to yield a manageable number of inter-related main research questions which form the basis for the methodology used.

These questions are listed below, accompanied by the methods adopted to answer them. These methods are discussed in greater detail later in this chapter.

Table 3.1   Main research questions

Question	Methods and Tools
How does transport affect people's ability to access services and participate in activities?	Q methodology study, interviews, analysis of web-based talk
How do different social groups make transport choices?	Interviews, desk research (inc. review of reports on research into transport & social inclusion, travel behaviour etc),
How will particular transport interventions impact on participants?	Interviews, desk research (inc. review of local transport plans, consultants reports etc), analysis of web-based talk
How do geographical dimensions affect transport choices and impacts?	Interviews, census data, travel to work data
How can transport be more inclusive?	Interviews, analysis of empirical findings, analysis of web-based talk
To what extent can transport investments promote social inclusion?	Analysis of all empirical findings/answers to previous questions

Research methodology

Transport and social exclusion: the absence of a definitive methodology

Despite the growing discussion of transport in the context of social inclusion and exclusion in academic and policy circles, there is still a lack of a definitive methodology for examining and investigating transport and social inclusion/exclusion. In order to provide a context for the adopted methodology which is described in subsequent sections of this chapter, this section outlines other approaches which have been employed to study the relationship between transport and social exclusion.

Two reports published in the past few years have used two slightly different approaches to investigate the relationship between transport and social exclusion: the Social Exclusion Unit (SEU) approach detailed in "Making the Connections" (Social Exclusion Unit, 2003) and the Hine and Mitchell approach described in the report 'The Role of Transport in Social Exclusion in Urban Scotland' (Hine and Mitchell, 2001).

Social Exclusion Unit approach   In February 2003, the Social Exclusion Unit of the Office of the Deputy Prime Minister published the report "Making the Connections: Final Report on Transport and Social Exclusion" (Social Exclusion Unit, 2003). This report was based on a study to explore the difficulties experienced by people in accessing work and key services. The study described itself as 'wide-ranging' and was based on a detailed review of literature and research; public consultation; five local area research studies; the results of questions commissioned from the Office of National Statistics Omnibus Survey to explore public views of local transport facilities and ease of access to services and visits to schemes that were considered to already be tackling the problems highlighted in the report. One of the main recommendations of the SEU report was the need for a new approach to accessibility planning[1].

However, while the research approach appeared to be comprehensive because of the number of techniques used, there are some doubts about its usefulness as a method for uncovering the structural dimensions of the relationship between transport and social exclusion. For example, while any initiatives which seek to understand and address the difficulties in access experienced by people in local communities are welcome, the effectiveness of the approach described as good practice in the Social Exclusion Unit report in revealing the real experience of accessibility is questionable. The report suggests that the mapping of access to East Surrey Hospital by public transport is an example of the work of a centre for excellence in integrated transport planning. However, the map provided shows shading representing journey times between peak hours on Monday to Friday. Charting access at the times of day when public transport services are most often available will not capture the difficulties of trip-making to the hospital in the evenings or at weekends.

Other research suggests that these can be the most challenging times for journeys to be made to hospital. The following quotes taken from participants in a survey of access to the John Radcliffe and Churchill Hospitals in Oxford (Rajé et al., 2003b:32) provide an insight into the constraints on access caused by timetabling in the evening and at weekends:

> "If (I am) late leaving hospital, (there is) pressure to catch the Oxford/Woodstock/Bladon bus at 1815. The small local bus between Bladon and Woodstock only runs intermittently or I have a 15 minutes walk to catch Witney to Woodstock bus".

> "On Sunday, when visiting a patient it took 1 ½ hours each way by bus from Summertown to the hospital (a distance of under 4 kms)".

This indicates that, while it may appear on the surface that access to a facility is good, there are dangers in interpreting such data without examining how it was sourced or measured. Indeed, the dangers of measuring the wrong factors in assessing attributes

---

1   Concerns about the merits of accessibility planning and measurement have been raised in Chapter 2.

such as performance or improvements are highlighted by the NHS (no date) which states, under the topic 'Measuring the Right Things' that:

> Several of the tools described on this website involve taking performance measures of a process. These tools are unlikely to be of any use to you if you have not made sure that you are using the appropriate measure for your particular situation. Even worse, if you have chosen an inappropriate measure you are in danger of being led astray and fooled into making the wrong decision.

It is clear then that, with respect to investigating transport and social exclusion, there is a need to ensure that appropriate methods are deployed which are sensitive to the nuanced, lived experience of people from different social groups. Such methods and approaches need to handle time and space dimensions from the perspectives of individuals in all potentially impacted communities and should not be dependent on the cursory reviewing of data. Without appropriate methods of measurement there is a danger that "what is measured, how it is measured, and how data are presented" (Litman, 2003) will affect how problems are defined and solutions selected. As Litman suggests "(a) particular solution may appear best when measured one way, but undesirable when measured another way".

Hine and Mitchell approach   In 1999, the Scottish Executive commissioned the Transport Research Institute at Napier University to explore the links between social exclusion and transport in urban Scotland[2]. The research adopted the following methodology (Hine and Mitchell, 2001):

- literature review: review of transport initiatives designed to address issues of social exclusion and four focus groups and in-depth interviews with urban residents
- three case studies (selected on basis of their transport links and socio-economic characteristics): involving household survey, travel diaries and assessment of local transport provision
- consultation: with transport providers to explore potential solutions to difficulties described in the first two stages

Arising from this three-stage study, Hine and Mitchell made a number of recommendations, including the need for increased targeting of subsidies and concessions; co-ordination and monitoring of public transport operations; increased co-ordination of transport, by transport authorities, funded by the public and voluntary sector; targeted, demand responsive transport services for specialized

---

2   The three case studies in this research were selected for their different urban locations: Leith – urban district located close to a city centre with good bus links, Castlemilk – an estate located on the periphery of a city, Coatbridge – a free-standing town with employment opportunities on the edge of town which are accessible by car but inaccessible for those relying on public transport. (Hine and Mitchell, 2001, 2003)

transport services; revised fares and ticketing arrangements that meet social needs and the provision of public transport in new developments.

Hine and Mitchell's approach (Hine and Mitchell, 2001; 2003) provided a qualitative insight into the difficulties faced by people in particular social groups, such as women, the elderly and people with health problems, when accessing services. Such understandings are important as they can assist in the development of policies that help overcome the barriers faced by members of these social groups. However, approaches that are primarily focused on seeing the world from a category viewpoint which places individuals in separate social groupings can mean that assumptions may be made about membership of a particular group implying that all people falling into that category have a common experience. Such an approach may be dangerous in the context of transport and social exclusion as it may result in myths about people's experience being perpetuated in relation to their social categorization when their experience of transport may not relate to the social grouping but be a common view across different groups.

Adopting a methodology

The two approaches outlined above have usefully collated information about groups who experience difficulties accessing key services. The Social Exclusion Unit methodology was mainly structured around a spatial aggregation perspective, while Hine and Mitchell's methodology was dominated by social categorisation. The two reports do not, however, provide a transferable methodology for charting the social structure that provides the framework in which transport difficulties operate: there is no evidence provided of how those who are considered to be excluded as a result of poor transport provision make decisions about their daily activities and how their community and its social capital affects the travel decisions they may make. A greater understanding of the impact that social capital may have on transport access can help provide insights into how transport impacts on people in various social groups. Such an appreciation of impacts, by extension, could provide the ground upon which more effective solutions to transport and social exclusion issues could be developed.

Having ascertained that there is no current defined methodology for investigating transport and social exclusion, the following sections describe the approach adopted for this research.

A need to look at the basics: the importance of individual perceptions in the study of transport impacts A review of the literature (e.g. TRaC, 2000; Lucas et al., 2001; Social Exclusion Unit, 2003) revealed that assumptions were being made by researchers about how people interacted with the transport environment and how transport impacted on people's lives. Following on from the findings of the literature review, this study seeks instead to take a step back in many ways to ask people how transport affects their lives and how they view transport, or more accurately, their need to travel, from the perspective of their neighbourhood's attributes and the social capital that characterizes their community.

This 'bottom-up' approach sets out to explore fundamental factors about how the individual connects to his community and how his access to services and opportunities within his community affect his need for travel and therefore his need to use the transport system. It was felt that only by developing an insight into these aspects of lived experience could understandings of the potential impact of transport interventions on different members of society be elaborated. As the research has been partly funded by the Department for Transport and the Office of the Deputy Prime Minister, it was considered appropriate to adopt such an approach which it was anticipated would enable the research to better meet the needs of a non-research, policy audience.

Research approach   The research was made up of three main components:

1. Review of literature: the review was cross-disciplinary and thematic, encompassing documents and online materials from academic, policy and government sources. The results of this phase of work are provided in Chapter 2.
2. Examination and interpretation of statistical data: this component identified key socio-economic and demographic features of each of the case studies. Some of the results of this investigation were introduced in Chapter 1 with the balance of the findings provided in Chapter 4 for the urban case and Chapter 5 for the rural case.
3. Empirical research: primary research was conducted to explore the transport experience of people from different social groups and their accessibility to services and activities. In addition, an exploratory Q methodology study was carried out to investigate people's perceptions about transport in greater depth. The remainder of this chapter concentrates on the design and execution of the field work, while the results are provided in Chapter 4 (urban case), Chapter 5 (rural case) and Chapter 6 (experimental Q methodology study). Chapter 7 places the findings in a wider context.

Using case studies

As Chapter 1 indicated, the research concentrates on two geographic case studies: Barton, an urban peripheral estate in Oxford and Charlbury, a rural town in West Oxfordshire. Table 3.2 shows that there are different focuses in each of the case studies. The urban case looks at the potential effects for local residents of planned changes to the large roundabout which provides access to the estate. It also specifically seeks views and insights into the experiences of elderly residents and young adults, particularly those with children, about their use of the transport system in general. The rural case looks at the potential impacts of a home zone for residents of the streets where it is planned. It also seeks to obtain the views of other residents of the town on their use of the transport system generally, giving particular regard to the differences in experiences of those with access to a car and those without.

In order to provide depth to the insights obtained from the two case studies, three other sources of information were also used. The views of a group of other residents of Oxfordshire were obtained through primary research conducted as a part

Table 3.2   Case studies

Case Study	Location	Main Study Groups	Intervention Examined
Urban Peripheral Neighbourhood	Barton, Oxford	Elderly/Young adults	Roundabout improvement
Rural Town	Charlbury, West Oxfordshire	Car Available/Car Not Available	Home zone

of this study[3]. In addition, the findings of two recently-completed empirical studies by the researcher were used as secondary data sources: a study of transport's impacts on residents of the ethnically-diverse cities of Bristol and Nottingham (Rajé et al., 2003a and 2003d) and a study of access to health care facilities in Oxfordshire (Rajé et al., 2003c).

Chapters 4, 5 and 6 provide the detailed research findings related to the urban case, the rural case and the Q methodology study respectively. Each of these sections relies on a combination of different informants' inputs. However, Table 3.3 summarizes the sources of the primary data inputs used in the overall study.

Table 3.3   Primary data sources and methods of informant interaction

Location	Number of informants by method			
	Interview	Focus group	Web forum*	Total
Barton	23	14	-	37
Charlbury	16	-	15	31
Other Oxfordshire	7	16	11	34
Total	46	30	26	102

* Number of people whose views were taken into account for this study i.e. not number of people using the forum

---

3   These participants were recruited from a number of sources. At the outset of the study, it was intended that a third case study would be included in this research. This case would have been based on the Cowley Road in Oxford, an ethnically-diverse community on a radial route into Oxford city centre where a major road safety scheme was planned. However, as the research progressed, it became evident that this location would not provide the depth of information needed to inform a viable case study because, largely as a result of the success of previous consultation on the road safety scheme, many residents approached to participate in this research stated that transport did not pose any problems for them. This is discussed further in Chapter 4 on the urban case study.

Nevertheless, since two focus groups were held in the Cowley Road and interviews and Q sorts were carried out with some local residents, it was considered appropriate to include these contributions in a group of non-case study specific participants. Other participants were recruited to this group through colleagues and friends of the researcher making a total of 34 'other Oxfordshire' contributors. These participants lived in West Oxford, North Oxford and Kidlington.

In the following sub-sections, the reasons for the choice of Barton and Charlbury as geographic case studies are provided.

Rationale for choosing case studies

A combination of issues came together to contribute to the choice of case studies: a) the desire to examine the effects of transport decisions at a micro-scale and the location of planned transport interventions whose effects could be considered and b) the recognition that experience of the transport system and, more importantly, accessibility, varies by geographic location (urban or rural). Each of these will be discussed briefly in order to justify the choices that were made. In addition, at the end of this section, the rationale for choosing two case studies, rather than one or several, will also be given.

The importance of planned intervention location to choice of case studies   As indicated in Chapter 2, previous social exclusion and transport research in the UK had examined macro-scale interventions such as public transport system impacts (e.g. TRaC, 2000). Indeed, empirical work by this researcher looking at social exclusion and road user charging had shown that, while the researcher may have wanted to discuss large schemes or interventions, research participants had much more local and personal concerns. They wanted to discuss issues such as an inability to get to hospital, lack of transport information, the deterrent effects of gangs of youths on buses or prostitutes at bus stops. Micro-scale effects such as these are largely absent from the literature. Yet, it is the day-to-day and local experience of the transport system that has the greatest impact on people's ability to access social and economic opportunities. In other words, it is micro-scale needs and effects that should be targeted through policies which seek to increase accessibility and lessen transport-related social exclusion. Such bottom-up approaches can more effectively meet the needs of people and communities and it is only through their adoption that transport-planning and policy-making can be a driver of social inclusion.

Given the desire to examine the local or micro-level effects of transport, planned transport interventions were sought which could be examined with a view to determining how they may affect local people's accessibility to key services and activities. It was also important that the chosen interventions were in, or near to, communities where the researcher would be able to spend substantial lengths of time in order to explore wider transport issues with residents. It was therefore considered appropriate to choose locations within close proximity to Oxford which would minimize on travel time and costs and allow the researcher to make several frequent and lengthy visits to the areas over a two-year period of fieldwork.

Barton was chosen because, in undertaking previous research[4] (Rajé et al., 2003b, 2003c), the severance of this peripheral urban estate from the city of Oxford had become apparent and raised the researcher's concerns that a planned roundabout

---

4   The earlier project was funded by the Department for Transport and looked at transport and access to health care in Oxfordshire. It specifically examined the potential of new technology systems to better meet the needs of people needing to access the John

improvement scheme at the main access junction to the estate may not be beneficial to the estate's residents. These issues are discussed in further detail in Chapter 4.

A desire to include a case study in rural Oxfordshire led to a search for a location which had a planned transport intervention which would impact on local people. It was also important that a number of transport options (other than the reliance on the car) were available to local people so that their choices and experiences within the context of rural dwelling could be explored. With a home zone planned for one of the residential areas of the town and a mainline railway station a short distance from its centre, Charlbury was considered to meet the case study location objectives. Chapter 5 provides greater detail about the Charlbury case study.

The recognition that experience of the transport system varies by geographic location   Transport and accessibility are likely to have more relevance for some people and places than others (Social Exclusion Unit, 2003). For example, transport networks are less dense in rural than in urban areas and it follows that there may be differences in the ways transport impacts on people's lives dependent on their location of residence. This research set out to examine the ways in which transport choices and impacts may differ as a result of geographic difference and, as a result, rural and urban case studies were considered to be appropriate. The following paragraphs give a brief insight into some of the issues around urban and rural residence and transport.

Urban residence and transport   The European Conference of Ministers of Transport (ECMT) recognizes that how people and goods move from one place to another in cities is a major factor in whether objectives for urban sustainability are met (ECMT, 2001). It underlines this by stating that assuring that the growing numbers of urban and suburban dwellers in all socio-economic strata have access to the services and activities integral to their daily lives, while minimising the negative environmental, equity, economic and health impacts of travel, is the principal goal and challenge facing transport and land-use policy-makers at this time.

While the desire to provide assured access to services for all urban residents may be a 'principal goal' as described above, it is important to note that within cities there are widespread differences in people's ability to participate in the daily activities of their society. Hamnett (in Cloke et al., Eds, 1999) describes modern Western cities as "frequently characterized by growing inequality – both between rich and poor and between different ethnic groups". Hamnett associates this with growing social segregation "between those with greater resources and choice, and those with limited resources and limited choice".

In terms of transport, the impacts of this social segregation can be seen in the observation that people on low incomes walk more than the national average and walking is more common in urban areas (Pedestrians Association, 2001). Due to the priority given to traffic movement over other activities, streets in many communities have become dirty, dangerous, unattractive places. Yet people on lower incomes are

---

Radcliffe and Churchill hospitals in the east of Oxford as patients and visitors from a number of locations in the county including Barton.

expected to walk in this environment. The Pedestrians Association states that the problems of a degraded public realm affect all communities, but they are most acute and cause greatest concern in urban areas and in disadvantaged neighbourhoods. It adds that:

> These anxieties are linked to the movement of people from urban to suburban and rural areas and from poorer neighbourhoods to richer ones. Dirty, dangerous and traffic-dominated streets can undermine the social, economic and cultural life of communities. This is true in all parts of the country, but particularly in urban areas and in disadvantaged communities. The historic failure to address these issues has contributed to problems of social exclusion, urban flight and neighbourhood decline. (Pedestrians Association, 2001 @ http://www.livingstreets.org.uk/page.php?pageid=58 accessed 210405)

Against this brief description of the potential links between urban dwelling and transport-related social exclusion, the choice of a deprived urban neighbourhood as a case study of a microcosm of experience which could be studied in depth was considered appropriate.

Rural residence and transport   Moving away from urban issues, fundamental demographic, social and cultural changes characterize rural areas (Shucksmith, 2000). Harper (1987) reports that rural hinterlands of urban conurbations have experienced a steady flow of inmigration, mainly after the Second World War, "emanating both from the surrounding rural areas and from the urban complexes themselves". As a result, "agricultural populations now coexist with urban commuters and the retired" (Harper, 1987). Harper states that the new population differs from the indigenous people "in their use of the environment, their social relationships and their attitudes to their surroundings".

Shucksmith (2000) asserts that this movement to rural areas is linked to new values placed on rural space, for example, clean environment, healthy lifestyles and community life. For Shucksmith, "the consequences of the imposition of such values on rural societies may be far-reaching" (Shucksmith, 2000:7). The net result of the movement of people, values and attitudes is a rural collection of people with diverse socio-economic characteristics and ways of life. Cloke (in Cloke et al., eds, 1999) regards rural areas as "fertile ground" for studies that focus on issues such as 'hidden others'. He states further that:

> Countrysides are rich in myth, and they represent territories where an overriding cultural gloss on life can mask very significant socially excluded groups. Issues of gender, sexuality, poverty, and alternative lifestyles are important in this context.

Inmigration to rural areas tends to be highly socially selective:

> 'Gentrification' has been evident in many areas of rural Britain, in so far as affluent people have migrated into the countryside and displaced less affluent groups (Phillips, 1993), primarily through competition for scarce housing. (Shucksmith, 2000:7)

Harper (1987) states that the process of residential change occurring within the rural hinterland "appears as a transition from the dominance of the agricultural worker to that of the Mobile Incomer" – this assumption of mobility of the newer rural hinterland dweller is important to the levels of public transport supply in the community and patterns of service provision which have entailed. Cloke (in Cloke et al., eds, 1999) suggests that "unemployment or underemployment, the scarce availability of affordable housing, the rationalization of local services into larger centres, and the shrinking of public transport services have all served to disadvantage low-income households in rural areas". For Shucksmith (2000), the rise of a rural professional and managerial "service class" in areas such as the south east of England has been the result of rural areas being "colonised" by home-workers able to operate at a distance from production activities and retirement migration.

In non-urbanized areas in Europe, access to transport services has decreased for small social groups with low car availability (European Environment Agency, 2001). The Countryside Agency (http://www.countryside.gov.uk/ruraltransport/ accessed 251004) describes transport as:

> (O)ne of the most critical issues of concern in rural areas. It impacts on people's access to employment, education and quality of life, on the viability of rural businesses, and on the character of the countryside itself.

The Agency states further that:

> Many people (in rural areas) cannot drive, due to financial constraints, disability or age. Some may also be stranded in their homes if the household car is in use. Many people feel they have to buy cars because of a lack of alternatives, even if they find it difficult to afford to do so. Some may simply not wish to use their car so often. For these people, an alternative service which provides access to shops, work or leisure can improve their quality of life and maintain a vibrant community.

Social exclusion in rural areas can be harder to tackle because the individuals concerned are geographically dispersed (Cabinet Office, 1999). In addition, the decline in services in rural areas has resulted in "jeopardising access to services for less mobile and socially excluded people" (Cabinet Office, 1999). For some, difficulties with transport impact on their life chances. Glendinning et al. (2003) report that, for young people, learning to drive and getting a licence were seen by 17-18 year olds as a prerequisite to living in a rural area. For some participants in Glendinning et al.'s study, the car was seen as a catalyst for accessing a better job. There is some indication that this view may be shared in policy circles too: the Cabinet Office (1999) report on rural economies states that access to transport is extremely important in rural areas, while recognising that public transport is unlikely to be able to meet all the needs of rural dwellers, implying that, for some, the car may be the only solution.

Given this background of rural dwelling being associated with access difficulties and car dependence, a rural case study was considered to offer the potential to yield descriptive information and understandings to provide contextual insights into the types of accessibility challenges some rural residents face. Charlbury was particularly interesting as it captures Cloke's previously-described concept of 'hidden others' effectively: the town is known as a desirable rural commuter haven, yet there are pockets of deprived residents in the area who are not within the direct gaze of policy makers.

The wider significance of the case studies

As we have seen, the literature indicates that place of residence, that is rural or urban, can affect a person's ability to meet the needs of daily life. It is important to note, however, that urban residence, and thus closer proximity to the transportation network, does not exempt a person from all negative effects of transport that a rural resident may encounter. Instead, the literature shows that transport can have different limiting impacts in different locations. By examining the microcosm of experience in one urban and one rural community, this book seeks to contribute to a wider understanding of how these impacts can differ by geography of residence.

Since this research is based on qualitative methods using purposive sampling, it is not possible to generalize the results. In designing the study, it was considered that the objective of understanding social processes meant that statistical representativeness was not a prime requirement. Instead, purposive sampling enabled the recruitment of information rich-cases for in-depth analysis. The advantage of such an approach is that it allows the researcher to identify specific groups of people who possess characteristics relevant to the social phenomenon being studied. In this research, the specific groups of concern were a) residents of a deprived urban estate in proximity to a planned transport intervention, within this group, two sub-groups were also examined: elderly residents and young adults, and b) residents of a rural town where a transport intervention was planned, within this group, two sub-groups were also examined: people with access to a car and people without access to a car. Across both case studies, differences in income levels were also important.

In order to set the case study findings in context, the research also purposively sought the views of other residents of Oxfordshire, none of whom lived in the two case study areas. This group of participants was probed to explore the range and nature of their views, experiences and behaviours with respect to transport in order to investigate whether these reflected the information obtained in the two case studies.

While the findings are not generalisable, they may have wider significance in as much as they are based on the exploration of particular issues with respondents who have particular features and characteristics. Thus, while it would be incorrect to suggest that all residents of deprived urban estates would experience the types of accessibility challenges that the participants in this research describe, it is possible to suggest that major junction improvements designed to facilitate the needs of inter-urban traffic may have effects on local residents which are similar to those described by participants from Barton. Similarly, it is not possible to determine the extent to which the contributions of Charlbury residents to this research reflect wider experiences of rural dwellers. However, it is possible to suggest that when a local transport intervention appears to be a solution in search of a problem, as in the case of the home zone in Charlbury, the reactions of residents may be similar to those of participants in Charlbury.

The case studies provide understandings of the meanings which people attach to actions and decisions that affect them in their contextual setting or social world. It is unlikely that the case studies have uncovered unique views and experiences[5] and, in the absence of a definitive source of evidence on transport-related social exclusion, they provide significant insights which are particularly useful to policy makers and planners in providing descriptive information and understanding of the context in which policies are to be implemented.

Number of case studies

In this section, the rationale for choosing two case studies, rather than one or several, is given. In the preliminary stages of this research, it had been intended that three cases would be examined. This was to meet the research brief which had been submitted for studentship funding. At that time, it was proposed that each case study would look at a particular aspect of the Government's 10 Year Plan for transport. Thus, one case would look at road user charging in Bristol, another would look at inter-urban travel along the Birmingham-Manchester corridor and the third would look at rural transport in Oxfordshire.

However, before fieldwork began, plans and provisions set out in the 10 Year Plan had started to be challenged in the policy and planning arena[6]. As a result, as Chapter 1 describes, the research objectives were revised to focus on local transport issues rather than the macro-scale policies of the 10 Year Plan such as congestion charging and provision of road and rail infrastructure. At this stage, it was still intended that three case studies would be employed. Each of these would focus on different transport interventions and different social groups. The choice of Barton and Charlbury has already been detailed. However, as footnote 21 indicates, a third case study of Cowley Road, a radial route into Oxford city centre was also planned. This case would have looked at a road safety scheme and concentrated on the views of ethnic minority residents.

Whereas the Barton case provided a fruitful location for the research, the Cowley Road 'case' was not, at the time of this research, viable as a full case study[7]. As indicated previously, once in the field, it quickly became clear that a decision needed to be made about whether this case study should be pursued amongst a community suffering from consultation fatigue, whether an alternative case study should be sought or whether the two other cases were likely to yield substantial findings to meet the desired outcomes of the research.

Since Barton had already generated a wealth of information and Charlbury was beginning to do so, it was decided in consultation with academic advisors, that the two case studies would provide a rich seam of data to meet the study's objectives.

---

5   For example, the other research on social exclusion and transport carried out by this researcher in Bristol, Nottingham and Oxfordshire also uncovered similar issues in relation to the use of the public transport system as the participants in this research raised. (See, for example, Rajé et al., 2003a and 2003b).

6   For example, the development of the proposed road user charging scheme was put on hold.

7   However, the materials collected in the pilot investigation of the Cowley Road have been incorporated into the study.

Indeed, there was some concern on reflection at that time, that three cases may have provided too much information for a research project of this type which is essentially limited in terms of fieldwork time and report size. This in turn raises the issue of whether one case, or several, may have been appropriate. The preceding discussion suggests that several case studies would not have added to the study and may have jeopardized the richness of insights that were revealed through the use of two case studies which could be concentrated on in-depth. One case study would have generated insights into a microcosm of experience in a particular area. But, by concentrating on only one case study, the different ways in which transport affects different people's lives would not have been revealed as successfully. In addition, the desire to examine the impacts of different transport interventions on local residents would not have been possible in one case study.

The need for flexibility with respect to case studies described here highlights one of the key advantages of qualitative research. It is flexible and can, more easily than quantitative research, be adapted. As more is learnt about the research phenomena and setting, it is not uncommon for there to be a need for modification and the possibilities inherent in the continuous process of design in qualitative research can be an advantage.

Conducting the research: techniques and considerations

Interviews

The main technique for obtaining the largest proportion of data for this research was semi-structured interviewing. This type of in-depth interview allows the researcher to explore individual views and experiences and is particularly helpful when looking at complex issues such as transport and travel needs. These interviews have an advantage over focus groups in that 'undecided' respondents will not be 'swayed' by those with stronger views, and they allow people who would lack confidence in a group discussion to participate.

An interview guide was drawn up (see Appendix 1), however, the National Centre for Social Research[8] (2002) reminds us that it is important that questioning is flexible enough to allow the interviewer to respond to the interviewee's concerns. As such, the interviews conducted for this study may be more accurately described as conversations with purpose. The researcher was responsive to each interviewee's comments and this meant that themes were sometimes discussed to different extents with different participants. By using these conversations with purpose, the research sought to provide explanation of attitudes and explore a range and diversity of views. The essence of the discussions was focused on transport, neighbourhood and social network issues and was ultimately aimed at providing an insight into the factors

---

8   The National Centre for Social Research is a not-for-profit company based in London that concentrates on work of public interest. The Centre conducts social research on behalf of a range of public bodies, including central government departments and agencies, local authorities, Universities, Research councils and Charitable trusts and foundations. (http://www.natcen.ac.uk/natcen/pages/au_ourresearch.htm accessed 280795).

that affect different people's transport choices and their accessibility to services and activities.

Responses to questions were written down by the researcher and additional notes, such as observations about surroundings, were made immediately after the interview. The decision to take notes rather than record the interviews was made early in the research process based on the researcher's previous experience of carrying out similar work in Bristol and Nottingham. The presence of the mini-disc recording discussions in that research had sometimes been disruptive for the interviewer (e.g. checking it was working, dealing with technical faults), as well as making some participants feel uneasy about talking while it was on. Some people had also refused to be recorded. Another important issue was that many interviews were held in conjunction with the Q sorting exercise which required the hand written recording of the pattern of distribution of a participant's sort and subsequent questions. It was considered to be tidier and less time-consuming for the participant if the researcher did not have to also monitor recording equipment, using a single document for the written recording of all sort and interview information together instead.

Using web-based talk

The interview material was complemented by focus group data from residents of Barton and other parts of Oxfordshire as well as information obtained by "listening" to "electronic chat", that is, using internet forums to understand local concerns. Two internet forums were regularly visited throughout the empirical research period to monitor local opinion in Oxfordshire (a) on access issues related to the city centre (www.oxfordshireforums.co.uk hosted by the publishers of the local papers, the Oxford Times and Oxford Mail) and (b) a Charlbury-based information site (www.charlbury.info) to obtain an insight into the types of topics and, in particular, the transport issues that concerned residents of Charlbury.

It was felt that, if it is accepted that people tend to talk about an issue when it is of concern to them, the examination of electronic sources could be considered to be helpful in developing a sense of concerns amongst a community. Also, as postings to discussion groups are dated, changes in concerns over time may be revealed.

Interestingly, this non-researcher-prompted naturally occurring electronic talk did prove to be a useful resource for developing local understandings. In addition, there were relatively frequent references to transport issues. The use of such sources is discussed further in Chapter 5.

Focus groups

Focus groups were the third method used to investigate participants' views. The questions in the interview guide in Appendix 1 were used to loosely structure these group discussions, however, emphasis was placed on allowing participants to interact and thereby capitalize on communication between them in order to generate insights into their experiences of the transport system.

In order to obtain shared views and experiences, as well as understandings of where people held conflicting viewpoints, focus groups were carried out with homogenous groups such as the elderly and Asian women.

All contributions were recorded by the researcher and additional notes made about issues such as non-verbal communication and conditions at the venue.

Q methodology study: an experimental approach to understanding lived experience of transport

In order to examine participants' subjective views of transport, a Q Methodology study was also conducted. Q[9] methodology was invented by British physicist-psychologist William Stephenson (1935). According to Brown (1996:561),

> (it) is most often associated with quantitative analysis due to its involvement with factor analysis. Statistical procedures aside, however, what Stephenson was interested in providing was a way to reveal the subjectivity involved in any situation, e.g., in aesthetic judgment, poetic interpretation, perceptions of organizational role, political attitudes, appraisals of health care, experiences of bereavement, perspectives on life and the cosmos, et cetera ad infinitum. It is life as lived from the standpoint of the person living it that is typically passed over by quantitative procedures, and it is subjectivity in this sense that Q methodology is designed to examine and that frequently engages the attention of the qualitative researcher interested in more than just life measured by the pound.

On June 28, 1935, Stephenson wrote a letter to the Editor of the science journal Nature introducing some of the main concepts of an alternative technique for applying factor analysis, thus initiating the development of what has come to be known as Q methodology. The letter eventually appeared in the 24 August 1935 issue of Nature and is reproduced here to provide background about the method and also to indicate that, despite the technique having been conceived 70 years ago, it has had little application in fields such as geography and transport.

Stephenson's letter: Technique of Factor Analysis

"Factor analysis is a subject upon which Prof. G. H. Thomson, Dr. Wm. Brown and others have frequently written letters to Nature. This analysis is concerned with a selected population of n individuals each of whom has been measured in m tests. The $(m)(m-1)/2$ intercorrelations for these m variables are subjected to either a Spearman or other factor analysis.

The technique, however, can also be inverted. We begin with a population of n different tests (or essays, pictures, traits or other measurable material), each of which is measured

---

9   The naming of the technique as 'Q' appears to be a deliberate attempt to distinguish it from more familiar R methodology (which identifies similarities across traits such as age, gender etc). "Q is more than just an alternative statistical method: it represents a fundamentally different philosophical approach to social science research and measurement. Among the distinguishing features of Q is that, in contrast to other research methods, it does not use concepts or measures that have been pre-specified by the researcher or require large numbers of participants to produce valid results" (Addams in Addams and Proops, 2000:15).

or scaled by m individuals. The (m)(m-1)/2 intercorrelations are then factorised in the usual way.

This inversion has interesting practical applications. It brings the factor technique from group and field work into the laboratory, and reaches into spheres of work hitherto untouched or not amendable to factorisation. It is especially valuable in experimental aesthetics and in educational psychology, no less than in pure psychology.

It allows a completely new series of studies to be made on the Spearman 'central intellective factor' (g), and also allows tests to be made of the Two Factor Theorem under greatly improved experimental conditions. Data on these and other points are to be published in due course in the British Journal of Psychology.

W. Stephenson, Psychological Laboratory, University College, Gower Street, London, W.C.1.June 28."

Source: Brown, S (2005) contribution to Q method listserv: Q-METHOD@LISTSERV. KENT.EDU from sbrown@KENT.EDU, Mon, June 27, 2005 12:19 pm

Q Methodology establishes systematic patterns by identifying individuals who share attitudes and gives a structure to subjective opinion and has the potential to uncover insights into major social groupings' construct of transport in terms of behaviour responses rather than social-demographic categories. For example, it may be that elderly Asian women may see their transport needs in a similar light to young white single mothers. This could have implications for transport policy and planning. For example, provision of a flexible mini-bus service may be more suitable to their common needs than a fixed route bus service, offering potential economies of scale related to operation of a flexible bus service with a greater demand when the needs of these two social groups are pooled together as against the financial unfeasibility of running a service for only one of the groups. Such needs across social groups may not have been revealed by other techniques.

Since Q methodology offers a way of revealing patterns and connections in opinions that cannot be revealed by non-statistical techniques, it was felt appropriate to adopt this technique and complement it with interviews with participants in order to obtain a clearer picture of the range of opinions amongst the people involved in the research. This combined method was considered to bring a "macroscopic people-oriented research design" (Valenta and Wigger, 1997:508) to the research that could be used to identify and categorize opinions and uncover underlying perceptions.

A reflection on the views of other researchers using Q methodology is useful in illustrating the technique's attributes in the context of this work. Barry and Proops (1999:345), discussing the benefits of using Q methodology for exploring "how the 'public' views environmental issues and policies", state that they "believe that information from Q could assist environmental policy making in two ways":

First, it would identify for policy makers the ways environmental issues are perceived by various groups, allowing the identification of common issues or perspectives in the population. Policies directed towards any such widely shared concerns would be likely to receive good social and political support, and be effective. While Q does not directly give an indication of the relative strengths with which the various discourses are adhered to by the population at large, the discourses identified can be related back to the individuals participating, to give at least the impression of what likely adherence there is in a wider population for each discourse.

Second, it would become apparent if different groups in society had markedly different perspectives on certain environmental concerns. This would suggest what policies would be likely to receive support, and from whom, allowing the policies to be formulated in a way most likely to generate wide acceptance. For example, a segment of society may see problems of unemployment as far more pressing than environmental protection. In that case, identifying environmental policies which simultaneously reduce environmental damage and increase the demand for labour (e.g. replacing labour taxes by environmental taxes) would help ensure the environmental policies received wider political support.

Q methodology offers a way of examining discourse on a subject from the perspective of the research participants:

> Investigating a variety of accounts…requires a methodology that is designed to identify the similarities and differences in accounts from within a particular culture…Q-methodology…generates diverse accounts that are not easily characterised as pre-defined attitudes or beliefs. (Also) often unexpected ideas or themes emerge through a cultural rather than an individual focus. (Risdon et al., 2003:377)

Steelman and Maguire (1999:2) describe Q-Methodology as a tool for facilitating public involvement and understanding participant perspectives, in their case, on national forest management. They describe the benefits of Q to systematic analysis of participant perspectives in the following extract:

> Surveys, contingent valuation, focus groups, and multiattribute utility analysis all have been employed by policy analysts to articulate the public's priorities among diverse goals (Fischhoff 1991; Gregory and Keeney 1994; Keeney and Raiffa 1976; Keeney et al. 1990). Surveys and contingent valuation suffer from difficulties in designing and administering the questions and interpreting the results (Keeney et al. 1990). Focus groups are often small and unrepresentative and no specific guidelines exist to elicit a systematic understanding of value-relevant information (Keeney et al. 1990)…An inductive, yet systematic, methodology is needed to provide information on public viewpoints, values and positions.

> Q-methodology has emerged to fill this void. Q-methodology promises to lend sharper, more systematic insight into the values and preferences held by the public. Oftentimes bureaucrats, researchers and analysts prefer to deal with 'facts' or empirically established data and therefore avoid addressing value issues and public preferences. This can occur because subjectivity, or an individual's personal point of view, is often thought to be difficult, if not impossible, to study with any degree of precision. Q-methodology provides researchers and analysts with a "systematic and rigorously quantitative means for examining human subjectivity (McKeown and Thomas 1988)".

The method is particularly useful because it enables the researcher "to identify groups of participants who make sense of (and who hence Q 'sort') a pool of items in comparable ways" (Watts and Stenner, 2004:3) through the use of a by-person factor analysis.

By providing a systematic method for investigating the subjectivity of individuals, Q methodology offers an opportunity to develop insights into public perspectives on transport and its social dimensions. A review of literature on Q methodology suggests that this is a relatively new approach in transport: the only published reports of studies using the method in the transportation context which have been found are a Q study of the environmental discourses related to the expansion of Amsterdam's Schiphol Airport (van Eeten, 2000), a study of motives for using the motor car (Steg et al., 2001) and an investigation of medium-distance travel decision-making in the Netherlands (van Exel et al., 2003, van Exel, 2003). Because the method's application is innovative and exploratory, it was considered preferable to present the detailed development, administration and findings of the study together in Chapter 6.

Data analysis

All notes were transcribed as soon as possible after each interview and focus group. The content of the resultant text was then analysed and common and disparate themes extracted. The researcher did not have pre-conceived categories for analysis prior to examining the data but allowed the topics therein to dictate the thematic groupings.

The postings to the internet forums were also analysed for themes and relevance to the research's topics of interest. The findings of this exercise have been woven through the two main results chapters (Chapter 4 – urban case, Chapter 5 – rural case) to provide depth to the interview and focus group data.

The Q study was analysed using PQMethod[10] software. A detailed description of the analysis and findings of the study can be found in Chapter 6.

Making contact: endeavouring for engagement

The researcher's previous experience indicated that it is difficult to carry out qualitative research in a community without a local "gatekeeper" who assists with recruitment of appropriate participants and advises on selection of venues (Rajé et al., 2002; Rajé et al., 2004a). In research carried out in Bristol and Nottingham with groups of people who tended to be less socially included, initial contact with such potential facilitators was made by visiting the field sites and talking to local people at key facilities[11]. In this way, contact was made with people who could provide access to key social networks in the local community.

A similar approach to recruitment was adopted for this study, relying on a number of methods of making contact with local people. Notices were put up in key locations such as the Post Office and community centre, inviting people to participate

---

10 PQMethod is a freeware statistical programme tailored to the requirements of Q studies (PQMethod Manual available @ www.rz.unibw-muenchen.de/~p41bsmk/qmethod/pqmanual.htm).

11 Such as community centres, post offices, local shops and other venues where people participate in activities (e.g. community translation service providers).

in the research. A notice was also placed on Charlbury's local information website. In addition, the researcher spent several days at a drop-in centre used by parents with small children and at a local information centre in Barton, asking people if they would be willing to take part. People were also approached on-street in each field site and asked if they would be willing to be interviewed. Finally, leaflets were distributed by hand to homes in Barton and Charlbury asking people to take part.

The use of incentives was also found to be desirable in previous work as participants considered that receiving a financial reward for offering their views indicated that their responses were valued by the researchers. All participants agreeing to take part in this study were entered into a prize draw for £100 worth of vouchers from a well-known high street retailer.

After contact had been made with a single individual and an interview subsequently held, it was anticipated that all other investigation of their personal network would be through a snowball sampling procedure since such an approach is described as "a valuable tool in studying the lifestyles of groups often located outside mainstream social research" (Atkinson and Flint, 2001). However, the snowball technique was not successful in facilitating contact with potential participants. The problems associated with the method are described in greater detail in the following section which looks at the limitations of the study.

Limitations of study

Snowball sampling   One of the main difficulties experienced in conducting this research was in making effective contact with people who were willing to participate. By their very nature, people who are less socially included are difficult to make contact with. Difficulties of engagement were experienced on a number of levels. Even when contact had been made and an appointment scheduled, some people were unavailable when the researcher arrived for the interview. Others made a number of repeated appointments but, at the allotted time, would report that they were too busy or otherwise unable to take part on that day. Also, despite an extensive leaflet-drop at 200 households in Barton and 100 in Charlbury inviting people to participate and offering the incentive of being entered into a prize draw for £100 in vouchers, no one contacted the researcher offering to be interviewed.

In addition, while it had been intended that a snowball technique would be adopted to explore the views of people connected by a social network, interviewees were generally not willing to provide names and contact details for people to be contacted with a view to inviting them to participate in the study. Comments made included "I wouldn't like to give you a name of someone, that wouldn't be right," "I don't know anyone," "I can give you my friend's name but I don't know his address or phone number," "I wouldn't like to say". Some participants took the researcher's business card and said they would ask their friends or neighbours to take part but none of these yielded a positive response.

The difficulties of using a snowball technique have been recognized by Atkinson and Flint (2001) who underline that referrals are dependent on subjective perceptions of initial respondents. In addition, the technique may have been less successful in this case than it had been in a previous study by the researcher (Rajé et al., 2002; 2003a;

2003d; 2004a) because residents of the two field sites appeared to be less likely to be members of community groups or active in their neighbourhoods than participants in the previous study who had often been initially involved in the research through existing community groups.

It would appear then that amongst highly atomized individuals, the snowball technique may not be particularly fruitful. It may also be the case that some of the most vulnerable and least empowered are the most difficult to reach by the snowball technique if the research is interview based and requires a considerable time commitment by a subject. The study that more successfully deployed the snowball technique by this researcher relied on respondents to a travel diary questionnaire supplying referrals who may also be willing to complete the mail-back diary: approximately 50% of the diaries that were returned in that research provided one or more snowball contacts (Rajé et al., 2004a).

The need for an evolving methodology: from focus groups and travel diaries to interviews   As previously mentioned, a multi-method approach was adopted for the empirical component of this research. While transport research has often been largely based on quantitative methods, measuring indicators such as average trip distance or number of trips per day, the relatively recent interest in the social dimension of transport has ensured that qualitative techniques have also entered the mainstream transport realm.

In order to capture the complexity of individual experience of transport and its impacts, qualitative techniques can provide the nuanced insights that quantitative methods can fail to offer. Conversely, quantitative methods can facilitate analysis which would be impossible through purely qualitative means. This study is largely qualitative, using semi-structured interviews, focus groups and the analysis of web-based talk as its main investigative techniques. However, these interviews methods are complemented by an exploratory Q methodology study, a method that uses quantitative techniques to analyze qualitative viewpoints. Having looked at each of the methods in greater depth earlier in this chapter, this section describes the need for adopting a dynamic, responsive methodological approach as the research evolved.

As set out in Chapter 1, the purpose of this research is to investigate the complexities of travel amongst different social groups and, in particular, the problematic of travel amongst marginalized groups. In so doing, this research seeks to produce an improved understanding of the extent to which transport investments can promote social inclusion. Once the research began, it became evident that while some of the issues above have been addressed to some extent in the transport and social inclusion/exclusion literature, there appears to be a gap in the fundamental understanding of how transport and travel are viewed by different people and the ways in which people feel transport affects their life.

Without an understanding of what it is people want from transport and their perceptions of how transport can improve their ability to participate in activities, the policy-making and academic communities may be developing proposals and schemes which do not meet local people's needs. It may indeed be the case that current understandings of the interaction between transport and social inclusion/exclusion have been largely influenced by the methodological approaches that were used to obtain insights. The main approaches used to study transport and social inclusion/exclusion in the UK have been focus groups and travel diaries. Indeed, such a combined approach had been planned as the main methods for this research complemented by supplementary in-depth interviews. However, experience of focus groups in the early stages of this study and previous research (Rajé et al., 2003a), left the researcher with some doubts as to the usefulness of the findings obtained through this method for the following reasons:

- It was difficult not to hear the "loudest" voices in a focus group – suggesting that there may have been other views in the room but that these were not being voiced.
- Much of the information obtained was anecdotal in nature and, while interesting, may not have reflected wider experience.
- There were problems in ensuring that attendees were motivated to participate out of interest in the subject rather than as a result of incentives being offered (some attendees tended to just sit in the room without contributing, even when specifically asked questions by the researcher).
- Where focus groups were arranged through an existing club or meeting group, the presence of people who were unable to participate but attended the existing club anyway (such as those with mental difficulties, young children and some elderly and infirm) could be quite disruptive.
- The venue could have a detrimental impact on the focus group's success. For example, there were difficulties in holding participants' attention in a focus group with elderly participants conducted in a large room where the researcher had no choice over the meeting venue – the researcher had difficulty hearing the participants and they had difficulty hearing her.

It also became evident that people who did participate were giving very similar comments and expressing what appeared to be a common set of perceptions about transport and how it affected their lives. However, it was impossible by focus group[12] and interview techniques to know whether there was indeed a commonly held set

---

12   Other researchers have drawn attention to the limitations of focus groups. For example, Gibbs (1997) outlines the following difficulties associated with the method:

- The researcher, or moderator, has less control over the data produced than in either quantitative studies or one-to-one interviewing.
- Focus group research is open ended and cannot be entirely predetermined.
- It should not be assumed that the individuals in a focus group are expressing their own definitive individual view.
- Focus groups can be difficult to assemble.
- It may not be easy to get a representative sample.
- Focus groups may discourage certain people from participating.
- Focus groups are not fully confidential or anonymous.

Source: Gibbs (1997) @ http://www.soc.surrey.ac.uk/sru/SRU19.html accessed 070705

of beliefs or whether researcher bias was influencing the researcher to only hear the stories she was more familiar with and thereby ignoring other points of view.

Similarly, when this research was conceived, the use of activity/travel diaries was considered appropriate. Previous experience (Rajé et al., 2003d; Rajé et al., 2004a) indicated that response rates to travel diaries are often low and that diaries are often returned incomplete. In order to overcome these problems, during the initial stages of this study, the researcher handed out the diary and provided a brief explanation at that time as to how it should be filled. She then arranged to collect the diary the day after it had been completed (to avoid non-return by post) and to interview the participant about the diary's contents at the time of collection. While this method helped ensure that a participant completed the diary and that the researcher could gain some insight into the activities and travel the participant had undertaken on a typical day, the diaries posed other problems:

- There was an unwillingness amongst people attending focus groups to take away a diary to complete the next day. For example, amongst elderly people who declined to take a diary comments were made that suggested that they did not feel that they had anything to put into a diary: "I don't do anything except come to this lunch club once a week," "I get depressed because I don't do anything each day," (attendees at Barton Lunch Club, 19 July 2004). When probed further, some stated that they were unable to write because of deterioration of their eyes and others were not willing to give the researcher their address to enable her to pick up the diary. There was a feeling that, in general, once one person in a group had declined, the others felt that they could also do so.
- At post-diary completion interview, some participants had not filled in any activities and when asked about this, they reported that they had not done anything on the diary day. Related to this perception of not having "done anything", the researcher asked one respondent, for example, whose diary consisted of travel and work-related activities only, whether she had cooked the previous day to which she replied, "No. I usually do but I just put a ready meal in the microwave yesterday". This statement reveals a couple of interesting points in relation to interpretation of diary information: the respondent did not perceive that warming a meal was actually cooking and, more importantly, she did not think that this constituted an activity. While this could be interpreted as a semantic difficulty, it reveals a more interesting finding which is that this participant only felt she should report what she felt were "substantial" activities despite being given a list of the types of activities that should be entered in the diary and being told that anything that took over 5 minutes should be reported. Similarly, some of the elderly who were unwilling to take a diary to complete had told the researcher during the focus group discussion that they go food shopping off their estate and go to the local shops for items such as milk and bread but they would like to be able to go to other places such as garden centres and the theatre. It is therefore difficult to determine how much their assertion that they 'do not do anything' is a true reflection of lack of activity or is, instead, a function of not doing the activities they want

to do. It has been commonly suggested in the transport research community that people do not return diaries because they have not been anywhere or done anything on the research day, however, the findings of this study may have revealed that respondents are actually modulating what is being reported and sifting out activities/travel when they feel that they are not interesting or significant enough to be reported.

As a result of the perceived inadequacies of the combined focus group/travel diary/ interview methodology for facilitating the development of an understanding of peoples' day-to-day experiences of travel and activity, a decision was made to work more closely with individual participants to develop a greater insight into their travel and activity needs, their social network and how it influences and satisfies these needs and how transport affects their lives. This represents a step back from actual analysis of activities and travel undertaken to gain understandings at a much more basic level. Such an approach may reveal the gap between common understandings about transport's impact on people that have become accepted in the literature and the actual needs and impacts that participants in this research reveal. The fundamental insight that this research sought to gain then was to establish how people in this study see transport affecting their lives. It also investigates the interactions between social networks, neighbourhood and transport. The Q methodology study that was designed for this part of the empirical investigation was introduced earlier in this chapter. The findings of the study are provided in Chapter 6.

Advantages and disadvantages of qualitative work

The main methods used for this research, interviews, focus groups and analysis of web-based discourse, are qualitative. These methods have been chosen for their capacity for revealing personal experience, that is, for accurately portraying or 'giving voice' to people's experience Cancian (1992).

The advantages of qualitative approaches in transport research are highlighted by Root et al. (1996) who state that cultural and emotional factors play a greater part than 'rationality' in influencing transport decisions. It is from qualitative data that insights into the contexts and cultures of choices can be analysed. The authors suggest further that qualitative information is valuable for analysing travel "as decisions about journeys must inevitably involve emotions and reasons, as well as economic calculations".

In order to develop an understanding of transport and travel behaviour, and of the need for and impacts of professional interventions in transport, it is important to capture the subjective reality of transport as it affects the individual. Qualitative methods of data collection can be sensitive to the unique personal experiences, perceptions, beliefs and meanings related to individuals (Sim, 1998). Altschuler et al. (2004) describe qualitative methods as appropriate to utilize when a concept is not clearly mapped: in the case of the impacts of transport on different social groups and the impacts of social networks on transport, there is a clear need for a closer charting of interactions than is available at present.

Qualitative research uses a small detailed sample to produce a plausible and coherent explanation of the phenomenon under study. The purpose is to examine a phenomenon or interaction and to understand it. Qualitative methods reflect the belief that intensive study of small numbers of cases generates more modest generalisations but better knowledge of individual cases. Qualitative methods allow fine distinctions to be made in the data during analysis because it is not necessary to force the data into a finite number of classifications as quantitative analysis requires. Qualitative approaches are dynamic, allowing the researcher to respond to changing circumstances and situations as the research progresses. In contrast, quantitative approaches are static as they depend upon a fixed instrument, for example, a questionnaire, to obtain data.

However, qualitative approaches do have drawbacks. The data generated is not in numerical form and requires interpretative rather than statistical analysis. Hence, the results are not usually statistically generalisable and the material can be cumbersome to deal with. Nevertheless, for exploring micro-scale issues and developing insights into social contexts in which policies operate, qualitative methods provide detailed understandings which can be fed into macro-scale policy making and planning.

Conclusion: using empirical investigation to develop new understandings

The methodology adopted examines lived practices and behaviours and, in so doing, attempts to develop a more nuanced and critical interpretation of what is stated by participants about transport than was available from the literature reviewed. The research approach was intentionally modest, seeking not to engage in sophisticated surveys, modelling of activities or other non-person-centred techniques, as its purpose was "to try and build an account" (Latham, 2003:2012) of an important aspect of public life:

> (a) that was respectful to the people and communities involved in its making; and (b) that had a certain truthfulness [a truthfulness consisting both of an intellectual rigour as well as a certain emotional resonance]... Such an approach, in dialogue with the more radical methodological accounts being developed by people such as Pratt (2000) and Thrift (2000a), can help make for a more dynamic and more empirically engaging style of human geography.

Having established the need for a methodology that sensitively reveals evidence that helps to inform and transform the literature by concentrating on micro-scale investigation which seeks to inform macro-scale policy and planning, in this chapter, in the next chapters of the book, we examine the urban and rural record of transport and social inclusion/exclusion as experienced by participants from the two geographic cases studies. We begin, in Chapter 4, with the findings of the urban case. Chapter 5 details the experiences of participants in the rural case. In Chapter 6, the exploratory investigation of participants' perceptions of transport's role in their lives is described. Chapter 7 then takes the empirical findings and sets them within a wider context.

Chapter 4

Transport and Social Inclusion: The Urban Experience

Introduction: locating the urban case study

This chapter provides an account of the urban experience of transport seen through a lens which views an understanding of social connections and neighbourhood ties as central to an appreciation of transport's impact on a person's life. The chapter builds on the themes drawn out in Chapters 1 and 2 in recognising the symbiotic relationship between transport and social relations in contemporary urban environments. The chapter uses the findings of the primary research carried out in Barton in Oxford as a basis for the understandings of transport and social inclusion that are developed as the chapter progresses. These findings are supported by other primary data collected during the current study in Cowley Road, a multi-ethnic area, on an urban radial route into Oxford.

The chapter starts with an overview of the urban case study. A discussion of the findings from the empirical research follows. This is accompanied by an interpretation of these findings in the wider context of transport and social inclusion.

Barton: urban periphery, main stream traffic and turning delays

Barton is a post war estate, with a population of over 4,000, situated on the north eastern outskirts of Oxford about 3 miles from the city centre. The estate is bounded by the city's ring road on one side and the A40 on the other. These dual carriageways bring traffic to the Headington Roundabout (known locally as Green Road Roundabout) which is also the junction where Barton's vehicles join the road network (Figure 4.1). It has been reported in the local media that cars and buses from Oxford's Barton estate have been suffering delays of up to 20 minutes during peak hours while trying to exit onto the city's busiest roundabout.

Housing on the estate is mixed but is largely composed of prefabricated houses, low rise flats and a few newer developments. Some houses have boarded up windows and there is graffiti on walls but this is by no means widespread. In some parts of the estate, there are blocks of garages. On-street parking is common, often with two tyres on the pavement. There is a school located very near to the entrance to the estate. Barton also has a parade of shops: a fish and chip shop, Post Office, pharmacy, newsagents and independent small food shop. The community centre is near the shops in the centre of the western side of the estate. At the other side of the estate, there is a school for physically and mentally handicapped children and a drop-in centre for parents to take their children to play.

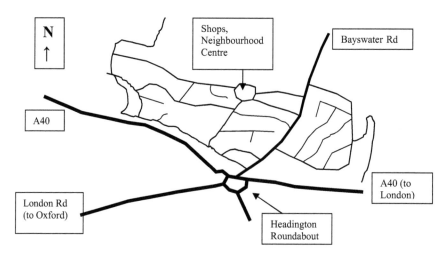

Figure 4.1   Diagrammatic map showing Barton Estate

A socio-demographic profile of Barton

Levels of poverty are high in Barton and Sandhills ward, reflected in the headline
statistics from the 2001 Census reported by Oxford City Council (2003) and based
on data from the National Statistics website. The City Council's report shows that
Barton and Sandhills ward has a higher proportion of under 16 year olds than the
City of Oxford as a whole and about the same level of over 75 year olds as the city
as a whole.

Table 4.1   Age profile of Barton and Sandhills ward (2001)

		Barton/Sandhills	**Oxford**
Population:		5881	134,248
Age profile (% of population:	Under 16	21.8	16.0
	Under 75+	7.4	6.6

*(Based on information from the National Statistics website_www.statistics.gov.uk: Crown
copyright material is reproduced with the permission of the Controller of HMSO, Oxford City
Council, 2003)*

The ward has lower levels of people from Black and Minority Ethnic (BME) groups
overall than the City averages (Barton 91% white, city 87.1% white). The number of

people from the African community is slightly higher than the city average (1.0%) and the proportion of Caribbean people is the same as the city average.

Table 4.2   Ethnic profile of Barton and Sandhills ward

		Barton/Sandhills	Oxford
Ethnicity (% of population):	White	91.0	87.1
	Indian	1.4	1.7
	Pakistani	1.1	2.0
	Bangladeshi	1.3	1.0
	African	1.2	1.0
	Caribbean	1.2	1.2
	Chinese	0.8	1.8

(Based on information from the National Statistics website www.statistics.gov.uk: *Crown copyright material is reproduced with the permission of the Controller of HMSO)*

With respect to housing tenure, Barton and Sandhills has the second highest percentage of households in the city renting from the Council (35.6%). Eight per cent of homes are privately rented (against a city average of 17.6%) and 50.2% are owner occupied (city average 54.9%). In addition, there are a higher number of households with dependant children and lone parents in the ward than in the wider city (30.8% in Barton, 24% in the city as a whole).

Barton and Sandhills ward has more people saying that they have a limiting long term illness (18.5% in Barton, 13.8% in the City) or are not in good health (10.2 % in Barton, 6.6% in the City). The ward has a higher level of unemployment (2.9%) and permanently sick or disabled people (5.2%) than the city averages (1.7% and 3.0% respectively). The ward also has a high percentage of people providing unpaid care for 50 or more hours a week and there are less people in managerial occupations and more in technical or semi routine work in the ward than the city of Oxford as a whole. The largest employment sectors in Barton and Sandhills are Health and Social Care / Education but Barton and Sandhills also has significant numbers working in industries associated with car repair and sales. There are also a higher number of people with no qualifications in the area (33.4%) than the city average (18.6%). The 2001 Census reported that there were 2,770 people in the ward in employment and 185 who work mainly at or from home.

As the information above illustrates, it is impossible to separate the statistics for Barton from those of the adjacent estate of Sandhills as both the census and indices of deprivation use the joint descriptor of the ward of Barton and Sandhills. Turning now to the Indices of Deprivation, the ward is consistently in the most deprived super output areas (SOAs[1]) across a range of domains in the Indices of Deprivation 2004[2] (University of Oxford, 2004). Barton and Sandhills is made up of 4 SOAs (EO1028513, EO1028514, EO1028515, EO1028516). EO1028513 and EO1028514 are ranked 4666 and 4511 respectively (where 1 is the most deprived of 32,482 SOAs) on the Index of Multiple Deprivation (IMD) i.e. in the most deprived 15% in England.

Figure 4.2 shows the relative deprivation of wards in Oxford against a colour-coded index. Barton and Sandhills ward is the area to the north east of the city centre (immediately above the label 'Headington' in Figure 4.2) which is darkly coloured indicating that it is in the 10-20% most deprived wards in England.

Looking at some of the deprivation index domains in greater detail, with respect to the domain "living environment" (which is based on the indicators: social and private housing in poor condition, homes without central heating plus air quality and road traffic accidents), EO1028514 falls within the most deprived 25% in England. With respect to the domain "barriers to housing and services" (which is based on the indicators: overcrowding, homelessness applications, access to home ownership plus road distances to GPs, food stores, primary schools and post offices), EO1028514, EO1028515 and EO1028516 lie within the most deprived 25% in England. In terms of the domain "education deprivation", EO1028514 is one of the most deprived in England ranked at 330 out of 32,482 (i.e. only 1% of SOAs in England are more educationally deprived than this one). EO1028513 is also ranked in the most deprived 10% and EO1028516 is within the 25% most deprived in England in terms of education.

Car ownership is related to household income and lack of access to a car has been used as a proxy measure for lower living standards (see, for example, Goldblatt, 1990; Bostock, 2001; Davey-Smith and Egger, 1992). The Office of National Statistics (http://www.statistics.gov.uk/cci/nugget.asp?id=1006 accessed 280405) reports, for example, that in 2002, 59 per cent of UK households in the lowest income quintile

---

1   Each SOA has a mean population of about 1500 residents and 500 households.

2   The Index of Multiple Deprivation 2004 (IMD 2004) is a measure of multiple deprivation at the small area level. The model of multiple deprivation which underpins the IMD 2004 is based on the idea of distinct dimensions of deprivation which can be recognized and measured separately. These are experienced by individuals living in an area. People may be counted in one or more of the domains, depending on the number of types of deprivation that they experience. The overall IMD is conceptualized as a weighted area level aggregation of these specific dimensions of deprivation. (Source: ODPM @ http://www.odpm.gov.uk/ stellent/groups/odpm_urbanpolicy/documents/page/odpm_urbpol_028470-01.hcsp#P25_ 3012 accessed 180805)

The IMD2004 provides measures of deprivation for every Super Output Area (lower layer) and local authority area in England. Separate indices at SOA level are provided for each of the seven domains of deprivation: (Income, Employment, Health deprivation and Disability, Education Skills and Training, Barriers to Housing and Services, Crime and the Living Environment). This allows all 32,482 SOAs to be ranked according to how deprived they are relative to each other. This information is then brought together into one overall Index of Multiple Deprivation 2004 (IMD2004) (Source: ODPM @ http://www.neighbourhood.gov. uk/page.asp?id=1057 accessed 270405)

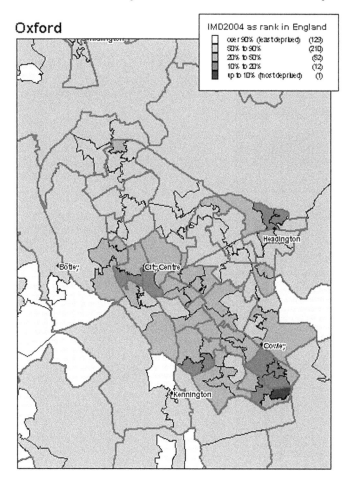

Fkgure 4.2   Thematic map displaying the IMD 2004 results for the city of Oxford

did not have access to a car. This was more than seven times the proportion in the top quintile group (8 per cent). High proportions of households without access to a car were found among single pensioners (69 per cent), student households (44 per cent) and lone parents (43 per cent). The Office of National Statistics suggests that, for many people, lack of access to a car can cause difficulties in getting to key facilities such as the shops or health services. In 2000/01, 11 per cent of households without access to a car said they had difficulty in accessing their GP. This compares with 4 per cent who had access to a car. In order to create a measure of the extent of low income in Barton and Sandhills based on car ownership statistics, a ratio of the local population to the number of cars in the area has been calculated. The results of this analysis are shown in Table 4.3 along with similar ratios for England, Oxfordshire and Oxford for comparison.

Table 4.3   Car ownership in Barton and Sandhills

Location	No cars (% of households)	1 car(%)	2 cars(%)	3 cars(%)	4 or more cars (%)	Total no. of cars in area	Population	Ratio of people in area to cars in area
England	26.84	43.69	23.56	4.52	1.39	22607629	49138831	2.17
Oxfordshire	18.18	42.67	30.54	6.47	2.14	320152	605488	1.89
Oxford	32.84	45.99	16.95	3.2	1.02	48604	134248	2.76
Barton & Sandhills	32.75	46.22	16.61	3.44	0.98	2208	5881	2.66

Source: Data from Census 2001 National Statistics website www.statistics.gov.uk

Table 4.3 shows that there is a higher percentage of people in Oxford without a car than in Oxfordshire as a whole and in England (ratio of people to cars in area is 2.76 for Oxford and 1.89 for Oxfordshire). The proportion of people without a car in Barton and Sandhills reflects the proportion in the city of Oxford as a whole (32.8%). However, the city of Oxford has a large student population (26% of the resident population in April 2001 were school pupils or full-time students compared to 5.1% of the population of England and Wales), many of whom live in or near the city centre where there are severe restrictions on parking which may act as a deterrent to car ownership. By contrast, Barton residents would not be restricted in terms of space available for parking, so it would be reasonable to assume that some other factor, such as restricted personal budgets, may be preventing ownership of a car.

The ACORN[3] profile for a randomly selected postcode in Barton neighbourhood OX3 8BT helps elucidate the socio-demographic picture of the estate:

Box 4.1 ACORN Profile for a Barton postcode

"Type 42: Council Areas, Young Families, Some New Home Owners (3 per cent of the population live in this ACORN Type)

Likely characteristics
These blue collar neighbourhoods contain many young families. They tend to be located in industrial areas with a bias towards the North, Wales and Scotland. Typical towns are Corby, Easington and Scunthorpe. The level of population mobility is relatively low with fewer than average recent home movers.

Heavy ITV viewing	High
Microwave purchases	Medium
2+ Car ownership	Low
Ownership of stocks and shares	Low
Buying home with a mortgage	Low
Population aged 0-14	High

Demographics
The demographic profile of these neighbourhoods is characterised by young couples with children. There are also above average proportions of households without children but with 3 or more adults. The proportion of single parent families is 88% above average. There are relatively few elderly people.

Socio-Economic Profile
The unemployment rate is 70% above average. The proportion of people employed in manufacturing is 63% above the national average. There are above average levels of skilled manual, semi-skilled and unskilled occupations; in

---

3   A Classification of Residential Neighbourhoods.

particular, the proportion of unskilled workers is twice the national average. 22% of workers are machine operatives – this is well over twice the national level. People are much less likely than average to travel to work by car, and more likely to travel by bus or on foot.

Attitudes

Were they to go on holiday, these people would be much less likely than average to want to try new destinations each time or to get off the beaten track. They are much less happy than average with their standard of living. They tend to look for the lowest prices when shopping and to budget very carefully.

Housing

53% of homes are rented from the council – 2.5 times the national rate of council rental. While the level of owner-occupancy is below average, this still accounts for 41% of homes, with 30% of homes being purchased. A significant proportion of the council housing stock was purchased by tenants during the 1980s. The housing in these areas is very homogeneous – over 93% of homes have 3-6 rooms and the two main dwelling types are semi-detached houses and terraced houses.

Durables

Car ownership levels are slightly below average; 47% of households have no car. Cars tend to be much older, smaller and less expensive than average. A number of Durables are purchased more frequently than average in these neighbourhoods – computer games and games systems, keep fit equipment, cookers, washing machines, tumble dryers and fridge freezers. 72% more homes than average are installing new central heating but rates of double glazing installation are below average.

Financial

Incomes in these areas are relatively low, the income profile peaking in the under £10,000 band. Ownership of all types of Financial products is very low, except hire purchase agreements where the penetration is 38% above average. Ownership of investment products is particularly low.

Media

Ownership of both satellite and cable television are above average. There are 3 dominant daily newspapers – The Sun, The Mirror and The Daily Record. The News of the World, The Sunday Mirror and The Sunday People are the most widely read Sunday papers with the Scottish Sundays also having strong readership levels. ITV viewing and commercial radio listening are both very heavy.

Leisure

People in ACORN Type 42 are almost 50% less likely than average to go on holiday. They go out to pubs and clubs frequently, but are much less likely than average to eat out. They are not at all sporty – only fishing has a significantly above average participation level. Bingo is extremely popular.

Food and Drink

People in these neighbourhoods are much more likely than average to do grocery shopping daily and on foot. They tend to be heavy users of freezer centres and of frozen foods, in particular items such as fish fingers and beef burgers. The diet here is not a healthy one as consumption of fresh foods, particulary fruit, is very low. These people are extremely heavy users of tinned steak and sausages. They also consume crisps, snacks, colas, bacon and cigarettes much more heavily than average. Consumption of most alcoholic drinks is below average, except for lager and vodka." (Source: ACORN © CACI Limited 2003 available at http://www.upmystreet.com/inf/msc/det/?l1=OX3+8BT accessed 170704)

Life in Barton: some empirical insights

Introduction

In this and subsequent sections of Chapter 4, the findings of the research carried out in Barton are described. These insights were obtained during a period of study in the area of over a year during which several people shared their experiences and views with the researcher. As detailed in Chapter 3, a combination of interviews and focus groups were used and, in this way, 37 people directly contributed to these findings. Amongst this group there were a number of principal research participants who provided in-depth details about their lives, often over a series of meetings. Further information about these participants is given in Appendix 2. Since the findings are qualitative, it is not appropriate to generalize them by designating them as the experiences and views of all residents of Barton. However, it is intended that the insights capture the experiences and views of the research participants and thus portray a picture of how their lives are lived on the estate and how they negotiate their accessibility and mobility needs.

A snapshot of Barton

Lying outside of the ring road and adjacent to an extremely busy roundabout, Barton appears to be effectively cut off from the rest of Oxford. There are very few services located on the estate and some of those that are there are threatened with closure. For example, the local pharmacist reports that there is very little economic activity in the area and that he may be forced to close (Personal interview, October 2002).

Barton was the subject of a 1995 BBC "Newsnight" report that showed youngsters "bus surfing" – riding on the backs of buses. In addition, the local media in Oxford has reported other similar incidents more recently[4]. Bus drivers have also had stones thrown at their windscreens and "youths have been 'displaying' stolen cars in Barton – performing dangerous manoeuvres such as wheel-spins and 'doughnut' 360-degree spins" (Lloyd, 2003).

Transport can have positive impacts on health by facilitating social support, for example, enabling better access to friends or family. On the other hand, transport can damage health through community severance producing a range of direct negative impacts on health, including reduced social support, reduced access to facilities and restricted access for disabled people. In addition, severance creates indirect health effects, for example disruption of social networks and reduced social support, thereby affecting health (New Zealand National Health Committee, 2003). There is a history of severance of the estate from the adjacent neighbourhood of Headington. In a history of Headington described in old postcards of the area (Jenkins, 2001), the development of Barton Road is described as:

> ...the first phase of the division of Barton from its mother village (Old Headington): the new road was doubtless in better condition than the old lane, encouraging the inhabitants away from Old Headington. Barton was of course soon to be severed completely by Oxford's first section of ring-road (the northern bypass, built from Headington roundabout to the Banbury Road roundabout in the mid-1930s).

After 1946, 1600 council houses were built on the estate. Yet with such large development, ease of access to services beyond the estate appears to have been largely

---

4   Examples of the types of activities reported in the Oxford Times and Oxford Mail (archived on the newspapers' website www.thisisoxfordshire.co.uk) include:

- Arson attacks on cars: "An official Crimestoppers Arson Alert has been declared by emergency services after the number of vehicle fires dealt with by Oxford's Slade fire station more than doubled, from an average of 10 a month to 22 in May. Of those, 12 were in the Headington Quarry and Barton areas." (19 June 2003)
- Missiles thrown at buses (1): "A 51-year-old bus driver was hit on the head by a piece of concrete thrown through the open doors of an Oxford Bus Company vehicle in Barton... In a separate incident, vandals threw an object which smashed the window of a bus in Pegasus Road, Barton." (19 March 2003)
- Missiles thrown at buses (2): "Attempts to stop vandalism and stone-throwing against buses on an Oxford estate are to be thrashed out at a public meeting in the town hall. The Barton estate and London Road, Headington, have been blighted by a spate of attacks in which missiles have been hurled at buses. Drivers have now threatened to withdraw their services in the interest of their own safety and that of their passengers." (15 January 2004)
- Missiles thrown at buses (3): "Bus services to an Oxford estate have been put in danger once more, after a bus came under attack again from a stone-thrower. It was the first incident in the Barton estate for several weeks, during which the window of a Stagecoach bus was smashed at about 8am on Wednesday in Stowford Road." (20 May 2004)

ignored: pedestrians have to use underpasses, cyclists and drivers are faced with the daunting roundabout and bus users are subject to delays associated with using the roundabout. A description of Headington and Barton in 1991 (Murray, 1991) gives one interpretation of the problems associated with an estate that is largely accessed on foot by an uninviting and unwelcoming underpass:

> Barton, over the ring road, presents a grimmer spectacle. Only reachable on foot by a dank underpass, on a ledge-like site slanting down to a brook choked with old prams, bottles and other rubbish...

While this description is austere and does not reflect the positive aspects of life on the estate such as the dramatic views over nearby farmland that the estate's position on a hillside affords (Plate 4.1) or the strength of community spirit that can be found on the estate (as indicated by the existence of community groups such as the Barton Resident Research Project[5]), it is useful as an indicator of the unattractiveness of the pedestrian environment that people have to negotiate if their only route to and from the services they need to access off the estate is via an underpass. This is particularly important if residents find alternative ways of accessing services difficult whether by public transport or by car through the Headington roundabout.

The legacy of the rolling back of the public transport system for many low income housing estates and neighbourhoods is one of broken links on a number of fronts: health, wealth, social being and general quality of life. Severance issues which have limited impact where quality public transport links exist become overwhelming barriers to mobility and accessibility where walking or cycling are the options.

At present, drivers from the Barton area have little choice but to use the Headington roundabout with right turns on to the London Road (A420) towards the city centre and towards North Oxford on North Way particularly difficult. The roundabout has three circulating lanes of traffic and the arm immediately before the Barton exit, the Oxford ring road, brings a heavy traffic flow from the north of the city to the junction. Traffic outbound from the city centre via Headington and from areas to the south of the city also transits the roundabout to access the A40 leading to the M40 towards London.

With a lack of services on the estate, there is a need to travel off the estate for trips such as food shopping, work and visiting the doctor or hospital. While a branch surgery operates out of the local community centre, it is only available for a few hours a week. It is indeed quite difficult to determine when the surgery is open, as information about the GP practice on the NHS directory of local services[6] lists the surgery as closed on all days.

---

5   The project's overall aim is to make Barton a better place to live. This will be done by employing 6 resident researchers for 12 months co-ordinated by one part-time project co-ordinator. They will be trained in consultation and research techniques and will consult the community of Barton on what residents would like to see included in a Community Action plan and a Resident Involvement plan.

6   http://www.nhs.uk/root/localnhsservices/gp/ContactDetails.asp?ot=15&id=K84009 &prmid=OX3%209LS%5E2&st=0 accessed 100403

Plate 4.1   View from North Way, Barton, towards the north

Source: Fiona Rajé

The impact of the uncertainty associated with the GPs' opening hours is summed up by a young female resident who stated during an interview that her mother often needs to see a doctor but does not know when they are open and has to walk down to the community centre to check despite having diabetes and arthritis. If the surgery is closed, she then needs to go to the main surgery which is on the London Road in Headington, requiring travel off the estate and through the Headington roundabout if she gets a lift. The trip on foot is undesirable because it requires the use of a pedestrian footway through an underpass of the A40 dual carriageway which is unattractive and makes vulnerable pedestrians, in particular, feel unsafe.

Reducing mobility and accessibility through poor transport links represents an intensification of severance: physical, social and resource severance are all features of the low income environment. Constraining mobility, and consequently accessibility, through poor, arduous and expensive transport links is unacceptable and highlights the need for attention to be paid to solutions that enable people to participate in key activities with relative ease.

Barton is, in some ways, hidden from view of policy makers and academics because of its frequent packaging with its affluent neighbour of Headington in analysis. This is summed up in a Small Area Survey of Barton published by Oxford City Council (Carter, 2003) which states that "the area is currently in receipt of Single Regeneration Budget funding and for some considerable time has been part of the Headington electoral ward. The major effect of being incorporated into the Headington ward is that data for the Barton area has been very hard to obtain". The small area survey also notes that the Headington ward is one of the more affluent wards in Oxford and that the consequent effect of including Barton within the Headington ward was that it concealed the nature and scope of the difficulties that residents of Barton experience.

While the ward boundaries have since been revised with Barton now being linked with nearby Sandhills, it is important to note that in order to effectively evaluate engineering solutions, there is a need for data to be readily available which realistically reflects the daily experience of local residents. By subsuming Barton with Headington, the policy and planning community has effectively hidden Barton's problems from view: the historical inattention to the needs of local residents could be construed as a form of severance of that community from the policy and planning environment.

Empirical research findings: key impacts of transport identified

Introduction

The research concentrated on the potential impacts of transport on young adults and the elderly. However, it is impossible to separate some effects of transport on these groups without extrapolating these concerns to the wider community. The following sections seek to describe through practical examples transport's impacts on both the target groups and the wider community.

Social capital, social change

Several participants described the neighbourhood as a place where social change had meant that people no longer looked after each other[7] as the following quotes from three elderly women indicate:

> "It used to be (a place where people looked after each other) but not anymore."

> "I can go back to 1948. There were four families moved in and we all remained good neighbours and friends. We stayed that way over the years but now people are dying off and you can't rely on your neighbours."

> "The young children aren't brought up to care about people. It's just the way now."

> "It's changed now. It used to be better."

> "People don't care anymore."

---

7   These sentiments were expressed by all except one interviewee (an elderly male on a relatively high income compared to the other Barton participants who travels to work off the estate in his own car). Members of both focus groups also highlighted what they felt was a decline in neighbourliness.

This sentiment was not confined to the elderly as this quote from a woman in her twenties who grew up in Barton shows:

"I did enjoy living here but don't now. The area's changed."

Nevertheless, when asked whether they enjoyed living in the area, several participants indicated that they did:

"Yes. I must do, I've been here 55 years."

"Me too. I came here 65 years ago."

"(It's) alright, this area."

When asked if it was an area where neighbours looked after each other, views were mixed:

"Yes. I've got very good neighbours."

"I can rely on people nearby."

"Not now, no one would know if you needed them."

"They do things for me, I do things for them."

"Neighbours don't seem to get together much anymore."

While people generally felt that others could be trusted, they often qualified this assertion with the following type of statement:

"That depends really on who it is. I can trust people I've known a while but you just can't trust everyone." (Elderly woman)

"Generally, yes. There's a minority who can't be." (Elderly man)

"Yeah, most of the time." (Twenty-seven year old woman)

Two of the younger participants did not feel that people could be trusted in their area, although both had lived there for several years and knew many people in the community:

"No. I wouldn't leave my handbag on the wall at the shops although I know everyone." (Twenty-one year old woman)

"I don't trust teenagers in this area. I've had a bad experience with my son's friends." (Thirty-six year old woman)

Transport: not dominant but important

For many participants, transport did not seem to be a major concern and only became a problem when they could not access a particular activity or service. When first approached to participate in this study, respondents were asked the deliberately general question of whether they would be willing to talk to the researcher about transport. Some looked rather bemused, making comments such as "What do you mean? I don't have a problem with transport"'; "Do you mean 'the buses'?"; "I just do what I have to do to get what I need"[8]. However, when the researcher probed further, asking them if they had, for example, encountered difficulties in accessing certain places, most respondents then started to describe their experiences, realizing that they did indeed have a view on the general theme of transport to express.

In order to test whether the perceived relative triviality of transport reflected a wider national tendency, views expressed in opinion polls were examined. The results of this analysis are described in Box 4.2.

Box 4.2 Investigating the relative unimportance of transport

To investigate whether the apparent lack of interest in transport expressed in this research was unique to the people approached to participate, national opinion polls were examined. The analysis revealed that the relative unimportance of transport in comparison to other issues in people's lives revealed in this study is also indicated in the findings of national polls conducted by social research bodies such as MORI. The pollsters' results show that members of the public consistently rate many other issues as more important than transport. Each month MORI's Political Monitor asks people:

a) What would you say is the most important issue facing Britain today? and
b) What do you see as other important issues facing Britain today?

The unprompted responses to these questions are then combined and trends in opinion over time are monitored. Taking March 2005's poll as an example (since this was the most recent month prior to the announcement of the General election in May 2005 when opinion polls may have been influenced by the numerous statements of rival politicians), transport/public transport was cited as important by 4% of respondents. Since July 1997 when the transport category first appeared in the Political Monitor, transport's lowest score has been 2%

---

8   While 68 participants made a personal contribution to the empirical research in Barton and Charlbury through either interview, focus group participation or web forum input, over the period of study in both areas, more than 200 people were approached directly in person at a number of venues and on street by the researcher and asked to participate. The responses described here are a snapshot of the types of reactions and comments of these prospective participants on initial approach. (This does not include the 200 households in Barton and 100 in Charlbury where letters inviting people to participate were also distributed which yielded no response).

(in months such as July 1997, December 1997, October 1998, January 1999 and February 1999) and as high as 22% (in January 2002). Transport/public transport tends to fall in the single-digit percentages, way below such issues as NHS (44% in March 2005), Race Relations/Immigration (33% in March 2005) and Education (30% in March 2005) – the most important issues that month. Crime and the EU are also seen to be more important generally than transport.

The analysis of views expressed in the opinion polls suggests that transport appears to be less important than other issues amongst the wider British public. Yet, despite the dominance of these other concerns in people's psyches, the findings of the empirical research described in this study indicate that transport has significant impacts on how participants are able to conduct their lives.

Research carried out on public transport and social exclusion in New Deal for Communities areas[9] also found that "although transport is not necessarily high on the agenda of residents", there appeared to be clear connections between transport and social exclusion (TRaC, 2000:9). Similarly, Lucas et al. (2001:34) report that it emerged, through the course of their study of the importance of transport in the lives of economically and socially disadvantaged groups and communities, that "transport is not a primary preoccupation of many low-income groups and that the role of transport in facilitating or eroding their quality of life often goes unrecognised". However, as the authors of the TRaC report had indicated previously, Lucas et al. (2001) found that poor transport provision was often seen to have implicit or knock-on effects in terms of disadvantages and exclusion research participants experienced.

Barton and buses

Interviewees pointed out that there was a perception amongst the wider Oxford community that the bus services to Barton are good[10]. Indeed, bus service frequency to Barton is good (for example, the Oxford Bus Company service 2/2A/2B operates every 5-12 minutes until late at night on weekdays and Saturdays, and Sunday services at 10 minute intervals). However, developing an understanding of how the buses are used by local people and, perhaps more importantly, their expectations of how they would like to use them, points to the services' drawbacks. These are important because they affect the range of activities people who are bus dependent can participate in. For example, one interviewee provided quite a detailed insight into her views on the bus service:

---

9   This Government initiative was launched in September 1998 as a part of the national strategy for neighbourhood renewal. It was designed to target money at the most deprived neighbourhoods to improve job prospects, bring together investment in buildings and in people and improve neighbourhood management and the delivery of local services.

10   Of 23 interviewees, approximately half talked about the prevailing belief outside of the area that Barton bus services were good.

People think you get lots of buses in Barton, but you get about 7 at once, then none for ages. I am exaggerating, but that happens regularly – usually it is 2/3! There are two different services, including one that is more accessible to pushchairs/ wheelchairs etc (Stagecoach) than the other, so that restricts choice even though there are many buses. I prefer the other service (City of Oxford Motor Services) as the drivers are politer! The fares are different - Stagecoach is cheaper…In Barton it feels like pot luck, and then more than one bus (2 different services at once). Getting off Barton in the morning to go to town is a nightmare.

The buses used to go round Barton in 2 directions i.e. 2A went one way around, 2b went the other way around. Not sure of the actual service numbers. This was before privatisation when there was only one service for the estate. (Now they only operate in one direction). What this means for people who rely on the bus service to go to the shops in the middle of the estate is that they can get there by bus, but not get home. As a result the elderly, parents with children and those with mobility problems are not able to use local shops which include a post office and chemist.

Community workers and activists have tried to address this. The bus companies' answers were that they were in competition with each other and that they would not be able to get round the estate the other way because of parking etc. When asked to vary their routes, they were not willing. However, I see on a regular basis that buses vary their routes when they want to get off the estate quick, missing the East pickups, or when there were diversions or road closures." (Forty-something female interviewee)

The views expressed in the quote above appear to be held by other research participants. A thirty-eight year old mother described similar sentiments. She stated that she had done an ad-hoc survey of buses outside her house on a Saturday because she said that "they often turn up in bunches" and the issue is that they are often late, which she felt must also be a problem at the other end of the route in Kidlington. She suggested that "you can miss the bus outside the house and catch an earlier bus by walking up the alley and through the underpass" to the London Road. When she calls the bus company to complain about late-running buses, she has been told that they get held up in Kidlington, coming into Oxford and through the city.

This is the essence of the problem people have with the bus service in Barton: the buses operate over a relatively long route through the city centre with Barton located at the end of the route, as a result the buses are often late and arrive together. Residents report that the drivers often re-route the buses within the estate avoiding certain stops either to make up time or because they can see another bus at a bus stop where they should stop[11]. With two operators, this can mean that a passenger with a ticket for one operator finds that the other one shows up while their operator's bus bypasses the stop. The unofficial re-routing within the estate also reportedly frustrates residents because the drivers sometimes use roads when they are re-routing where people would like to have a bus service run but have been told that one cannot because of the traffic calming measures that have been introduced on that roadway.

One interviewee felt that a better use could be made of the resources and that the running of the buses in one direction through the estate (which she said changed

---

11   This observation was described by 8 interviewees.

some years ago) means that making trips by bus on the hilly and large estate is quite difficult or impossible. She added that, "There is a common perception that bus services are good to Barton but that all depends on where you want to go".

This theme was repeated by other interviewees. One suggested that there was a definite need for a bus service within the estate and referred to a time in the past when more flexible, minibus-type services operated in Barton enabling access to the central area from all parts of the estate:

> People from the east side have difficulties getting to the Centre (located in the middle of the estate). (Also) Thames Transit nippers used to be around here and they were ideal for peoples' needs on an estate. (Barton Neighbourhood Centre Manager)

Another interviewee, a young mother who lived on the western side of the estate, described how she uses the bus system. She stated that while there are many buses on the estate, it is easier for her to walk through the underpass off the estate to London Road to catch a bus into Oxford since getting on a bus on her street means she will have to travel all the way around the estate first before getting to London Road. She felt that the bus service to Oxford may be good but it is impossible to go to other places such as the Asda supermarket at Wheatley (where she suggested many people would like to shop) and there are no buses to Sandhills where the children attend school, so people either have to walk, although "the lazy ones drive".

The impacts of a lack of direct bus links to other areas were also highlighted by a 36 year old mother describing her 18 year old son's difficulties finding suitable activities to participate in to keep himself "out of trouble". She stated that:

> He stays in his room a lot playing games rather than going out with his pals who come round to ask him to go and hang around. He says there is nothing to do in Barton and he doesn't want to hang around and get into trouble. He goes to Blackbird Leys to go bowling once a week but has to go with a friend in a car as there are no buses that go there. He also goes to DJ sessions at a church on Cowley Road once a week. That's not so bad since he can go by bus to St Clement's and then walk back up the Cowley Road to get there.

The difficulties associated with a lack of bus services to destinations residents wish to visit makes day-to-day activities quite complex. For example, the difficulties associated with hospital trips have already been described but shopping journeys can also be tedious - the trip into Oxford can be made by a single bus journey but a trip to the Templar's Square shopping centre in Cowley (where anecdotal comments from residents suggest that goods are more reasonably priced than in the city centre) requires the use of two buses.

Young adults and the elderly: distributional impacts of provision

Another of the key findings emerging from the work in Barton was the way in which provision of mobility related facilities in public space (e.g. street furniture) for members of an entire community could meet the needs of one social group while being abused by another social group. Specifically, the circular routing of buses through the estate means that people living on the western side of the estate can take the bus to the local shops (post office, newsagent, fish and chip shop and food shop), neighbourhood centre and satellite medical facility in the centre of the western side of the estate but cannot take the bus home as the bus only operates in one direction. Similarly, those living on the eastern side of the estate can go home from the shops/ neighbourhood centre/GP by bus but cannot get there by bus. Respondents reported that this was particularly hard on the elderly who may not be able to walk as far as the shops or walk uphill and that some people must end up going without, while others were reported to have to take the bus in one direction and a taxi in the other[12].

Related to this issue, it was also reported that some older people are often seen 'struggling up the road', having to stop frequently to recover as they make their way to get their pension or milk and bread at the centrally-located shops at Underhill Circus[13]. On pension days, in particular, older people are seen talking while sitting on a low, narrow wall outside the post office.

Participants reported that wooden benches had been removed from the vicinity of the shops as younger people had vandalized them[14] but lamented that they had not been replaced, for example by concrete benches. One elderly respondent stated that older people should be treated with dignity and not have to sit uncomfortably on walls when they are tired. She associated sitting on the wall with the activities of the youth in the area (who she did not attribute to be the sole source of disruptive activities on the estate, blaming adults just as much for dropping litter, speeding and other anti-social activities) and added that she felt older people should be regarded with more respect and provided with appropriate support for their needs (e.g. benches to sit on if they had to walk within their neighbourhood). She referred to the grassy area in front of the shopping parade, where the wooden benches had been, as 'a waste of space' which was 'only used for dog fouling'. She suggested it could be converted partially for cars to park when people were going to the shops, as the cars at present park with two wheels on the pavement outside the shopping area, blocking the pedestrian walkway, causing the road to be congested and making it difficult for people to cross the road on foot between the cars.

Splintering the public realm: using local public space for corporate gain

The concept of "splintering urbanism" was developed by the UK urban planning scholars Stephen Graham and Simon Marvin who were responding to "what we feel is an urgent need: to develop a more robust, cross-cutting, international, critical, dynamic and transdisciplinary approach to understanding the changing relations between contemporary cities, infrastructure networks and technological mobilities" (Graham and Marvin, 2001:33). The authors argue that "a parallel set of processes are

---

12   These issues were raised by most of the participants in Barton regardless of age. However, 6 of the older interviewees (out of a total of 23 interviewees) concentrated on this theme.

13   Five interviewees reported their concern about older people's access to the neighbourhood centre.

14   The removal of benches was mentioned by 3 interviewees. One focus group participant also raised the subject.

under way within which infrastructure networks are being 'unbundled' in ways that help sustain the fragmentation of the social and material fabric of cities" (Graham and Marvin, 2001:33). MacLeod (2004:28) provides an overview of some of the features of the concept:

> Blending several theoretical perspectives and deriving their analysis from a truly impressive range of cities stretching across the global 'north' and 'south', Graham and Marvin position the emergence of features like gated communities, US-style privatized Business Improvement Districts, self-enclosed shopping malls, and edge city developments within a broader context of political economic transition. In particular, and importantly, they locate such trends within the shifting contours of state power and the practices of and limits to urban and regional planning.

The concept of fragmentation of the public realm is relevant to discussions of transport and social inclusion since any "splintering" which may occur would be counter to the objectives of lessening social exclusion. To this end, in this section we examine one of the features of Graham and Marvin's splintered urban environment in greater depth: the gated community, a residential area with restricted access:

> Through the establishment of designated perimeters (usually in the form of walls or fences) as well as controlled entrances, gated communities are intended to prevent intrusion by non-residents. For some scholars, they are deemed to be precipitating a private world that shares little with its neighbours or the larger political system leading to a fragmentation that "undermines the very concept of *civitas* – organized community life" (Blakely and Snyder, 1999). (MacLeod, 2003:5)

While not as prevalent in European societies as in many other regions of the world, the gated community is showing a rising presence in the UK. There are now over 1,000 gated communities in England with most being found in the wealthier south east and London in particular (Atkinson and Flint, 2003). The physical separation of one residential area from another has an infamous precedent in Oxford. In the 1930s, rapid growth of the motor industry brought an influx of immigrants from other parts of the UK to Oxford. There was a resultant pressure on the city's limited housing resources:

> The council estate at Cutteslowe became notorious in 1934 when developers of an adjoining private estate built walls to prevent the council's tenants from using its roads: it was alleged that the tenants were former Oxford slum-dwellers, although most of the houses were inhabited by newcomers to the city. The council was not able to compel the demolition of the walls until 1959. (Crossley, 1979 @ www.british-history.ac.uk/report. asp?compid=22805 accessed 270505)

One of the newest gated communities is being built in Barton (Plate 4.2). The gated Barratt Homes development "Jazz" is located on the site of the former local pub, The Fox, adjacent to local authority-owned flats and is being sold as:

> A modern gated development...The development is within close proximity to the Headington Roundabout and has easy access to the A40 and links to the M40. Buses to Oxford Central and London a short walk away. (http://www.barratthomes.co.uk/searchres. cfm_accessed 281004).

Plate 4.2   Gated development adjacent to local authority housing, North Way, Barton

Source: Fiona Rajé

The apartments are being marketed without reference to the estate upon which they are built, their location being advertised as "Headington, Oxford" – the more socially salubrious adjacent neighbourhood. The marketing information indicates that the development's main attribute appears to be that it is located near to the main inter-urban road network for ease of access to the Oxford-London corridor. The Barton estate has seen other private developments being built within its boundaries but the establishment of a gated community represents another factor contributing to the further fracturing of the local community fabric.

The literature of the post-apartheid South African city describes gated or walled communities as "security villages" (Jürgens and Gnad, 2002:337). There may be some merit in viewing the development in Barton in such a light. Villages tend to be isolated with access to many facilities and opportunities being dependent upon car access: this is a characteristic of the Jazz development. Similarly, building housing with restricted access in an area that is commonly associated in the media with crime intensifies the perception of personal risk to new residents without the security of the gates and walls of the security village. The very fact that the development is gated implies to a purchaser that the area around their new home is not a space to be explored but to be accessed by car from the conveniently located trunk road network. By extension, making social connections with local residents outside the gates may be equally liable to associations with dubiety.

Atkinson and Flint (2004) argue that gated communities are not only an example of residential segregation but are also symbolic of a contemporary turn towards segregation and social withdrawal which necessitate urgent policy intervention:

> In contrast to the view that gated communities provide an extreme example of residential segregation we go further and argue that the time-space trajectories of residents suggest a dynamic pattern of separation that goes beyond the place of residence. Gated communities appear to provide an extreme example of more common attempts by other social groups to insulate against perceived risk and unwanted encounters. Patterns of what we term time-space trajectories of segregation can thereby be seen as closed linkages between key fields, such as work and home, which enable social distance to be maintained and perceived risks to be managed by elite social groups. We conclude that gated communities further extend contemporary segregatory tendencies in the city and that policy responses are required which curtail the creation of such havens of social withdrawal. (Atkinson and Flint, 2004:875)

The emergence of a policy discourse on gated communities raises concerns about the objectives of the local planning community. MacLeod (2004:20) reports that "some commentators imply a causal link between gating and social exclusion". By granting planning permission for a gated development, regardless of any clauses that may have been associated with the permission to help assuage negative impacts[15], brings into doubt the vision of the local planning authority. Oxfordshire County Council's social inclusion scrutiny review clearly states that promoting social inclusion is a key role of the authority:

> 'Social inclusion' is not just 'jargon', but refers to the core work of the Council: helping people to fulfil their potential and to overcome the disadvantages that they might face. It is vital that good quality services are provided to all people, especially those who are potentially vulnerable and need support. Social exclusion, whether through low income, poor educational achievement, illness and disability, isolation or other circumstances, is a loss to the whole community, and as a Council we have a responsibility to tackle both the causes of social exclusion as well as the outcomes. (Oxfordshire County Council, 2004:3)

However, the report goes on to reveal that it found a need to weave social inclusion issues through all Council policy and activity. It was critical of the lack of a corporate social inclusion strategy, a deficit of resources to coordinate social inclusion

---

15   It is understood that when permission was granted for the developer to demolish the existing pub and build apartments on the land, an agreement was made for the housebuilder to provide a new pub in Barton. Subsequently, the building company abandoned plans to build the new pub. Negotiations between the local authority and developer were on-going during the research period and it has since been reported that an agreement has been reached whereby the housebuilder will pay £140,000 of the £300,000 required to refurbish the sports pavilion on Barton's recreation ground. The balance of funding will be sought through an application to the National Lottery Fund. (Sources: Oxfordshire County Council website www.oxfordshire.gov.uk and "Developer will help fund £300k refurbishment" Oxford Times/ Oxford Mail website www.thisisoxfordshire.co.uk accessed 220105)

promotion, the absence of a joined-up approach to social inclusion and expressed a need for greater corporate commitment to the social inclusion:

> The Review found that although many officers were committed to broad principles of social inclusion, there was not a common understanding of what that meant to the Council, or what the Council's aims were for disadvantaged people. There is insufficient lead from the Executive or the County Council's Senior Management Team on co-ordinating social inclusion activity or providing a strategic focus. This makes it harder for individual service managers and officers to pursue social inclusion activity, or to get guidance on their social inclusion priorities. (Oxfordshire County Council, 2004:3)

Given the above, there may be an unintentional lack of awareness of the ways in which a gated community may impact a local community negatively amongst the planning officers of the Council. It is imperative against such a background that empirical studies of impacts of new types of developments should be carried out and findings fed back into future decision-making within the Council as well as being shared with other authorities. Evidence-based planning can do much to preclude the negative impacts of decisions that have not taken full account of consequences on the wider community. Pressure from developers to secure land adjacent to road networks and pressure on planners to secure investment in road improvements by developers can cloud judgement, obscuring professional sensitivity to softer impacts which may have more far-reaching effects on local people. In this case, such as sanctioning the socially exclusionary use of land formerly occupied by the only pub on the estate. The absence of a local pub precipitates the need to travel away from Barton to go to a pub and the closure of the pub has removed one of the only spaces for social gathering from the neighbourhood.

Along the road from "Jazz" is "Renaissance Park" another Barratt Homes development, not gated but also marketed with a distinct emphasis on its convenience for access to the inter-urban road network:

> An appealing development…with access to the M40 – London and Birmingham – A40 to Whitney (sic) – and Oxford City Centre (http://www.barratthomes.co.uk/searchres.cfm accessed 281004)

Staying with the issues related to the planners' decision to allow the gated development and the neighbouring housing site to go ahead raises another concern about the apparent disconnection between the authority's statements that it promotes public transport usage and less dependence on car travel. The marketing of the two developments makes it clear that the car-owning public is their target market. The premise of car-based travel associated with the new housing runs counter to the Council's policy on transport and development:

> Oxfordshire County Council's Structure Plan reinforces PPG13 - the Government's planning policy guidance on transport - by aiming to reduce the need to travel by private car through land use planning policy…More generally, the Structure Plan policies seek to ensure that developments are located and designed so as to be easily accessible by walking, cycling and public transport. (Oxfordshire County Council, 2000:25)

Oxfordshire County Council's Residential Design Guide... is intended to inform and guide developers to provide developments which encourage more sustainable travel by minimising the need to use cars particularly for shorter trips to local facilities. (Oxfordshire County Council, 2005b:ch1 p3)

Arguably, the two housing sites are located "to be easily accessible" by walking and cycling: that is, if one does not feel uncomfortable walking through underpasses to access facilities outside the estate, having to dismount from a bicycle to use an underpass or face the challenge of negotiating large volumes of circulating traffic at the Headington Roundabout. Similarly, both developments are near to bus stops. However, the buses pass these stops as they enter the estate and passengers boarding here would have to travel through several other streets on their journey back to the main roundabout, out of Barton and on towards Oxford city centre. Once again, it should also be pointed out that the buses only operate along the one route from Barton, to Oxford and on to Kidlington, resulting in the need for interchange to access some destinations, while others, often relatively nearby geographically, are effectively inaccessible by bus. Therefore, the private car again becomes the most suitable solution to the in-migrant's transport needs. It also protects him from perceived potential perils beyond the gates of his manufactured community.

However, despite the actions of the developer, Barratt, in overtly marketing these properties in terms of their proximity to the inter-urban road network and the concealment of the development's location under guises such as "Headington" and "Northway" rather than Barton (which can only serve to undermine the fabric of the local community), the housebuilder promotes itself as "Britain's leading urban regenerator" (The Oxford Times, 06 May 2005: 47). In an article entitled "Barratts regenerate local brownfield sites", a mythology of intention appears to be peddled:

Housebuilder Barratt...is transforming derelict land and recycling redundant buildings to create new communities around the UK...Barratt Maidenhead has successfully transformed the former site of the derelict Fox pub, in Northway, Oxford, into its stylish and popular Jazz development...

We have successfully recycled all kinds of sites, which have made good use of valuable land resources, helped to meet the strong demand for new homes and also brought life back to urban areas, producing a wide range of benefits for local communities and the environment...Regeneration can reduce the need for new infrastructure, produce sustainable residential developments and help re-form communities nearer their workplaces, lessening car dependency. (The Oxford Times, 06 May 2005: 47)

Despite the noble aims expressed by Barratt group chief executive, David Pretty, in the quote above, this research indicates that a small community of car-dependent professional commuters are likely to live in the gated development. Working away from the area, they would have little opportunity to mix with anyone beyond the gates and local people would gain nothing by having the new residents living in their neighbourhood.

How this development may bring life back to this peripheral urban area or produce a wide range of benefits for the local community and environment is not readily apparent. What does appear to emerge, instead, is a causative connection between the proximity of the urban road network and the availability of brownfield land to be developed under the guise of regeneration. If lessening car dependency was truly the developer's objective, a site with greater propinquity to the public transport, cycling and walking networks would have been more attractive. Thus, in a competitive and highly-lucrative housing market, the road network enables exploitative development to take place, that is, development that goes against the principles of social and environmental sustainability.

This raises concerns about the acceptability of such enclaves in an area which has already been singled out as in need of regeneration (i.e. in need of the development of a sustainable community). It would appear that rather than contributing to the regeneration of Barton, this is an example of selective social exclusion with the transport system allowing enclave-dwellers the flexibility to look beyond their own locality for social, employment and other life opportunities.

In summary, the granting of permission to build a gated community in a deprived neighbourhood may be interpreted as a form of complicity between institutional actors, housebuilder and local planning authority, in perpetuating and extending socially divisive and exclusionary features in the built environment. To local people, planning decisions such as this imply a lack of engagement of public service providers with estate communities. Residents feel, as a result, that decisions have been imposed upon them with little understanding of their circumstances and that they have little or no say in decisions about their estate. As a result, the local authority may become associated with the arbitrary exercise of power on an estate, rather than being seen as on the side of the residents (Page, 2000).

Negotiating day-to-day life

For some participants, negotiating daily life involves navigating the consequences of their own lack of access to the transport system as well as the impacts of other people's mobility on their ability to participate in activities and access services. Some examples can help to illustrate the dichotomy of such experiences further:

Car availability and mobility: a hidden displacement effect   The flexibility and range of choice bestowed by availability of a car has indirect, external consequences. An example from the study in Barton can help to illustrate how private transport can bring about such inequity effects. The Roundabout Centre on Waynflete Road is a bright and clean drop-in facility for parents to take their young children to play in a safe environment. It is also a place to meet other parents and have refreshments. There are organized activities and parents can play with their children using the materials and toys that are provided. In addition, there is a sensory room for relaxation in the centre.

During one of many visits to talk to users of the centre, a volunteer described Wednesday sessions to the researcher as being "always particularly busy". There is a music session on a Wednesday morning which attracts several more people than on other days. She explained that the "middle class come to the session" because "it is really good and unique". These people do not live in Barton but come to the centre by car. The volunteer stated that, as a result, some of the local mothers did not feel comfortable going into the music session but tended to hang around on the periphery in an adjacent room, feeling that they were unable to participate.

It is important to point out that the centre is relatively easy to access by car since it is located at the east side of the estate, off the first road on the right when one enters Barton from the Headington roundabout. In other words, people from outside do not have to travel very far into the estate to use the facility. Thus private transport is allowing people to come into Barton to avail themselves of a facility and activities which are provided for the local community: people from outside the area are able to travel in the comfort of their private vehicles to use the facility that mothers on the estate walk to. This is an example of what Smyth and McDonald (2001) term "consumer choice" with respect to access to facilities and opportunities coupled with the inherent flexibility of individual choices that a car bestows resulting in the effective marginalisation of those without access to a car.

The parents in cars from outside are very unlikely to come to Barton by bus or even to walk around the area because of the negative perceptions of the estate that exist in the wider Oxford community. In this example, the private car is providing access for people off the estate but, in so doing, is indirectly affecting access on the estate to a local activity/facility. Thus accessibility by car to the estate may impact on accessibility to local services for local people.   This may be a hidden displacement effect.

To help illustrate the type of person who may be affected by such a displacement effect, a brief description of the way in which one young Barton mother uses the centre provides an interesting insight (Box 4.3).

Box 4.3 The weariness of walking: using a 'halfway house'

Sue's story

Sue is a 27 year old mother of three, one of whom is a toddler aged 2 who was playing at the Roundabout centre at the time when she was interviewed. Sue uses the drop-in centre when it is open on a Monday and Wednesday between 1000 and 1200 as a stopping off point so she does not have to walk all the way home after taking her other two children to school on the adjacent estate of Sandhills. She lives on Barton Village Road which is at the extreme western edge of Barton – as far away as you can get and still be within Barton in relation to Sandhills. She said she walks nine miles a day, making three return trips to the school: one to take both children, one to collect one child at 1130 and another at 1500 for the 3rd child. Although she did not complain about her responsibilities for the children, she described herself as sometimes being 'tired of walking'. Her husband works away from the area during the week, so she tries to do all her shopping when he is home to take her to the supermarket by car on a Saturday.

This brief illustration introduces the use of intermediate places of shelter when distances to be travelled are too great by slow modes. The substituting of the Roundabout Centre as a 'halfway house' or refuge enables Sue to negotiate her responsibilities for her children by juggling the time she has available to travel on foot over relatively long distances.

Returning to the almost invasive presence at the Centre of mothers from outside the area, their attendance and ability to do so because of their access to a car raises issues of disparity and social justice. The highly mobile mother has a freedom to chose where she wishes to take her child by car. In contrast, the walking mother has much more limited scope or choices for her child. Bostock reports that walking is a crucial part of the daily experience of poorer women (Bostock, 2001):

> The current public health agenda tends to emphasise the positive effects of walking as means to increase physical activity as well as reduce obesity. This fails to recognise that, for some segments of the population, walking is compulsory and a source of both physical fatigue and psycho-social stress. At best, it could be said to have contradictory health effects for such groups: positive features include exercise while negative effects create fatigue and stress. At worst, walking may be health damaging. (Bostock, 2001:11-12)

The author goes on to describe the pathways by which compulsory walking with children may undermine health and well being:

> Firstly, women point to the psycho-social pressures of managing the demands of children worn out from walking. Secondly, mothers report physical fatigue themselves as a result of long journeys by foot. Thirdly, lack of motorised transport restricts mothers to areas often lacking in health, retail and other social resources. This is compounded by living in places that are often neglected, depressed and intensify mothers' sense of social exclusion. (Bostock, 2001: 12)

It would be fair to say that Bostock's findings do reflect the experience of Sue in Barton and that the more mobile mothers that she encounters at the local Roundabout Centre probably serve to increase any psycho-social stress she may be experiencing. This introduces issues of self-esteem to the picture. Taking personal appearance as a measure, the mothers from Barton interviewed at the centre tended to be casually dressed for a busy day in jeans and sweaters with coats and comfortable shoes, such attire enabling them to play with the children and also to walk comfortably to school, perhaps take the bus to the shops in Headington and then carry bags home. In contrast, mothers arriving by car from elsewhere were much more likely to be wearing rather chic labels on their co-ordinated and slightly less utilitarian clothing. For the Barton mothers, the outward appearance of the mobile mother may have been an important factor in delineating the differences between their respective lives and lifestyles. Consequently, feelings of inferiority and low self-esteem could leave the local mother feeling inadequate and unable to participate in a local activity, thus physical access by the mobile mother may result in the indirect effect of impinging on the psychological access by a local mother. In this way, transport and mobility of one has caused the social displacement of another.

Stretching limited budgets by walking   Staying with walking as a mode of travel amongst low income mothers, another research participant with three children and without access to a car reported that she and her nine year old daughter "are happy to walk" and do so for most journeys, despite the bus stop being immediately outside their house. By walking with her daughter, she estimates that she saves about £10 per week which she can then use for food. In contrast, however, she found that her eleven year old son was unwilling to walk and always asked to travel by bus. With a dearth of available studies on walking as a mode of transport amongst low income mothers, Bostock's findings are once again useful. The author suggests that mothers may use their bodies as a means to bridge the gap between responsibilities and resources (Bostock, 1998; Bostock, 2001). In the case of our low income mother in Barton with an income £141/week, walking is a way of minimizing public transport costs and thereby creating additional space in a budget that is already over-stretched through day-to-day living expenses and debt (Kempson, 1996).

The challenges of accessing key services: an example   In order to elaborate on how transport can impact on people's lives, this section describes the experiences of a thirty-something mother who was interviewed in the course of this research. This vignette relates to access to hospitals since it has been identified that a key barrier to improved health and well being is access to health services (Social Exclusion Unit, 2003). Poor transport connections negatively affect health quality and Alice's[16] story, provided in Box 4.4, is an insight into some of the barriers to hospital access being experienced amongst residents of Oxfordshire. This vignette has been chosen because it represents issues that are faced by normal people, dealing with circumstances that could affect any one of us. In other words, the accessibility challenges are likely to be replicable for others both within Oxfordshire and beyond.

For people like Alice, it is likely that the provision of sophisticated demand responsive transport solutions may not help her juggle the demands on her time or help her traverse the space she needs to in order to keep life going for herself and her family. But demand responsive transport may be useful to help move her husband between hospitals for his appointments, easing the pressure on her time and making use of seats on vehicles which may be travelling between the two facilities anyway.

Re-examining entrenched perceptions and 'stylised fallacies'

The Office of National Statistics (ONS, 2004) reports that "lower income is not necessarily related to low levels of social capital". However, traditionally, persistent presumptions or 'stylised fallacies' (Hodge and Monk, 2004) have meant that lower income appears to have been used as a proxy for the term 'socially excluded' and this ONS finding from the most recent UK General Household Survey suggests that such usage may not always be appropriate. In the context of transport, this study's investigation of the social capital dimension of travel seeks to establish whether it is indeed the case that amongst marginalized groups social networks provide the support

---

16 All names of participants have been changed to protect their anonymity.

Box 4.4 Barriers to hospital access: an insight

Alice's story

Alice is a 36 year old mother of two toddlers living in Barton. She is married but her husband has been in hospital for the past 18 months following a road accident on his way to work one morning early last year. His shattered pelvis has left him requiring a catheter and his head injuries mean he has no short term memory. The medication to deal with his injuries has made his weight balloon to 18 stones and he is unable to walk more than 10 metres without having to stop. She is allowed to take him home to at weekends. In addition, she has to take him to all his medical appointments, which are numerous because of the complexity of his injuries and at different facilities in Oxford. She provides transport between hospitals as the authorities say he does not meet their criteria for hospital transport. She applied for a disability parking sticker as she finds it hard to have to walk with him from long distances (if she finds a parking space at the hospitals at all) to the buildings, this is made worse by having two children who may also need to be looked after if accompanying her. The application was turned down because Paul 'is able to walk' – no regard appears to have been given to the difficulty with which he walks or the strain this puts on the family unit. She says she had stopped driving 10 years ago because he did all the driving but, after the accident, as soon as she realized how much she needed to do each day and how hard it was to do it by public transport, although she was frightened, she went back to driving. She feels that there is much more traffic now on the roads than when she used to drive but recognizes that she needs to drive to allow her to have flexibility she needs to look after the children (e.g. pick them up from her Mum's after she has finished work). She says without a car, she would find it very difficult, particularly in the winter, to take the children home at the end of the day and also to visit her husband each day and provide his transport needs.

---

system necessary to facilitate ease of access to facilities and services as is suggested by the following extract from the report by the Office of National Statistics:

> High neighbourliness and a satisfactory relatives network were in fact more prevalent among households with incomes less than £250 per week compared with those with incomes above that level. However, the lower income households were considerably less likely to give and receive favours from neighbours (high reciprocity), to enjoy living in their areas, and to feel safe after dark, though their likelihood of having been a victim of crime was not very different. Lower income households were also rather more likely to report low social support and high local problems.

It does appear to be the case that for some of the lower income earners in this study, levels of social capital were, as suggested above, relatively high. One participant in Barton, for example, described a sense of satisfaction with her social life, was employed and active in her community. She earned less than £10,000 per annum, supported three children and her partner who was unemployed and had chosen to exclude himself from the social welfare system structure by being unwilling to sign up for any benefits. She described her involvement with various friends in the area, exchanging favours with neighbours and visiting relatives living outside of Barton as well as reaching out to people who lived alone.

Turning to another commonly-held view, lack of access to a car is a recognized measure of low socio-economic status (Goldblatt, 1990; Davey-Smith and Egger, 1992; Bostock, 2001). Conversely, there is often an assumption that ownership of a car equates in some way to being socially included (see, for example, Bostock, 2001). However, one young woman in Barton interviewed for this study does not appear to reflect this notion. Jan is twenty-two and has lived in the area all her life. She lives alone and has an annual income of less than £5,000. She has a car but it is often off the road. She drives to Bournemouth three times a week to look after her ill mother for whom she is main carer. She states that the rest of her time is largely spent doing housework. When asked what she felt the main transport issues affecting her were, she said "(They) need lights at Green Road roundabout. They need to take down the trees there because they obscure your vision. There's no chance to see what's coming otherwise. The only way out of Barton is via the roundabout unless you travel across country but it's a long way round." She does not have a telephone but reported that she had spoken to friends and relatives on an on-street payphone in the past two weeks. She described a relatively isolated life saying "I have only one friend I rely on but I don't know where he lives. He doesn't have a phone and I don't know the exact address. He lives in Blackbird Leys." When asked whether he would be willing to give her a lift to Bournemouth to see her mother, since her car was not working at the time of interview, she explained "I think he would. He's kind but I wouldn't ask him though".

For Jan, having a car is vital for providing support to her mother and in this way serves an important social function. However, conversation with her suggests that she does not know anyone in her local neighbourhood and that she travels off the estate to go shopping by car. In this way, the lack of adequate facilities and suitable shopping opportunities locally coupled with the availability of a car, albeit one that is unreliable may mean that she has not made social connections in her neighbourhood. Since she spends much of her week away from the area and does not work, she has little opportunity to build relationships and a support system which could assist her when she has difficulties such as a broken-down car. It appears that for this participant, Acheson's contention that "lack of transport may damage health by denying access to people, goods and services" (Acheson, 1998:55) may not be relevant. On the contrary, access to private transport enables her to care for a family member at a distance but her consequent mobility may be to the detriment of her ability to establish social networks within her community. Her description of feelings of social isolation and of having very little to occupy her when she is at home may indicate that she is vulnerable to the damaging psychological effects of poor social networks such as loneliness.

Perceptions of crime: impacts on transport-related behaviour

Concerns about crime can dissuade people from walking, cycling or using public transport (renewal.net, 2002). This research indicates that concerns about crime may also extend to another transport-related activity, parking. On several streets in Barton, houses have driveways where residents can park their cars. However, on other streets, mainly where local authority flats can be found, parking provision can be found in remote garage blocks or communal spaces. These parking areas have come to be associated with malevolent activities and, as a result, drivers tend not to park in their designated spaces/garages, parking on-street and on the pavements instead:

> Parking on the roads in Barton is a problem. There's lots of garage blocks but they've become criminal areas, so no one goes near them. (Fifty year old male participant)

The narrowing effect of on-street and on-pavement parking in turn causes difficulties for pedestrians and other vehicles, particularly the buses:

> I saw a bus have to pull out to get round a parked car and it couldn't get by without hitting the mirror on the car. (Seventy year old female participant)

> It's difficult getting out my road...I just have to ask my husband to take care and put his foot down as we can't see traffic coming. It's also made difficult because the two houses at the end have those people carrier things and you can't see past them when they are parked up on the road. (Sixty-three year old female participant)

By choosing to park as close to their front doors as possible, drivers are seeking to lessen the probability that their vehicle will suffer criminal damage. The impact of this parking behaviour is to displace walkers from pavements and make circulation of traffic difficult.

In a report entitled 'The Cost of Policing New Urbanism', Bedfordshire Police's Force Architectural Liaison Officer describes a typical conflict related to disagreement about parking and permeability of communal spaces between planners' designs and the police's crime reduction principles.

> (P)lanners frequently seek to 'improve' the street-scene by concealing parked vehicles in off-plot, sometimes remote, courts/garage areas. Courtyards create communal space, which directly contradicts the principle of creating defensible space. In social housing, such communal space - in theory owned by everyone and in reality controlled and influenced by no one - has a disastrous record. This is often compounded with any number of pedestrian routes through the facility. Attempts at providing natural surveillance by locating flats on top of garages do not, in the main, significantly reduce the prevalence of auto-crime and perceived disorder. As regards permeability, police architectural liaison officers will generally seek a legible and coherent movement network, beyond which the greatest gains are made by reducing, as far as is reasonably possible, the number of dwellings on through-routes. This creates more defensible space, significantly increasing the potential for residents to take ownership, and exert influence and informal social control over their environment. Implicit in New Urbanism on the other hand, is a belief that permeability is inherently 'good', and should therefore be maximised...This typically

results in a 'spider's web' of inter-connecting roads and linkages, with bollards or other measures to obstruct cars (and police patrol vehicles). (Knowles, no date) @ http://www. operationscorpion.org.uk/design_out_crime/design_main.htm accessed 050505

As the quote above implies, the design of the built environment can make communal spaces more vulnerable to crime and thereby increase perceptions of criminality. Another factor contributing to fear of crime in Barton is the presence of indicators, in some parts of the estate, of a lack of care for the area such as graffiti and vandalism[17]:

> Some criminologists suggest that the presence of vandalism and graffiti not only impacts on fear of crime, but also on the level of crime itself. The 'broken windows' theory, developed in the United States, has identified possible links between disorder, fear of crime and more serious crime. This theory proposes that if a broken window is left and not repaired, the other windows will soon be broken in response to the message that 'no-one cares'. It is argued that this in turn creates a perception that crime in general is on the increase, and as a consequence people will be less inclined to use public places. With fewer people using public places, there is less deterrence to crime, which will rise. Hence the perception of rising crime becomes a reality. (DfT, 2003b:2)

By introducing changes to the communal spaces which have been provided for parking, the detrimental effects of displaced parking may be lessened and additional benefits may also be brought to the wider community. Applying the concept of 'defensible space' in Barton may contribute to a lessening of opportunity for criminal activity and concurrently bestow additional benefits of increased neighbourhood power, ownership and participation. The architect and planner Oscar Newman

---

17   Though not widespread throughout the area, pockets of the estate appear to have been subject to vandalism and have graffiti on the walls. In these parts of the estate, the impression of an apparent lack of care for public space is exacerbated by the build up of household detritus in garden areas and roadsides e.g. old washing machines, cookers, broken bicycles, cardboard boxes were seen piled up in some areas. Against this backdrop, potentially dangerous vandalism has also been reported. To give an insight into the types of activities reported, one such incident is related here:

"Residents in a block of flats on an Oxford estate face a dangerous journey in and out of the building after vandals smashed hallway lights. People living in Brome Place, Barton, claim the four-storey building is a "death trap" at night because they cannot navigate the concrete staircases without lights, which were destroyed by vandals on November 16. They are angry because, although the damage has been reported to Oxford City Council, which owns the building, new lights have still not been installed...The vandalism is the latest in a catalogue of problems caused by gangs at Brome Place. In the past, residents have complained of arson, drug use and damage caused by teenagers playing football in the corridors. Now they are urging the council to fit CCTV and extra security to prevent vandals getting into the building...A city council spokesman said workmen had responded to tenants' calls and had been to the flats three times. He said: 'The council is very concerned about vandalism at Brome Place. Our crime and nuisance action team is working with residents and police. We need information to identify the vandals.' It was believed that youths had obtained a key to the front door to the block. The council had installed a new entry system and residents would be given new keys." (Owen, 2002)

suggested that a lack of commonality and civility among neighbours increases our vulnerability to crime and results in a withdrawal of the public from streets. To counter this trend, Newman created the concept of 'defensible space' in the early 1970s, suggesting that defensible space does not automatically oust the criminal, it just renders him ineffective. He added that:

> What 'Defensible Space' also does is give low-income families a self-respect they never had before; and an opportunity, in the case of our housing integration programs, to become part of the social mainstream. It gives people a new respect for the work and territory of others by giving them territory of their own to prize and to wish to see respected.... 'Defensible Space' is not about fencing, it is about the reassignment of areas and of responsibilities—the demarcation of new spheres of influence. (Newman, 2003 @ http://www.defensiblespace.com/book.htm accessed 050505)

Another related example of the ways in which the design of public space may contribute to malevolent activity can be found in Barton. There is an extensive network of alleyways on the estate, linking residential streets via fenced, walled and sometimes over-grown passages. Anecdotal comments by participants in this study suggest that these hidden spaces may be used for undesirable activities, for example, by groups of teenagers to smoke and behave rowdily, by drug dealers to ply their trade and by opportunist thieves to steal handbags[18]. Consequently, some participants avoided the alleys, while others asserted that they were not afraid to use them but they knew people who were.

During the period of the research, a boy of ten taking a short cut back from the post office one afternoon was the subject of unwanted sexual advances by a man in the alley between Aldbarton Road and Barton Village Road[19]. This incident provides

---

18   Five interviewees commented on the types of activities that may be found in the alleys. In addition, focus group participants, all elderly, appeared to not even consider using such spaces, alluding to their fear of crime rather than describing a particular activity.

19   "Parents on alert after sex attack" by Staff reporter, Friday 29 April 2005 @ http://www.thisisoxfordshire.co.uk/oxfordshire/archive/2005/04/29/TOPNEWS1ZM.html accessed 090705)

The mother of a 10-year-old boy has spoken out about her son's ordeal after he was sexually assaulted in an alleyway on an Oxford estate. The woman, who wants to remain anonymous to protect his identity, said her boy is so upset he has not been able to go to school...The youngster was walking on the Barton estate on Tuesday (Apr 26) at about 4.30pm when a middle-aged man surprised him. Police have not given details of the assault, but it is understood that the man approached the boy from behind and touched him inappropriately. The youngster managed to break free and run home, but the attack has sparked fears for the safety of other young children on the estate. The boy's mother praised her son for the way he handled the attack. She said: "He went to post a letter for me. He was playing with his phone and did not hear the man approach. The man grabbed him but he was brave. He screamed and said he'll call the police then escaped and ran away. "He came running to the house and was really upset. He could hardly speak as he had run so hard, and was saying call the police. He was really shaken. I was appalled".

The alley where the attack took place is about 50 yards long and connects Aldbarton Road to Barton Village Road on the Barton estate...Local schools have been told about the attack, and people are being warned to take particular care...Simon Leigh, 39, who lives next to the

an example of the latent dangers intrinsic to public space that is hidden from the protective gaze of community members. In order to produce safer places for walking, space needs to be open, lit, over-looked, well-used and, therefore, defensible. Instead, the alleys of Barton are an example of transport infrastructure which has become hazardous because of its inherent design and resultant under use.

The potential of personalized travel planning

Individualized travel marketing such as TravelSmart[20] programmes arose from a desire to encourage modal shift (DfT, 2002b) by presenting individuals who were seen to be open to change with alternative travel options. A vignette from this research (Box 4.5) points to the potential of personalized travel planning for wider and more prosaic applications, not as a catalyst for modal change but as a way of encouraging people who walk, cycle and use public transport to broaden their knowledge of what is accessible along the transport corridors that are currently available to them.

While the vignette is helpful to illuminate how important social capital and networks can be to the decisions an individual makes, it is used here to illustrate how individual transport knowledge could be supplemented to deal with structural changes which could have far-reaching effects for someone who is already a single mother of two children. Specifically, when Oxford Primary Care Trust moved the family planning clinic in 2004, within five months, there was a 25 per cent reduction in patients using the service (Owen, 2005). Tracey was obviously one of the people

alley in Aldbarton Drive, said: "The first I heard about it was when a neighbour brought my son back home. Now he is barred from going in the alley and has to play where we can see him. We even leave the front door open to be sure. We have told him to kick, run and scream as loud as he can if anyone approaches him."

20   Sustrans, the UK sustainable transport charity, describes TravelSmart programmes "as ways to change the way we travel". Sustrans states that TravelSmart is a cost-effective technique for increasing walking, cycling and use of public transport – thereby reducing car travel. It delivers real change by making people more aware of their daily travel choices through a process known as Individualised Marketing. Sustrans states that "Individualised Marketing is an innovative approach to changing travel behaviour through direct contact with households. It encourages people to make greater use of alternatives to car travel by offering them personalised travel information, advice and incentives to try out new ways of getting around". (http://www.sustrans.org.uk/default.asp?sID=1091003006653&pID= and http://www.sustrans.org.uk/default.asp?sID=1090849616969 accessed 270705)

While in its relative infancy in the UK, TravelSmart Australia has been in operation for a number of years. This initiative brings together the many community and government based programs that are asking Australians to use alternatives to traveling in their private car. The TravelSmart Australia website gives an overview of its approach:
TravelSmart asks you to think about your travel needs.
*   Use alternative transport to the car, for example using walking, cycling and public transport.
*   Reduce the negative impacts of the car on traffic congestion and air pollution.
*   Recognize the health benefits of incidental exercise such as walking or cycling.
*   Choose shops and facilities that are near you to reduce the need to travel and to support your local businesses. (http://www.travelsmart.gov.au/about.html accessed 260705)

Box 4.5 A candidate for personalized travel planning?

Tracey's story

Tracey is a 21 year old white single mother of two African Caribbean/white children. She and her children moved back to Barton in November 2003 after she split up with her boyfriend in Carterton, West Oxfordshire. She chose to go back to the area where she had grown up, although she had also been offered housing in the Summertown or Headington (both areas seen as considerably more desirable to Oxford residents than Barton), because she has family and friends there. She also felt that people may have been 'racist' in other places '…but people don't mind around here that the children are mixed'. As a mother of two boys under five, life is not easy and time is particularly precious. Yet, Tracey fits in work as a volunteer on the estate and tries to go to the gym in the evenings as often as possible. Her gym trips are very much dependent on a babysitter's availability and she negotiates the timing of these trips around the babysitter's schedule. Sometimes she calls on her mother to help out. Going to the gym involves a bus ride towards the city centre but she is happy to travel because it gives her some time to herself. For food shopping, she does not like to go to the Co-op or Somerfield in Headington because she feels they are expensive and it is not easy to carry heavy bags on the bus from these shops. Instead, she relies on her mother to give her a lift to Asda or Tesco, since both these supermarkets cannot be accessed by bus. When asked whether there was anywhere she would like to go to but was unable to because of transport, she expressed some concern that she has not been able to go to the family planning clinic since it moved from Manzil Way, off Cowley Road, in April 2004. The clinic was transferred to the Radcliffe Infirmary site north of the city centre and she feels it is now too difficult to get to.

---

who agreed with the Primary Care Trust's sexual health development manager's statement:

> We now know that clients in east Oxford, and in Rosehill, Barton and Blackbird Leys areas, find it too far to travel to the RI (Radcliffe Infirmary), and we've found they have not been attending the clinic at its new location. (Owen, 2005)

In response to the decline in clinic users, the Trust decided to launch new satellite centres which will open once a week at community centres in east Oxford, Rosehill and Barton. Taking Tracey's case as an example, however, and without entering the debate on whether the decision to re-locate was in the best interest of the key target groups in deprived areas on the east side of Oxford (with high rates of teenage pregnancy – Owen, 2005), Barton is served by buses which travel through the centre of Oxford and north along Banbury Road to Kidlington. Banbury Road is parallel to Woodstock Road where the Radcliffe Infirmary is located. Walking from a bus stop on Banbury Road to the Infirmary would take about five minutes. Thus, while Tracey perceives that it is too difficult to travel to the new clinic's site, it is likely that she is simply unaware of the location of the clinic in relation to the main bus route from the area where she lives. Indeed, accessing the clinic would not involve the deterrent effect usually associated with the requirement to interchange, something that she must have done during trips to the former family planning clinic location. The trip to the new site may be longer in terms of time and distance travelled by bus than a trip to the old location but the new trip would definitely involve less walking or waiting time than the previous journey since there are no direct bus services to Cowley Road from Barton.

For someone like Tracey, affected by the relocation of an important health care service, it can be argued that there is a call for personalized travel planning. If she had been offered the services of someone at her last visit to the old clinic who could have talked her through the ways in which she could travel to the new site, it is likely that she would not have discounted it's location as too difficult to access because she would have realized that it is within easy walking distance of the main bus route to and from her home. For someone who is already a bus user, personalized approaches to conveying information about destinations that are within easy access of the transport corridor can do much to expand travel horizons.

Within the NHS there is a trend towards centralization of services. Rather than providing photocopied maps of new service locations as appears to be current common practice, it is likely that the services of someone to work out a personalized route to and from the new location would result in a greater acceptance of the service centralization. Such an approach has been beneficial in the legal sector where there was a danger that a change in service location could mean a fall in court attendance. Specifically, in Warwickshire, a number of courts have recently been closed. As a result, witnesses may now have to travel to towns they are unfamiliar with to give evidence. An officer within the Witness Care Service has now taken on the responsibility for investigating how a witness may travel to the new site and provides them with bus and train times where public transport services are available or arranges for taxis from more isolated locations. This role of conduit of information has greatly increased the likelihood that a witness will attend court than if they had to work out themselves how they would need to travel (Representative, Witness Care – Warwickshire, personal interview, March 2005).

With respect to employment, a web-based tool has been developed to link job opportunities with transport opportunities. The EMIRES[21] project was funded by the European Commission to develop and demonstrate a network of Regional Service Centres offering personalized, dynamically generated packages of intelligent, value added services. One of the project's demonstration sites is located in the Central and East Sutherland area of the Scottish Highlands where a lack of local jobs and lack of transport to work and interviews had been identified as barriers to employment. The EMIRES service was set up for users "to obtain personalized information on suitable job vacancies that they can get to by public transport (and providing information on the public transport service they need to use)" (www.emires.net accessed 140805).

---

21 Economic Growth and Sustainable Mobility Supported by IST at Regional including SMEs. (www.emires.net)

An online prototype of the UK EMIRES Regional Service Centre is available at www.emiresscotland.org:

> This application looks at the same lists of Job Vacancies as JobCentre Plus and the same lists of training opportunities as Learn Direct, so it is guaranteed to be current and up to date. It can combine these sources of information with Public Transport data to provide users who rely on public transport with a more focussed and personalized search for jobs and training. Public Transport information is provided by Highland Council data and includes Demand Responsive Transport (DRT), (also known as Dial-a-Ride) services within the East Sutherland area as well as local and intercity fixed route bus and train services. This allows job seekers from outside East Sutherland to gain information on accessible opportunities within the area, as well as allowing local residents to find suitable training and vacancies in neighbouring towns outside the East Sutherland area which they can get to using public transport. If the recommended public transport journey includes DRT (Dial-a-ride) then details of how to book this will be provided. A by product of the system will be management information which will highlight to Local Authority transport planners where there are gaps in the public transport provision. (www.emiresscotland.org accessed 140805)

For those with internet access, this is a convenient and functional tying together of data sources to enable improved accessibility to information about employment and transport opportunities. For those people without access to the internet, this personalized data source will be inaccessible without facilitation through either a call centre or a dedicated officer. However, adaptation of such a tool may furnish the needs of other sectors beyond employment, such as the health and legal described earlier, where changes are planned.

As the illustrations above have indicated, there can be simple yet powerful benefits in searching for solutions and adopting policies which work together across governance domains. Such an approach can be a practical tool for inclusion. As we have seen, personalized transport planning offered to a person who is about to be affected by a change of service delivery location could preclude a resultant downturn in usage of the service. Thus, the ill effects of geo-spatial exclusion resulting from unfamiliarity with the wider transport system may be minimized.

Before leaving this discussion of personalized travel planning, it is important to introduce a note of caution about the reliability of information available to help plan peoples' journeys. As part of the Government's 10-Year Plan, the Transport Direct programme was announced as a new, comprehensive, national transport information service, covering all modes of transport. Its slogan is 'Connecting people to places' (http://www.transportdirect.gov.uk/).

In order to test the system's applicability, the on-line planner was used for a simulated return trip by Tracey from Barton to the Radcliffe Infirmary. Off-peak journey times were chosen and two different origins in Barton were used, one near to the shops at Underhill Circus and the other at North way in proximity to the main road into/out of the area. However, rather than providing the option of using the direct bus service that operates to and from the estate, the journey planner suggested, for both return journeys regardless of origin, a trip involving a walk towards Headington (with no mention of how to get there, i.e., via a pedestrian underpass) to take a bus into central Oxford and then walk to another stop to interchange to another bus heading towards Kidlington. Interestingly, this second bus originates in Barton. Given the rather tedious nature of the planner's suggested options, a trip from Barton to Kidlington (i.e. between the two ends of a direct bus route) was also tested. The journey planner once again recommended a walk/bus/walk/bus trip with city centre interchange. These findings suggest that it may be more helpful to rely on a person with a good mental map of local bus services and the technology than some of the technology that is currently available. Also, it is necessary for the Transport Direct journey planner to take account of detrimental impacts of interchange and undesirability of some walking trips. In addition, there are no directions provided for the person who is advised to walk: if they are using the system, it is likely that they may be unfamiliar with the area and thus benefit from simple directions.

Identifying dynamics and projecting forward: the baseline scenario, policy changes and transport interventions

Introduction

To provide an insight into the types of challenges faced by residents, some of the difficulties accessing services and facilities they have described are provided below:

- a library – located only about 2 km away at Bury Knowle in Headington: the elderly have suggested that they would walk there but are not comfortable going through a park where people have been mugged, as well as not wanting to use the underpasses in Barton to travel off the estate in order to go to the library.
- food shops – some residents who are dependent on buses to get to the supermarkets in Headington state that they find it hard to carry large loads on the bus. However, others have coping mechanisms such as relying on friends or relatives for lifts to/from the supermarket or saving the trip until they can spend £25 or over at one of the supermarkets which then delivers the bags free of charge.
- schools – there is no longer a secondary school on the estate. Students now have to travel by bus (which parents state is at full fare before 0900) to Headington to school. This journey is at peak time and buses can be delayed at the Headington Roundabout.
- GPs' practice – people can use two surgeries in Headington, those who are registered at Bury Knowle Surgery can also see a doctor at Barton Neighbourhood Centre where a satellite practice operates (although people describe not knowing if it will be open on some days, particularly if the receptionist is on holiday or away as no other cover is sent from the main surgery) but those who are registered at Manor Surgery (about 1 kilometre further from Barton than Bury Knowle) have suggested that it can be quite difficult to get to the surgery as it is located on a side road which requires them

to walk uphill from the bus stop.
- Hospitals – the John Radcliffe Hospital is located on a hill in Headington. Those who are able and willing to walk there say that it is much easier to do so than to get there by bus which would require the use of one bus towards the city centre and then another back out to the hospital. Some elderly residents have had to go to the Nuffield Orthopaedic Hospital, also in Headington, and describe the walk with mobility difficulties from the bus stop on the main road to the hospital (located about a kilometre away from the stop) as difficult.

The examples above are provided as contextual background for the discussion of the potential impacts of the Headington roundabout redesign which follows. In this section, the findings of the research in relation to the roundabout are discussed within a wider social context which takes account of the potential of policy changes and transport interventions to promote social inclusion.

Barton: how planned roundabout redesign may impact on members of the local community

Drivers from the Barton area have little choice but to use the Headington roundabout with right turns on to the London Road (A420) towards the city centre and towards North Oxford on North Way particularly difficult. The roundabout has three circulating lanes of traffic and the arm immediately before the Barton exit, the Oxford ring road, brings a heavy traffic flow from the north of the city to the junction. Traffic outbound from the city centre via Headington and from areas to the south of the city also transits the roundabout to access the A40 leading to the M40 towards London.

Currently 6,000 vehicles use the junction in peak hours and there has been one accident there a month over the past 3 years, making it the county's biggest accident blackspot. In 2004, Oxfordshire County Council approved plans to improve the roundabout. The Council plans a £2m scheme (Figure 4.3) involving introduction of traffic signals and a 'hamburger' design: a new lane through the middle for A40 traffic from London to Kidlington in the north with associated bus priority measures:

- a bus lane on the A420 London Rd eastbound to reduce delay to buses leaving Oxford city centre
- traffic signals at the junction of Bayswater Road and Waynflete Road with priority for buses leaving these roads
- giving buses traffic signal priority on the A40 westbound on the approach to the roundabout

While the design does not include traffic signals on the Barton arm of the roundabout (Bayswater Rd), council officers are said to believe "lights at the other four junctions should give Barton drivers sufficient time" (Ffrench, 2003). How much easier it will be for drivers from the Barton estate to egress under the new scheme remains to be seen, although the removal of some circulating traffic should be beneficial in providing additional turning opportunities, at least in the short term after opening. It is important though that the needs of people using the Barton arm of the roundabout

Figure 4.3 Proposed roundabout layout

Long-Term Measures

FABER MAUNSELL

Green Road Roundabout - Hamburger Proposal

Proposed Road Layout

- Signalised approach
- Signalised approach
- Direct A40-A40 Access
- Left Turn Slip
- Bus - Presignal
- Signalised approach
- Left Turn Slip
- Signalised approach

Benefits of Proposed Scheme

- Reduces delays for local buses when combined with Waynflete Road signalised junction and the A4120 Eastbound bus lane

- Bus pre-signal reduces delay for Park and Ride and long distance buses on the Oxford bound A40 approach

- Reduces peak period congestion for all traffic at the roundabout improving the environment of the local area

- All pedestrian and cycle facilities will be maintained

- Reduces Personal Injury Accidents

Drawing Key

- New Cycle Lane
- Existing Cycle Lane
- New Bus Lane
- Existing Bus Lane
- Carriageway
- New Build-outs
- Road Closure

are re-visited by scheme designers in order to ensure that this option presents the best solution to their prevailing difficulties: it should be recognized that turning delays currently being experienced are contributing to the exclusion of local residents from access to key services at present. If turning towards nearby local work and other social opportunities in central Oxford is difficult, whether on the bus or in a car (and with walking routes requiring use of underpasses), some people must be missing out on participating in the normal activities of residents of their society. In this light, it is unsurprising that local youths have become involved in activities such as 'bus surfing' since there appears to be little else for them to do locally or in easy access of the estate.

Interestingly, the least difficult turn that can be made from the estate's arm of the roundabout is away from the city centre on to the A40 towards the M40 and London, suggesting that estate residents may find it easier to search for employment opportunities away from Oxford and as a result feel no connection with the central area that should serve this urban estate.

By surrounding the estate with two dual carriageways and making egress extremely difficult, traffic engineering has effectively cut the estate off from its parent city. The solution that consultants have designed is likely to penalize this arm of the roundabout in comparison to the other arms, since all other arms will have traffic signal control. In addition, the resulting isolation will be worsened by a lack of safe pedestrian routes off the estate: the proposed scheme does not include any ameliorative measures for pedestrians.

The challenges of negotiating the Bayswater Road (Barton) junction of Headington Roundabout were described by one participant as follows:

> It is really difficult to get off Barton because of the roundabout. It certainly, in my experience, is the most difficult exit and entrance. This is being addressed, but the current situation has existed for many years. There are long queues to get off in the morning and even at other times. Trouble is when it is busy, you can't get off, and when it is quiet, the traffic from the other entrances beats you to it. (Forty-something female interviewee)

Another participant indicates that he feels that the planned roundabout improvements do not offer substantial benefits for residents of Barton:

> Thinking of the roundabout, I always wonder what driving instructors teach their students about using the roundabout. I did an advanced driving certificate a few years ago and there's no way you could stick to the Highway Code when you use the roundabout. The Code says you must not enter if there is traffic from the right. You'd wait days if you stuck to that rule there.
>
> I've seen the plans for the roundabout. They look impressive, you know, all computerized models and things but I really think it could've been planned better for people in Barton." (Fifty year old male interviewee)

Concerns about the needs of local people in the context of proposed changes to the roundabout were also expressed by another male participant from Barton:

I think cycling isn't given priority. I went to the roundabout exhibition and consultation but no one took account of what I was asking. They just couldn't answer whether the cycle/bus lane coming from London was to be shared or also used by taxis too. I think priority should be given to pedestrians and wheelchair users, then cyclists and then cars but it is wrong to make changes that may affect large housing areas badly. I know it is difficult to take account of all people's needs and clearly you have to give priority to the largest users but they seemed, at the consultation, to be just giving lip service and that's why they couldn't answer the questions. I think what they've planned is good but I'm not sure it'll do anything good for people in Barton who are facing real problems getting out. Putting a road straight through the roundabout helps the straight through traffic greatly but how it helps local people is unclear. Also, I think that underpasses are often undesirable to use and its kind of unfair putting up a sign telling cyclists to dismount in them. I mean what would car drivers say if they got to a junction and were told to get out and push the car? I think the problems for Barton have been raised a number of times with the consultants but what can they do? It feels like it is all decided anyway to be honest. (Thirty year old male)

As the quote above illustrates, concerns about the roundabout re-design were not only expressed in relation to the impacts on car users. Other participants take up the roundabout theme in the following quotes:

I have used the main roundabout subway for 25 years and have always been ok. Well, 20+ years ago my pram was hit by a motorbike in the subway. However, I am not put off by the smell and graffiti – it is much better now - or the fact that there may be someone in the subway with me. Residents of Barton and Risinghurst (estate across the A40), find the subway difficult, particularly if there is a group of youths nearby. While I have never had any difficulty and usually feel able to say hello, I appreciate how hard it must be for the many people who feel vulnerable. I do believe that this results in the elderly and people from minority groups not using the subways. (Forty something female)

I can't see how it'll make a difference with the design I've seen. Where do Barton people go? I can't see it working. I can't see how the lights will work for Barton people. I've seen them make changes to it over the years. Now you can't see over the roundabout since it was made bigger. We're like an island now since they put in the bypass. We used to be able to walk across the road. (Seventy year old female resident)

The roundabout is quite scary, you have to be aware of others. Junkies use the underpasses. (Twenty-one year old single mother)

I'm not even sure what they're going to do. I walk the kids to school using the underpass. I'm happy to use it, although it smells and the lights are sometimes not working. (Thirty-six year old single mother)

While the do nothing situation already affects people, with the deterrent effect of current delays at the roundabout making access to places outside the area difficult, the roundabout improvement does not appear to hold any benefit for residents of Barton. By extension, it is arguable that, in terms of social justice, large-scale investment in an improvement which enables more traffic to transit the junction should also seek to address the prevailing problems faced by local people and not concentrate solely on maximizing the throughput of inter-urban and non-local traffic.

Over several years, the older participants in this research report that this roundabout has been increased in size to the present size where they state that it is now impossible to see beyond the junction and that it has only made their area even more "cut-off" from the surrounding neighbourhoods[22]. The notion of physical severance ties in to the main indirect effect of the proposed roundabout improvement scheme, that is, the nature of consultation conveys a negative message to local residents by the planning process. Amongst participants in this study, there was a range of knowledge about the scheme. Some people had heard about it, some had seen plans and some had attended meetings about the scheme; others had not heard about it, felt that the Council would do what it had decided anyway or simply had no opinion on the subject. Those who had seen plans and/or attended public meetings felt that the plans were well-presented visually but that there was either little opportunity for their personal concerns to be addressed through the consultation process or that the consultants who had designed the scheme would not be making any changes to their plans to take account of local input.

For local residents, an inability to participate effectively in decision-making and an attendant lack of choice in changes that happen around, and thus to them, can underline their impotence in the social processes that affect them. A consultation process that appears to be deficient in terms of inclusiveness could serve to highlight to residents the institutional power of the local authority over local people. This is a significant way in which the planning of changes to transport infrastructure can serve to undermine wider social inclusion objectives.

An empirical insight into more effective consultation: the case of Cowley Road

As outlined in Chapter 3, when this research was originally conceived it had been intended that there would be three case studies with Cowley Road, a radial route into Oxford city centre being the third case. However, as the research progressed, it became evident that this location would not provide the depth of information needed to inform a viable case study. Indeed, it was the success of an extensive and recent consultation exercise on a transport scheme for this road that meant that when local residents were approached to participate in the current research, they stated that they had no new comments to make, transport did not pose any problems for them or that they simply were not interested.

Nevertheless, by talking to local shopkeepers, some road users and Asian women who were willing to attend focus group discussions, it was possible to ascertain that there was a general view that, in terms of the planned changes to the road space, people's opinions had been effectively garnered and incorporated into the designs. With Cowley Road located a couple of kilometres from Barton, the contrasting approaches to consultation within the same local authority are of interest. The Cowley Road consultation exercise is described briefly here in order to highlight the ways in which the deployment of participative approaches can facilitate more efficient design that targets local needs.

---

22   Four interviewees highlighted the changes in the roundabout over time.

**Plate 4.3   Making a feature of consultation in the affected community,
              Cowley Road, Oxford**

Source: Fiona Rajé

The Cowley Road area of Oxford has been the subject of recent consultation,
involving the public in the design of a road safety and environmental scheme.
This consultation was inventive (involving, for example, the use of video[23]) and an
example of best practice with innovative measures being assessed as part of a very
wide ranging consultation process engaging the local community[24] (DfT, 2004c:6).
Plate 4.3 shows the long-running display, inviting feedback from the local community,
of the final scheme design in a vacant shop window in a prominent position on the

---

23   To view the consultation video, see http://www.eastoxford.com/
24   An extract from a response by a resident of the local area to criticism of measures
being introduced on Cowley Road (in a letter to the Editor of the *Oxford Times*) helps illustrate
the positive reaction of one local person to this engagement process:
"…It must be really hard to understand the Cowley Road development if you've not yet
looked at the shop window opposite Honest Stationery explaining what's going on. If he's
only cycled and not walked, and missed the long public consultation exercise carried out
by East Oxford Action employing local people, then he must think it's sent to bamboozle
us. I didn't participate in the preparatory work (wish I had now, looks like it was fun!) so
I've been catching up by reading the shop window…" (Liz Hodgson, "Road safety picture
will make sense when unfinished jigsaw is complete", Letter to the Editor, *Oxford Times*,
08 July 2005 p15)

Cowley Road. Qualitative research as employed in the Cowley Road consultation is useful in informing the design of interventions and has been underused by the policy and planning profession in the UK. It is a more normal practice for engineers and planners to design a proposal or number of options and then present these to the affected public:

> In a typical public infrastructure process, a few design options are prepared in advance by design professionals and presented at public forums. Unstructured feedback is then gathered using microphones and flip charts and is used in an unspecified way to determine which one should be selected. This limited-involvement and restricted-choice paradigm, termed Decide, Announce, and Defend (DAD), reinforces the distrust that many stakeholders hold toward public planning processes (Campbell-Jackson, 2002). Loud voices, mobilised resistance groups, charges, and counter-charges typify many such public meetings. They are only half-jokingly referred to in some circles as "karaoke nights". (Bailey and Grossardt, 2004:547)

Involving the targeted population at the inception stage of design and proposal development allows the engineers and planners to hear, and take account of, how people say they use the environment that is being re-designed as well as serving as a humanizing reminder that highlights that their plans impact on the daily lives of people in the community.

The contrast between the consultation reported by participants to have taken place in Barton and that which was carried out a couple of miles away in Cowley Road raises some important issues. With the same local authority institution being responsible for both exercises, the differences in quality and nature of consultation may be attributable to a number of factors. While it is not possible to determine why there was such a profound variation in the quality of consultation, a few suggestions can be made about potential contributory factors.

It may be that the individual transport planning officer managing the scheme design process may influence consultation: those that are more proactive looking for effective methods of two-way communication with the affected public while the less interested do minimal consultation to satisfy statutory requirements. It may also be possible that the presence of a large ethnic minority community in the Cowley Road area may have led to a search for innovative and overtly non-discriminatory methods of consultation whereas areas with less diverse populations such as Barton may have suffered from a less finely-tuned approach to local participation and consultation. Equally, it may be that there were existing social structures, community groups and networks in the Cowley Road area which helped facilitate effective consultation when no such organisations were available in Barton. It is also possible that the consultant engineers chosen to design the schemes had different approaches to consultation and these resulted in the differences in effectiveness. These are all possibilities which reveal the need for consultation to be seen not just as a task on a project management timeline but as an essential and actively-planned part of the project's development.

Conclusion: urban concerns, urban solutions

This chapter has described the ways in which transport can impact on people living in Barton. The study looked at how people's perceptions of their local area may affect their desire to travel (monitoring) and at how the provision of mobility related facilities in public space (e.g. street furniture) for one group may be abused by another group (distributional impacts of provision). The chapter has suggested that there is disconnection between the stated social inclusion objectives of the County Council and some of the planning decisions which the authority makes. The apparent lack of community engagement in such decisions renders local residents powerless in the face of institutional power, that is, it serves to perpetuate their vulnerability to social exclusion. Transport has been seen in this chapter to impact at a number of levels: on communities and individuals and on social inclusion and exclusion. The next chapter turns to the rural case to look at the impacts of transport on residents of Charlbury in West Oxfordshire.

Chapter 5

Transport and Social Inclusion: The Rural Experience

Introduction: locating the rural case study

In this chapter, we explore transport's impacts on people's lives from a rural perspective. The chapter uses the findings of the primary research carried out in Charlbury in West Oxfordshire as a basis for the understandings of transport and social inclusion that are developed as the chapter progresses. These findings are supported by secondary data from a previous study of access to health care in Oxfordshire. The chapter begins with an overview of the case study and then moves on to a description of the research findings. The implications of these findings are then discussed.

Charlbury: small rural town, mixed social composition with 'hidden' socially excluded, car dependent but with public transport options

Rural Oxfordshire was chosen because of its location in relation to the city of Oxford. It is near-rural area where there has been inmigration by urban residents. These residents form households with high levels of car ownership, resulting in a drop in demand for public transport services from the villages they move to. Falling demand leads to falling supply, leaving no/low-car-owning residents (such as traditional agricultural families) with an impoverished or non-existent public transport service. The impact of such migration and associated decline in local services is summed up by a resident of The Bartons, a group of villages in rural Oxfordshire, responding to questioning about transport to hospitals in the Oxford area:

> If these services (car clubs/dial-a-ride) exist in this village (Middle Barton), they are a well-kept secret. This village is now run by, and for the benefit of, a 'yuppie' elite to the exclusion of 'ordinary' people. We are retired people on a very low income yet we qualify for nothing. (Rajé et al., 2003a)

The South East Region has the highest level of car ownership in England. DEFRA (2002b) reports that:

> (M)ultiple car ownership amongst the rural well-off gives them easy access to facilities in towns and, in consequence, must weaken support for local services. The excluded minority in rural areas who do not have a car suffer more in the South East than they do elsewhere in England. Attempts to reduce car use through taxation will impact adversely on the rural poor who struggle to afford to run a car that may be essential in their locality.

Fifty per cent of parishes in Oxfordshire are without a village shop and 46% without a Post Office - worse than the national average of parishes for England. Oxfordshire has 54% of its parishes without a school, again higher than the national average and 92% of the area's parishes are without a bank - slightly worse than the national average. Health care provision in Oxfordshire is worse than the national average for England, for example, 86% of its parishes are without a doctor based in the parish and 84% of parishes without a pharmacy - worse than the national average. In terms of transport, 79% of parishes in Oxfordshire (the worst rate in the South East region) are without a daily bus service, against a national figure of 75%. (DEFRA, 2002b). As such, rural Oxfordshire has been chosen because of the tension between its relative proximity to the urban centre and the apparent lack of local service provision in the rural area resulting in trip-making at present which is largely dependent on the car. Secondary data is also available for this area on patterns of trip-making to hospitals in the Oxford area.

Charlbury, the specific field site in rural Oxfordshire, is about 15 miles northwest of Oxford and is one of the only rural towns in the area with a mainline rail station (Figure 5.1) and was chosen to allow an exploration of how people make choices about travel depending on whether they have a car available or not. In addition, although the town is largely made up of private dwellings, there are areas of local authority housing. One of these areas has been earmarked for implementation of a home zone and this research sought to look at residents' views on this intervention as well.

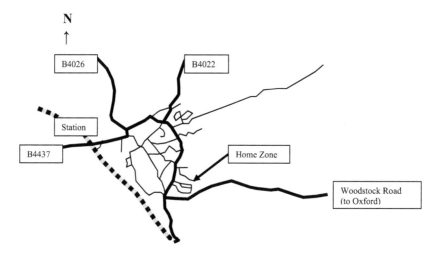

**Figure 5.1   Map showing location of proposed home zone, railway station
and main routes in Charlbury**

Bordering the Cotswolds on a hill overlooking the Evenlode River and Wychwood Forest, the main activities in the town are farming and associated trades. There is a railway station in the town with services to Oxford and London in the south and

Worcester and Malvern in the northbound direction. There are also bus services to the nearby market towns of Witney and Chipping Norton, as well as to Woodstock and on to Oxford. The journey time to Oxford by car is around 25 minutes off-peak, while peak period trips can take around an hour or longer. The rail journey time is approximately 15 minutes and the bus takes about 35 minutes off peak and 60 minutes at peak times.

There are a number of small, local shops in the town including a butcher's, pharmacy, book shop, flower shop and post office, as well as a Coop store. The railway station is about 5 minutes walk from the centre of town. The doctor's surgery is beside the Coop store in the centre of town. Housing is mixed but mainly composed of old Cotswold stone terraced and detached houses. There are some streets of older bungalows and other housing built in the mid to late 20th century. In addition, there are some areas of sheltered housing and a group of housing association and local authority houses.

A socio-demographic profile of Charlbury

Charlbury is in West Oxfordshire district, the least deprived of the 5 local authorities in Oxfordshire, ranked 347 (out of 354 local authorities in England) or within the 2% of least deprived authorities in the country. The ward of Charlbury and Finstock has a population of 3,777 (Census 2001). There are 1,599 dwellings in the ward and 11.8% of these are social rentals.

Table 5.1   Age profile of Charlbury and Finstock ward (2001)

		Charlbury/Finstock	West Oxfordshire
Population:		3777	95,640
Age profile (% of population:	Under 16	20.0	20.0
	Under 75+	8.4	7.0

(Based on information from the National Statistics website www.statistics.gov.uk: Crown copyright material is reproduced with the permission of the Controller of HMSO.)

Table 5.1 shows that the ward has the same proportion of under 16 year olds as the wider district of West Oxfordshire. There are a larger proportion of over 75 year olds in Charlbury and Finstock that there are in West Oxfordshire as a whole.

As illustrated in Table 5.2, nearly every resident of Charlbury and Finstock ward described their ethnicity as white in the 2001 Census. This reflects the wider trend within the population of West Oxfordshire district.

On the Index of Multiple Deprivation (IMD) the town has been allocated into three Super Output Areas (SOAs) which also include the nearby village of Finstock: Charlbury and Finstock (EO102877, EO102878 and EO102879). All three fall in the 20% least deprived SOAs in England. However, Charlbury and Finstock is one of

Table 5.2   Ethnic profile of Charlbury and Finstock ward

		Charlbury/ Finstock	West Oxfordshire
Ethnicity (% of population):	White	98.9	98.4
	Indian	0.2	0.2
	Pakistani	0.2	0.1
	Bangladeshi	0	0.1
	African	0	0.1
	Caribbean	0	0.1
	Chinese	0.1	0.2

(Based on information from the National Statistics website www.statistics.gov.uk: Crown copyright material is reproduced with the permission of the Controller of HMSO.)

the ten wards in Oxfordshire with the highest proportion of people under 20 living on a low income (Oxfordshire County Council, 2005b). The 2001 Census reported that there were 1,874 people in employment in Charlbury and Finstock and 233 who work mainly at/from home.

Journey to work data analysed by Oxfordshire County Council indicates that Charlbury lies in an area of Oxfordshire that has medium interaction with Oxford (Oxfordshire County Council, 2005a). This indicates that while some residents of Charlbury commute to Oxford, others travel to alternative destinations for work, both within and outside of the County.

Chapter 4 described the links that have been made between car ownership and household income and the common practice in the transport community of using lack of access to a car as a proxy measure for lower living standards. Some people appear to be more likely to belong to a household which does not have access to a car (such as pensioners or students) and thus may be more vulnerable to any ill effects that absence of a car may cause. In order to create a measure of the extent of low income in Charlbury and Finstock based on car ownership statistics, a ratio of the local population to the number of cars in the area has been calculated. The results of this analysis are shown in Table 5.3 along with similar ratios for England, Oxfordshire and West Oxfordshire for comparison.

Table 5.3 shows that there is a higher percentage of people in Charlbury and Finstock with access to at least one car than in West Oxfordshire, Oxfordshire or England. Similarly, there are 1.65 people for every car in Charlbury as against an average of 2.17 in the rest of England. This indicates that residents of Charlbury are more likely to have a car than the national average and, therefore implies that, in line with the commonly-applied assumption of a relationship between lack of car ownership and low income, they are also expected to be higher income earners. However, rurality of residence is also relevant to car ownership with rural-dwellers more dependent on car travel (Cabinet Office, 1999; Boardman 1998; Glendinning et

Table 5.3   Car ownership – Charlbury and Finstock

Location	No cars (% of households)	1 car(%)	2 cars(%)	3 cars(%)	4 or more cars (%)	Total no. of cars in area	Population	Ratio of people in area to cars in area
England	26.84	43.69	23.56	4.52	1.39	22607629	4913831	2.17
Oxfordshire	18.18	42.67	30.54	6.47	2.14	320152	605488	1.89
West Oxfordshire	13.12	42.40	34.34	7.58	2.56	55763	95640	1.726
Charlbury & Finstock	12.89	44.43	33.54	6.57	2.57	2283	3777	1.65

Source: Data from Census 2001 National Statistics website www.statistics.gov.uk

al., 2003). Nevertheless, with much of West Oxfordshire also being rural, Charlbury's car ownership rate is still slightly higher than the average for the surrounding district, indicating that another factor other than rurality, such as higher income, may also be in operation.

Yet, while these findings and the Index of Multiple Deprivation would suggest that residents of Charlbury are relatively affluent, there are people who do not fit into that category living in the town. The ACORN[1] profiles of two distinct postcodes within the town are helpful in providing an insight into the two disparate communities in Charlbury.

The first shortened profile (http://www.upmystreet.com/inf/msc/det/?l1=ox7+3px accessed 190205) is for Church Lane, Charlbury (OX7 3PX). This is a centrally located street with St. Mary's Anglican Church at one end and made up of old, stone, terraced houses with on-street parking.

Box 5.1 ACORN profile of Church Lane

Type 14: Older professionals in suburban houses and apartments

(1.48% of the population live in this ACORN type)

Likely Characteristics
This type is well represented in Outer London (Bromley, Barnet and Kingston-upon-Thames) and Manchester (Trafford), Aberdeen, Stirling and Home County towns such as Guildford and St Albans.

Family Income: High
Housing – with mortgage: Medium
Interest in current affairs: High
Educated to degree: Very high
Couples with children: Medium
Have satellite TV: Low

These are affluent people living in largely suburban areas. Households tend be a mixture of couples, families and singles, but with fewer children and more retired people than the UK as a whole. People tend to be well educated, and employed in senior managerial and professional occupations.

Property is a mixture of houses and flats. The houses tend to be large, with four or more bedrooms, with slightly more semi-detached than detached and terraced. Flats are a mixture of purpose built and converted, some of which are privately rented. Reflecting the slightly older age profile of the people in this type, more of the houses are owned outright.

---

1   A Classification of Residential Neighbourhoods.

Car ownership is high with two cars being very common. One of the cars is likely to be a high value company car.

These affluent individuals have high incomes as well as high levels of savings and investments. They are also characterized by high credit card limits and high credit card usage. They make investments using financial advisers and brokers, as well as directly using the Internet. Internet banking is very common. All the major broadsheets are read, and interests include fine arts and antiques, theatre and good food and wine. Eating out is also popular.

The second profile (http://www.upmystreet.com/inf/msc/det/?ll=ox7+3ss accessed 190205) is for Sturt Close, Charlbury (OX7 3SS). This is one of two streets on the eastern side of the town where a home zone is proposed. The housing stock is local authority built semi-detached and terraced dwellings built in the 1960s.

Box 5.2 ACORN profile of Sturt Close

Type 49: Large families and single parents, many children

(1.33% of the population live in this ACORN type)

Likely Characteristics
This type is found in most major urban centres including Belfast, Londonderry, Motherwell, Falkirk, Newport, Ipswich and Walsall.

Family income: Low
Housing – with mortgage: Low
Interest in current affairs: Very low
Educated to degree: Very low
Couples with children: High
Have satellite TV: High

These are some of the poorest young families in the country. They have exceptionally high numbers of children and a very young age profile. The level of single parents is three times the national average.

Housing is mainly three bedroom terraces, or sometimes semis, rented from the council. For the larger families, this means some overcrowding.

Unemployment is very high with a significant number of young people never having worked. With many single parents not working, the number of wage earners is low and so, inevitably, are incomes. A number of households are in debt.

People have to be careful shoppers. Clothes come from catalogues, street markets or supermarkets. Like other younger people, what spare money they do have is spent on going out to pubs, cinema and nightclubs. Otherwise, they spend their time at home watching TV.

While the two profiles above evoke starkly contrasting images, they do capture some of the extremes of living experiences of local residents observed during this research. It is also the case that the second profile captures the circumstances of a largely hidden sector of Charlbury's population. Visitors to the town tend to see the central area with its caramel-coloured stone terraces and specialist shops rather than the less aesthetically-pleasing bungalows and other ex-council houses on the eastern fringes.

Life in Charlbury: some empirical insights

Introduction

In this and subsequent sections of Chapter 5, the findings of the research carried out in Charlbury are described. These insights were obtained during a period of study in the area of about eight months during which several people shared their experiences and views with the researcher. As detailed in Chapter 3, during this time, direct contact was made with 31 participants. Of this group, 14 were principal research participants who shared more detailed information about their lives, sometimes over several meetings. Web-based resources were also used to gain a greater understanding of life in the town and rural Oxfordshire in general. As in the urban case study, since the findings are qualitative, it is not appropriate to generalize them by designating them as the experiences and views of all residents of Charlbury. However, it is intended that the insights capture the experiences and views of the research participants and thus portray a picture of how their lives are lived in the town and how they negotiate their accessibility and mobility needs.

A snapshot of Charlbury

On the surface, Charlbury appears to embody the essentials of the quintessential rural idyll. It is a small town with mainly Cotswold stone buildings in the central area and larger houses hidden behind lush foliage on the outskirts of town. On a Saturday, people can be seen meeting in the streets, chatting and exchanging pleasantries. The commercial activity is dominated by estate agencies and specialist shops such as a delicatessen, a butcher's and a florist's. There are also a post office, pharmacy and Co-op shop in the centre and a general store on the eastern side of the town.

However, Charlbury's historical edifices and pleasant vistas belie what appear to be structural divisions amongst the residents of the town. This statement from one of this research's participants alludes to the social schism, "I don't know much about the people over there (Sturt Close and Hughes Close in the eastern section of Charlbury). I know they tend to work on the check-outs at the Co-op." The chasm that appears to exist between the people living in the privately-owned/privately-rented housing on the one hand and the ex-local authority/housing association housing on the other is concerning. There would appear to be an entrenched perception that people from one part of Charlbury make no social contribution to the town other than to supply labour for more mundane jobs. By stigmatising the other residents, who they do not actually know, in this way, the more financially and socially included participants in this research virtually denied the existence of the hidden others in their town.

As a corollary, in conducting this research, it became clear that the researcher must always be careful in forming opinions based on what they are told. Specifically, amongst the respondents who were involved in this study during its initial stages, the main transport concerns expressed related to issues of parking, rail and, to a lesser extent, bus travel. None of these respondents[2] drew attention to the home zone that was being planned for their town: indeed, one wonders whether they had even heard about it. Without seeking out respondents who lived in the area where the home zone was proposed, the research may not have uncovered the views, needs and experiences of another important group of Charlbury residents.

Empirical research findings: key impacts of transport identified

Introduction

The research concentrated on the potential impacts of transport on those with and without access to a car and on the ways in which a proposed local traffic calming scheme or home zone may affect residents of the zone. The following sections describe transport's impacts on these target groups while also taking account of the impacts on the wider community. Other transport issues that were revealed during the course of the empirical work are also explored.

Community and space, place and participation

Participants' description of the community they live in and the texture of the town's sociality was largely positive. For example, when asked if this area was a place that they enjoyed living in, all participants replied that it was. Similarly, in response to the question "Would you say this area is a place where neighbours look after each

---

2   There were 8 interviewees at this stage of the fieldwork, none of whom mentioned the home zone.

other or not?", all participants felt that it was. A mother of three living in the centre of the town summarized her feelings about the area thus:

"Community spirit and good facilities go together. It is one of the reasons we chose to live here. One of the things we like is that it is rural but it has facilities we like to have. It has a nice community spirit here which we didn't know about before we came here. There's lots of overlap of different communities. People do still meet on the street and stop and talk and people talk at the school which is great. That's when you meet people and on a Saturday morning. You could never say there's nothing to do. My friends who live in Hampshire were amazed when they visited by the number of notices about things going on outside the Corner House." (Forty-five year old married mother of three)

Participants were asked whether they felt that people could be trusted. All respondents felt that people could be trusted but a few indicated some dubiety about the extent of this trust:

"On the whole, yes." (Thirty year old married male)

"People on the whole can be trusted but you can't take it as read." (Retired male)

"I would always trust until proven otherwise." (Fifty-five year old female)

However, despite the generally positive depiction of their community, some residents did express concerns about certain social issues such as vandalism:

"There's loads of vandalism . They're all on drugs round there (indicating towards the playground area)." (Elderly female resident, Sturt Close)

"You get vandalism round here." (Elderly female resident, Hughes Close)

"The town council believes it is only one family, well element, that causes the trouble. They have taken control of the playground making it a no-go area for anyone else. The ones that control it are about 19-20 and it has now been decided that Cottsway Housing authority will take control of the open space but they don't know what to do with it. It may be that they decide to put a house on it but it has access problems." (Middle aged male resident, central Charlbury)

"Things are bad enough here with kids breaking things. If they put those trees in, they'll vandalize them too...We don't want more vandalism. There's nowhere for the youth in Charlbury." (Elderly female resident, Hughes Close)

Interestingly the references made to vandalism of public space above all related to the Sturt Close/Hughes Close area where the home zone is proposed. In other parts of the town, people expressed concerns about vandalism to personal property:

"Our car was vandalized by having a key run all over it - every single panel and the bonnet and boot too. The estimate for repairing it is over £1,000 and as it's an elderly M reg Ford Escort (nothing flash) the insurers have declared it a write off. We need this car and cannot afford to replace it, so it looks as though we shall have to pay for the repairs ourselves - just what you need before Christmas. This is also the second time this has happened to us in 12 months, both times on Market Street. I know that other people have also experienced the same type of damage." (Forty-five year old female resident, central Charlbury)

"Before I moved in December I lived on Sheep Street for 9 years...During that time I had a back light cluster smashed (witnessed, and went to court), a rear panel kicked in, 2 wing mirrors broken off, at least 2 aerials snapped, 3 bonnet badges broken off and stolen, and a wiper arm bent. Not a bad score! I won't mention the other inconveniences involving traffic cones, foodstuffs and unmentionables. I even started to think that it was something personal...I doubt if it was, or that it has any purpose or is particularly targeted." (Middle aged male resident, central Charlbury)

The incidence of vandalism of the playground at Hughes and Sturt Closes draws attention to another aspect of public space and the implications of the ways in which it is used. It appears that to some extent a resident's ability to participate in the decision-making processes that affect his day-to-day life may affect the way in which he uses the environment in which he lives. In addition, it would appear that a resident's degree of choice is linked to propensity or vulnerability to social exclusion, that is, if he does not have the choice to move home, he needs to negotiate the drawbacks of the place he finds himself in. Being "stuck" in place may mean people, such as teenagers with time available and a lack of interests, leave marks such as graffiti or vandalism to define their own spaces within public places. However, this renders the public space less desirable for others, with a cycle of destructive use of public space resulting and causing exclusion of others.

Against this background and without a taking back of the area that is being abused, residents may feel vulnerable in their neighbourhood but also feel unable to change the way the public space around them, including the roadways and pavements, are used. The deteriorating public realm serves, instead of being a generator of social closeness and inclusiveness, to fracture fragile social networks and produce divisive shards within the community. A neighbourhood characterized by such unstable groundwork is less likely to be able to act cohesively and generate the social connectivity that may influence decisions that affect local residents.

Access to activity: implications of store relocation and expansion

During the period when fieldwork was being conducted in Charlbury, one of the main concerns being voiced by residents was about the relocation of the Co-op store to a new, larger site within the town. People were concerned about traffic impacts of the relocation as well as the possible effects on local small businesses of the expansion of the supermarket's services. The discussions of the proposal on the Charlbury internet forum (http://www.charlbury.info/) are useful for this research as they provide an indicator of the types of travel decisions residents were making prior to the store's relocation and expansion in late 2004. For example, in a contribution made in May 2004, a local resident writes that she travels by car to the town of Witney for food shopping and, consequently since she is there, she also buys incidentals such as newspapers which she could have bought at home in Charlbury:

"I think the big question people need to be asking here is do we want Charlbury residents to do their weeks shopping in Witney or in Cahrlbury (sic)? My husband and I go to Witney and 'as we are there' we pop to newsagents in Witney to buy our magazines, thus losing News And Things the chance of a sale. We might go to a Witney butchers or buy our lottery tickets in Smiths, our sons nappies in Boots, there again, losing Fiveways (local shop) and the butchers and chemists a sale. With the new Co-Op I will do all my shopping here in the Town and that will mean using ALL of Charlbury's shops more regularly. My car being at Spendlove (car park in Charlbury) will not add impact becuase it is quite often parked there when visiting the vets or Dr's surgery. We are not adding a Boots or WH Smiths, or even a Tesco superstore, all that is happening is our existing Co-op is moving to more suitable premises. 2 shops already sell magazines, 4 sell bread.....is it really likely that the Co-op growing in size will actually put these people out of business??? It is blocking the Co-op that will lose any chance we have of viablility (sic), giving out the message that residents don't need shops. Well we do. If people want more art galleries or an antiques shop or 3, then fine, let Charlbury fade into a dormitory town where the residents are all weekenders and the only visitors are ramblers. I would rather see people live their whole lives here (as I have) and see visitors here being people from Finstock and Fawler who are coming to use our Co-op and our other shops." (http://www.charlbury.info/ accessed 200904)

This quote is instructive as it implies how residents' patterns of trip-making may threaten the viability of rural retail activity. The availability of a car to the couple above allows them to make the journey to another town on a regular basis for shopping. It is difficult to determine from the quotation whether the availability of the car is the primary reason why they chose to travel to Witney or whether the perceived lack of suitable sources of goods in Charlbury caused them to search for alternative shopping locations. Indeed, it may be some other factor comes into play in the decision to go to Witney regularly such as combining the shopping trip with a visit to relatives. However, it may be inferred from the suggestion by the writer of the quote that she would shop locally if the new supermarket was open that the lack of sufficient availability of goods at present appears to be an important driver of her trip-making decision.

This provokes related, wider concerns: does being cognisant of the availability of a car make an individual more selective about the choices they can make with respect to accessing the accoutrements of daily life? Do people search more extensively through a number of options and destinations because they are more mobile as a result of car availability? How does the availability of the car to some residents (and the subsequent range of decisions they can make) affect the choices offered to residents who do not have access to a car? Are these residents more vulnerable to the vagaries of those with cars whose actions may ultimately result in the loss of local services through loss of revenue and low levels of usage? These questions all relate to the issue of transport and, often hidden, social exclusion in rural areas where some residents without cars find trip-making and access to services particularly difficult:

"I oppose the idea of moving the bus route in order to generate parking spaces apparently championed in these pages, by those who now doubt have a car to use. Older people do not all have cars and find it hard to walk longer distances. Young people such as my stepson would have been unable to get to work without the buses. If you wanted more parking spaces then why not look for a residence with such before moving to your current and presumably unsatisfactory home." (Contributor to Charlbury Forum, August 2004, commenting on a call for removal of buses running through the town available at http://www.charlbury.info/ accessed 220904)

For those without cars available in the quote above, the writer points to the difficulties of accessibility that can result.

Parking perversity

Writing in The Guardian, in an article entitled 'Station parking is club for elite', Clark (2004) characterizes the rural local railway station car park as an exclusive club. Clark cites the magazine Country Life as declaring that a "parking space is among the status symbols most sought by provincial commuters" and uses Charlbury station car park as an example of a car park that can be full by 7am "as early risers set off for work in the City". It is indeed the case that the designated bays at Charlbury station are usually full with over-spill parking along the access road a daily phenomenon (Plate 5.1). One research participant described the station as "Charlbury Parkway" because of his perception that he often had to walk away from the station, along the access road, perilously close to departing commuters' cars as they rushed home in the evening.

Plate 5.1   Spill-over parking on railway station access road

Source: Fiona Rajé

The impact of the high levels of parking at the station and the perception amongst some station users that the cost of £2.50 per day to park is too much has meant that the local authority has introduced parking restrictions on the roads in Charlbury that are nearest the station to dissuade drivers from parking there. These restrictions have, however, been viewed by some local residents as derisory as they allow parking on one side of the road except for one hour each week day (see Plates 5.2 and 5.3), clearly as a barrier to all day parking by commuters. As a consequence, local people who have no off road parking are inconvenienced and three were taken to court over the matter of tickets issued for parking on the street. The judge chose to quash the charges, recognizing the peculiarity of the parking restriction.

Plate 5.2   Parking restrictions on the east side of Church Lane

Source: Fiona Rajé

Plate 5.3   Parking restrictions on the west side of Church Lane

Source: Fiona Rajé

Local operator, national operator: concerns about bus services changes

During the period of study in Charlbury, the franchise for bus services from the town was lost by Worths buses of Enstone (nearby local village) to the national company Stagecoach. Prior to the announcement of the change, people had given accounts of their reasons for satisfaction with the services provided by Worths to the researcher. They perceived the service as reliable 'it gets you home even in the snow' (Fifty-five year old female interviewee) and suggested that the drivers made every effort to meet their needs as much as possible. When the changes to the services were announced, expressions of consternation were made by bus users as the following quotes indicate:

"It's worrying, at first glance, to see the County neglecting local family businesses in favour of the conglomerate that is Stagecoach, with their questionable background and not entirely reliable reputation. How on earth did this happen? Gareth (Thu Oct 14)"

"I just hope this doesn't harm Worths. That wonderful company has faithfully served Charlbury all my life and long before, and I for one would have voted to keep them every time. Stagecoach are a national company with no interest in us what so ever and nothing to lose financially by providing a dubious service, Worths on the other hand are in Enstone and knew that if the service was lacking then we'd come and tell them so!! And I've never had to!! Stagecoach Oxford on the other hand have offered me, late busses (sic),rude drivers, bad drivers, route alterations with no notice, time alterations with no notice and so many cancelled busses (sic) it's a shame. Thank you OCC for rewarding all of Worths hard work over the last god knows how many years with chucking them over in favour of a company that doesn't have a local interest, or need the money. Typical of England nowadays. Kate (Sat Oct 16)"

"Not a bad frequency, but a shame that only Chippy (Chipping Norton) gets the late night buses. It would be better if the last bus of the day (23.40 out of Oxford) could detour via Charlbury. Richard (Sat Dec 4)"

"Well, the revised timetable has more buses on weekdays, but fewer in the peak times. This alone makes the bus less useful to me (daily user of the 70 service).I wonder if December 13th will also see a marked increase in fares? I also worry about reliability, Worths have failed me once in over 3 years....with a swift follow up apology. I know of colleagues in Woodstock and Begbroke who chose the Worths bus rather than the current Stagecoach due to the unreliable service. I will give the new service a fair chance...I have no alternative but their customer service will hear from me if they fail to live up to the service we have received from Worths. Ian (Fri Dec 10)"

(quotes from charlbury.info forum 'Stagecoach' accessed 131204)

These views suggest that local people feel that decisions have been made that affect them without their involvement in the decision-making process. The comments also highlight the issues that these participants deem to be important when using a bus service: reliability, services at the times they would like to/need to travel, safety and fares. It is also instructive that they perceive that the small, local operator cares for their needs whereas they have doubts about the interest of the national operator in local people, suggesting that it is more concerned about financial gain than people.

Trains and timetables: the challenges of rural rail reliability

It is not only the bus operator that changed during the study period. The train services through Charlbury became the responsibility of First Great Western Link, replacing Thames Trains. After a timetable change towards the end of 2004, there were increased reports of unreliability and information failure. In an entry entitled "Railway reliability collapses" one resident sums up the problems experienced:

> One month after the introduction of a new timetable, Charlbury's rail service has seen a drastic fall in reliability. Though the newly-introduced trains are more comfortable, they have proved unable to keep to time, causing knock-on delays on the single-line railway. On occasion, the stop at Charlbury has even been omitted so the train can make up time. Passengers have been turfed out at Oxford and told to wait for the following train.

> Train breakdowns and unadvertised closures for engineering work have accentuated the misery. Indeed, the service got off to a bad start on its first day in December, when services were cancelled and replaced with a fleet of Oxford black cabs.

> Long-serving rail staff are now regularly voicing their exasperation to passengers. One member of staff at Oxford station angrily told a platform of complaining Cotswold Line customers: "As far as I'm concerned, we were going downhill anyway and since FirstGroup took over we've got a lot worse."

> As well as reliability problems, the new trains have a serious problem with bike accommodation. The cycle storage, at each end of the train, has to be unlocked by the guard and is awkward to operate. Combined with the end-of-carriage doors, this means that trains are frequently delayed at stations while passengers get on and off.

> Though there may be no 'quick fix' for the train design, the problems have been exacerbated by First Great Western Link's inability to provide accurate information. Display screens are frequently wrong, while late-night trains have been replaced by buses with no warning at stations. There are no posters to tell cyclists where to stow their bikes - with the resulting confusion delaying trains still further. The chaos on the line has forced some Charlbury commuters to catch earlier trains in order to reach work on time. Local people are understood to be bombarding First Great Western and its managing director, Alison Forster, with complaints about the service. The current franchises are set to run for another 18 months, at which point they will be replaced by one single Great Western franchise. Among the bidders is a consortium of London-Scotland firm GNER and Chiltern Railways, the highly acclaimed operator of trains from East Oxfordshire to Marylebone. If it hopes to retain the franchise, First will have to raise its game - and fast.

(Richard Fairhurst @ http://www.charlbury.info accessed 170105)

It would appear that the views expressed above are held by other users of the Cotswold Line which serves Charlbury. The Cotswold Line Promotion Group (CPLG) reports of a 'revolt' which took place at Oxford Station:

The Cotswold Line Promotion Group is deeply concerned to hear that a situation was created which resulted in a revolt by passengers at Oxford station on the evening of Wednesday 12th January 2005…(T)he Group understands that the 1552 Adelante service from London to Worcester Shrub Hill was running late and it was decided to terminate it at Oxford, without any apparent thought about what was to happen to the 200 or so passengers who wanted to travel to stations on the Cotswold Line. They were merely advised to wait for the following train, which is the notorious 2-car 1722 departure.

This train duly arrived and some 400 people struggled to get on board, to such an extent that the Senior Conductor deemed it to be an unsafe situation. Requests were made for some people to get off, but nobody moved. Even a threat that the train would go no further unless some got off was ignored and passengers sat (or stood) tight. Eventually, a 3-car train was produced and passengers then transferred to it, but even so, some still had to be left behind when the train departed some 40 minutes late, having blocked platform 2 at the station for this period. This effectively delayed trains on the Cotswold Line for the remainder of the evening.

(Cotswold Line Promotion Group, 14 January 2005 @ http://www.clpg.co.uk/ newspassenger%20revolt.htm accessed 170105)

The experiences of users of the Cotswold Line were raised at a House of Commons debate on rail timetables by the local Member of Parliament, David Cameron, at the beginning of February 2005:

Mr. Cameron: I thank the Secretary of State for that reply but is he aware that, on the Cotswold line, the new timetable has been a disaster? A daily commuter who lives in Charlbury wrote to me to say that her trains arrived on time only twice in the first four weeks of the new timetable's operation. Some trains did not stop at the advertised stations, and overcrowding, lateness and delays have become endemic. Will the right hon. Gentleman look at that line specifically and help ensure that timetables in rural areas are both deliverable and delivered? Is he aware that there is a suspicion in those areas that the new timetables favour urban areas and let down rural commuters such as my constituent?
Mr. Darling: The hon. Gentleman's latter point is not correct, but performance on the Cotswold line since the changes has been lamentable and is totally unacceptable. I have been given a long explanation as to why that is, but, unless the hon. Gentleman is a trainspotter, I shall save him from listening to me reading it out. The long and short of the matter is that the problems are capable of being fixed and First Great Western is in the process of doing so.

(Hansard, 01 Feb 2005 @ http://www.publications.parliament.uk/cgi-bin/ukparl_hl?DB =ukparl&STEMMER=en&WORDS=charlburi+&COLOUR=Red&STYLE=s&URL=/ pa/cm200405/cmhansrd/cm050201/debtext/50201-04.htm#50201-04_spnew6 accessed 250205)

The dissatisfaction expressed in the quotes above and in the previous sub-section about the quality of public transport services in Charlbury indicates that there are issues that need to be addressed by the operators and the County Council. In a community where car ownership levels are high, there is a potential for many of those who are disenchanted with bus and rail services to become even more dependent upon car travel, if they have access to a car. This works counter to the local authority's policy of promoting non-car modes (Oxfordshire County Council, 2000 and 2005) and points to the need for integrated planning and proactive management of transport to meet the daily needs of the system user reliably.

In a rural town such as Charlbury, some residents appear to be particularly motivated to use public transport, having moved to the area specifically because of the railway station being there (as discussed in the next sub-section). However, habit can be a major inhibitor of behavioural change. Individuals settle into routines of travel behaviour in terms of the trips they make, the modes they use, the destinations they visit and so on, that become habitual and entrenched (Stanbridge, 2002). Losing the patronage of people who were motivated to use public transport, as a result of operational vagaries and poor service quality may mean that, if they are not part of a captive market (i.e. those who have no alternative but to use public transport), they are permanently lost as public transport users to car-based travel. By extension, loss of patronage may result in loss of services which are no longer financially viable and a net increase in travel-induced social isolation of residents through withdrawal of services may occur.

Transport and residential choice

Some respondents described having chosen to move to Charlbury because of its transport connections:

> "One of the reasons we chose to live in Charlbury is that it has a train station. It is possible to live here without a car and, even if we had a car, we wouldn't have to use it for work. I work from home and Laura gets the train to Oxford." (30 year old male who moved to Charlbury in June 2004)

> "Several people moved to Charlbury because it has a train station. I did 4 years ago when I commuted to London for 6 months until I found a job in Oxford. I was a member of Friends of the Earth and used to take my bike with me on the train to London". (36 year old male who moved to Charlbury in 2000)

Even amongst people who had moved to the town several years previously, good transport connections had been a key motivating factor. For example, a 50 year old female participant stated that when she and her husband moved to Charlbury 20 years ago "the main reason we moved to Charlbury was because we didn't have a car and there was good public transport here. I didn't drive and still don't, so that still applies".

While people who chose to move to Charlbury often did so because of transport[3], in-migration as a result of the railway station was characterized by one local interviewee as detrimental to the town:

> "The worst thing that has happened to Charlbury is the train station. Since services there were improved many years ago, incomers have come here, people who've moved here to

---

3   Overall, 7 out of the 16 interviewees linked choice of Charlbury as a residential location to transport network connectivity, in particular the availability of mainline rail service from the town to Oxford and London.

commute to Reading, Oxford and London. We didn't want them to come and before the train station, they didn't." (Fifty-something female resident)

Local talk, local concerns

The voices expressed on the internet forum above have been helpful in pointing to some of the transport issues that were preoccupying local people over the period of the empirical research. Analysis of the postings on this forum was useful for developing an insight into current local opinion on transport. The results of this analysis are shown in Box 5.3.

Box 5.3 'Listening' to electronic 'chat': using an internet forum to understand local concerns

The potential of electronic 'chat'

In an effort to obtain an insight into the types of topics and particularly transport topics that concerned residents of Charlbury, the web-based forum on the Charlbury information website was a valuable resource. This naturally occurring electronic talk made relatively frequent reference to transport issues and provided another useful insight into people's concerns. If we accept that people tend to talk about an issue when it is of concern to them, the examination of electronic sources is considered to be helpful in developing a sense of concerns amongst a community. Also, as postings to discussion groups are dated, changes in concerns over time may be revealed.

All postings to the forum between 6 March 2003 and 28 January 2005 were analysed with a view to exploring the value of electronic discussion groups to develop local understandings. During this 23 month period, there were 133 topics posted on the discussion group. Amongst several issues raised, 16 of these topics were directly related to transport. This does not include those postings that related to vandalism of cars in the area. The 16 transport topics were made up of a total of 129 postings with the topics 'Stagecoach', 'The Trains', 'Up to 700 daily movements to and from the proposed new Coop site' and 'Speed Bumps' generating the highest numbers of posts amongst the transport related topics at 22, 21, 21 and 18 respectively. Together these 129 transport-related postings made up the largest number of entries on any one theme. The only other topics yielding similar or higher numbers of postings overall (and thereby serving as a useful barometer for issues generating discussion) were largely related to communication issues (digital radio, broadband, mail). The generator of greatest discussion was 'Earthquake/Tsunami relief' with 33 posts.

Topic	No. of posts
Earthquake/Tsunami relief	33
The play	28
The post again	26
New Co-op	23
Internet Broadband	20
Broadband News	19
Digital radio reception	19
Save the Corner house	19

These findings are interesting not only as an indicator of the transport topics that have taken local interest but also as much for what they do not say. No mention is made on the forum about the proposed home zone in the town although interviews with local people in the area where it is planned suggest that there are concerns about this scheme. The area where the home zone is proposed is made up of local authority housing stock and residents on these two streets have been described by a local councillor anecdotally as being 'poor'. He adds that the people on the other side of the town are seen as the 'nice' people of Charlbury. Using his terminology and reflecting upon the discussion forum, it may be that this is an example of how the 'connected' make use of tools of connectivity to express their needs and views while the 'poor' or excluded do not have the ability or choose not to avail of such media.

There are examples amongst the postings of local people organising themselves through the forum to make representations to the train operating company about the poor service they feel they are receiving. In this way, the forum acts as an informal meeting place for like-minded individuals who may have, in the past, met at a community centre or been connected through social relationships within the town. Amongst an increasingly-mobile society, several participants in this research stated that they had chosen to live in Charlbury because of its transport connectivity through the train service to London. It follows then that while they may live in the same town, commuters with complaints about their train service may find it much easier to meet those in a similar situation through an electronic medium than they would in seeking out others through other means locally. Thus the electronic forum is being used as an organising tool for the expression of impacts that transport is having on a particular sector of Charlbury's residents. Indirectly and perhaps more subtly, it is also serving to underline the exclusion from this mode of expression of another sector of the town's social mix: that is, the residents of Sturt and Hughes Closes do not make use of the electronic media to organize a response to an issue which some of them state that they are not supportive of.

The potential of a rural car club: solving transport and social concerns?

Although one of the couples interviewed stated that they had moved to Charlbury because of its good transport links, an insight into their lives (Box 5.4) reveals that some of their leisure transport needs are not being suitably satisfied.

Box 5.4 Balancing the satisfaction of latent travel demand with environmental concerns

Laura and Adam moved from Oxford to Charlbury when they got married in June 2004. They wanted to live where Laura could commute to Oxford and Adam could travel to London relatively easily once every fortnight when he was not working from home. They are happy in their rented cottage and enjoy cycling and walking on the "masses of footpaths and rights of way" around the town. However, Laura admits that there are some activities she would like to do but cannot because of transport problems such as attending evening classes. They would also like to be able to travel to somewhere other than Oxford on a Sunday but, since the buses do not run that day, their only choice is to take a train to Oxford if they fancy a day out. The weekend before they were interviewed, they had been to visit Laura's relatives in Cornwall. While they would have liked to have travelled by train for that trip, engineering work had meant that the outward trip would take several hours and there was no service on the day they needed to return home. The couple rented a car instead. This is something they said they do three or four times a year: to visit friends and relatives, to carry heavy items and to be able to travel to places that are difficult to reach by public transport. Indeed, although they state that they definitely would not need a car for travel to work purposes, they are now considering buying a car. Adam summarizes the duality of his thoughts on the issue: "(We've been) talking about buying a car. It would be for leisure use, for example, it would give us stuff to do on a weekend like go to a country pub, to National Trust properties, even places like Blenheim. I think if we had a car, many other destinations and options that we don't see at the moment may open up to us. But I really like walking around and it is better to have active streets with lots of people on them. You feel more comfortable in communities when people walk around and say hi to each other. Local transactions and exchange make it feel a more comfortable place. I go to the shops here everyday – actually, everyone knows me now in the shops. Otherwise if everyone is in cars, the streets are dead.'

For this couple who describe themselves as "feeling strongly about environmental issues" (Adam) and express feelings of satisfaction about their neighbourhood "It's a peaceful area" (Laura), the need to maintain social networks and access activities beyond the local community is forcing a reconsideration of their car ownership status. Their willingness to rent cars when needed indicates that this couple may be ideally suited as users of a car club. They do not have daily need for a car but would like to have the flexibility to be able to participate in activities beyond the neighbourhood that access to a car club vehicle would allow. Also, the appeal of not committing to full time car ownership is likely to be particularly attractive to someone who stated that:

> "I like not having a car. It feels like I'm doing something positive about the environment. I promised myself when I was young that I would not have a car before I was 30, well, I'm 31 next birthday and we are actually considering getting a car, not for work but for leisure." (Adam)

The concept of rural car clubs was championed in the Rural White Paper, which recognized that for many people living and working in rural communities, using a car was the only practicable means of undertaking many journeys. The "on-line guide to what works in neighbourhood renewal", www.renewal.net, provides a summary of the car club concept:

> Car clubs involve common ownership of a mix of vehicles which members can be book for specific trips. Members are charged an annual membership fee and then pay for each journey on a time and mileage basis. Overheads are low because the costs of purchasing, maintaining and running the vehicles are shared by the members. Car clubs have the potential to provide access to a car for the many people who may not need a car every day but who depend on one for particular journeys. They also help to reduce traffic congestion, parking problems and air pollution. (renewal.net, 2005a:5)

Renewal.net's report on rural car clubs goes on to describe some of the findings of research carried out on a national initiative to promote and support the development of such clubs funded by the Countryside Agency. The research indicated that "car clubs appear to appeal to a wide range of social classes with a broad spectrum of incomes", "early adopters tend to be keen abut the idea, fairly 'green' and/or active in other community initiatives" and the "main motivational factors for joining relate to lifestyle and environmental issues" (renewal.net, 2005a:6). Against these criteria, it would appear that the couple described here could be potential early adopters. In addition, renewal.net reports that the evaluation of the national rural car club initiative found that:

- Individually the clubs have between one and four cars
- They operate across 31 rural communities with populations of between 4,000 and 23,000
- Individually they cover between one and 16 villages or small towns
- Cars are generally used on average for a period of five hours, although the range is between one and 34 hours
- The average mileage covered per hire is around 20 miles, with a range of four to 548 miles.

These findings indicate that the scope of membership, fleet size, geographical coverage and usage varies. This suggests that there may be benefits in exploring whether a rural car club may be most economically and efficiently run only for residents of Charlbury or whether there would be economies of scale in extending coverage to encompass adjacent villages such as Finstock or Enstone.

Lift-sharing: building on social capital, building social capital?

Some of the participants in this study described their reliance upon friends and relatives for regular and one-off trips:

> "I come to this shop (local Londis store) to get my bits and pieces but I go to Witney for my main shop. I go with a friend. (Also) my sons live nearby and my grandson. They give me lifts." (Retired female non-driver, Sturt Close)

> "I've got my son to drive me places. I get my daughters to take me to the hospital when I need to go." (70 year old female non-driver, Sturt Close)

> "My friend comes from another village to take me places." (Eighty-two year old female who can no longer drive, Hughes Close)

For some, infirmity and ageing meant they were no longer able to use their car, for others, a car was simply not available to them. The community has responded to some of the social needs of the elderly by providing trips to different homes on a Sunday for tea to those who would not have an opportunity to meet others normally. There is also another group which gives elderly people lifts to the memorial hall on a Wednesday for lunch. While provision of such lifts may enable some older people to meet others, the service does not satisfy all their travel needs nor does it meet the travel needs of other local people. The Charlbury Caring Community Car Scheme serves to fill the gap between public transport services and private car journeys as it provides a car service for local residents by volunteers using their own cars. Trips are organized on request but tend to be made to hospital and other health care appointments. Anecdotal evidence from a previous study of trip-making to hospitals (Rajé et al., 2003b) suggests that there may be a certain amount of stigma amongst young people about using such services. However, through more widespread usage and acceptance of such schemes, they may be mainstreamed and the likelihood of any aversion to using them may be duly lessened.

Another related concept that could help satisfy latent travel needs amongst the rural community of Charlbury is the use of a more formalized model of lift-sharing. During the period of research, a new resident in the area posted a request on the Charlbury information forum about the possibility of travelling with another local person to work outside of Oxfordshire, indicating that there may be a latent demand for shared trip-making. There are a number of websites available in the UK for people to find others with whom they can make both regular and one-off trips. Some of these such as http://www.mylifts.com/ and http://www.shareacar.com/ are aimed at commuter trips. A particularly user-friendly website can be found at www.liftshare. org which enables people to make links with other users for all trip types:

You can share a car for any journey - getting to work, doing the weekly shop, taking the children to school, going to the match at the weekend, travelling to a festival, event or show, getting to or from university, visiting friends or getting to the airport. (http://www. liftshare.org/welcome.asp)

With an active information website already in place in Charlbury at www.charlbury. info, a hyperlink from the community's information site to the lift-share website would be a practical way to facilitate ease of access for potential lift-sharers. The benefits of such an intervention are that it:

- Saves you money - travelling with others enables you to reduce your transport costs by up to £1000 a year.
- Reduces the number of cars on the roads - resulting in less congestion, less pollution and fewer parking problems
- Provides a real solution to the transport problems of rural areas
- Gives employees and employers more transport options
- Reduces the need for a private car (http://www.liftshare.org/welcome.asp)

It is clear from this study that local people seem to travel to Witney and Chipping Norton regularly. By sharing lifts on these two routes, people would be able to pool together their resources, make trips when public transport was not available and lessen the number of individual car journeys to and from these destinations. An additional benefit would be that by making contact with other people in the local area, new acquaintances may be made, possible friendships formed and there may be positive spin-off effects of increased social networking and development of the community's social capital. In a town such as Charlbury, where there appear to be a barely-hidden chasm between different groups of residents, a lift-sharing scheme could bring together sectors of the community who would not necessarily naturally find a common focus with a spin-off effect of helping to instil a sense of community pride amongst those involved.

Making non-car options attractive

The difficulties experienced by some residents of Charlbury in using the trains and buses have been rehearsed earlier in this chapter. This brief section captures the positive comments made by participants about their experience of using the transport system. Insights into the factors that users describe as enhancing the transport system's amenity can assist in targeting investment to the most appropriate and beneficial features for the customer.

One of the main issues that public transport system users complain about is the lack of availability of information (Social Exclusion Unit, 2003; Rajé et al., 2004a). In Charlbury, a simple solution has been adopted: local bus and train timetables are displayed on a wall in the centre of the town. This information is in a place where it can be easily seen by residents and visitors to the area since it is beside the main shopping street. The provision of public transport information that is easily accessible also serves the useful purpose of providing those who are largely-car dependent with a ready source of information about alternative modes should they be willing to consider, or forced to use, an alternative mode:

> "I think the transport information on the wall in the town centre is really good. Although I've never used the buses, my car had to have its smashed windows fixed in Witney last week and I did look at the bus times to see how easy it would be if I needed to take a bus to Witney." (Forty-four year old single female car driver)

However, provision of easily-accessible public transport information is of little use if the services or routes offered do not meet the trip-making needs of local people. One participant highlighted how a relatively-recent change to the bus timetable had facilitated access to greater employment and leisure opportunities for some residents:

> "By providing a subsidized service to Witney, people who hadn't previously been able to work are now able to go there to work. The subsidized service runs back later than the last service used to and means that people in Charlbury have the option of working a full day and then coming home. I think this has given people more employment opportunities. I hope the service continues because old people also use it to travel to and from the market in Witney every Thursday." (Fifty-five year old female with access to a car)

From this account, the subsidy has opened up opportunities for rural community members to participate in activities which are not available locally.

It is often the case that people describe the alternatives to the car as unattractive. A benefit of park and ride is that it allows those who prefer to use a car to do so for a part of their journey. But, even within the park and ride system, there are features that make some sites more attractive to use than others. Take, for example, the views of a user of the system:

> "I'd be keen on everyone being able to use a good public transport system like the standards at Water Eaton Park and Ride which are a great experience. You feel like they value you as a customer there. I'm much more likely to use Water Eaton than Pear Tree because of the facilities – toilets etc." (Forty-four year old female)

The interviewee here sees the standard of facilities at the new Water Eaton Park and Ride site as a benchmark, not only for park and ride sites, but also for all public transport services. She attaches great importance to people being valued for their custom and suggests that the high standards that she has experienced at this site should be emulated throughout the transport system.

How parking policy in Oxford may affect residents of Charlbury

The research revealed that parking policy in Oxford can affect the decisions people living in Charlbury make about where they travel to and how they get there. An exchange of views made by contributors to an Oxfordshire internet forum, writing about the proposed expansion of the Westgate Shopping Centre in central Oxford, helps illustrate how Oxford's parking policy can affect its economy and the social lives of residents of the wider county:

Participant A: ...Oxford is rubbish for shopping, Reading and Milton Keynes and even Cheltenham is so much better...

Participant B: ...Does it really matter? The shops will be the same as anywhere else in the country. What benefit will it be to the people of Oxford? What is the point in building a shopping centre when access to the city is so restrictive and the actual city centre has become so uninviting?

Participant A: The Westgate multi storey car park is so ugly, we might as well have shops there and an underground car park and bus station and get the buses out of Queen Street and George Street. Why should I keep having to travel for a decent shopping experience, more cars on the road, more pollution. (Source: Oxfordshire Forums, September 2004 @ www.oxfordshireforums.co.uk/pop_printer_friendly.asp?TOPIC_ID=15770 accessed 150904)

While the above commentary provides an interesting insight into views on the need for improved shopping facilities in central Oxford, in terms of this research it is more interesting to examine the implication by Participant A that having to travel to destinations other than Oxford contributes to congestion and the perception expressed by Participant B that access to Oxford is restrictive.

Looking at each of these views in further detail, the contributor links a perceived need to travel by car to alternative destinations to a concern about congestion. Other studies have also shown that there is a high level of concern about congestion among the UK public. MORI (2001) states that the single most important transport issue for the public reported across the country is congestion. There is other evidence to support this finding. For example, Foley et al. (2005) report that traffic congestion is one of the quality of life concerns of residents in the South East of England. MORI's study found that 71% of people who drive into congested major town or city centres are prepared to pay something by way of a congestion charge and, of these, almost a third are willing to pay £5 or more. With reference to social exclusion, the survey found transport is perceived as critical to life as it is seen as the key to freedom, independence, access to work and social opportunity. Thus, the internet forum participant points to a possible internal dilemma: on one hand, he would like to be able to participate in activities in the city centre and access them with ease; on the other, he feels that there are socially undesirable effects such as pollution and congestion associated with travelling by car to other destinations because Oxford does not offer opportunities of which he would wish to avail. It is likely that a person with his views would be averse to paying a charge to enter the city of Oxford. However, if he felt that opportunities and activities available in the centre had been improved, he may be much more willing to pay to access them with relative ease, rather than making longer journeys which he perceives to be more environmentally-detrimental.

We turn now to the issue of access to Oxford raised by Participant B and specifically to the contribution of parking policy in the city to the ease with which rural residents may participate in activities in the centre. Interviewees in Charlbury were asked about their views on parking policies in Oxford and whether these affected the choices they made about travel. Responses were varied. Amongst respondents with access to a car, some expressed no desire to go to Oxford:

> "I never go to Oxford, I don't like it." (Elderly female resident, relies on lifts from family and friends or uses bus)

> "I don't go shopping in Oxford. I go where I have relatives and there's good out of town shops like Wycombe and Aylesbury. If I visit my sister in Thame, we go to the big shops by car in Aylesbury. There's no need to deal with Oxford then." (Female car driver aged 42, mother of 2 children)

Some participants with access to a car described perceived disincentives to parking in Oxford. Price, congestion and difficulty in locating a space all appeared to be contributing factors:

> "I go into Oxford far less than I used to. I'm split on this, we should use the park and ride but I want to go where I want to go. There's no charge for parking in Witney. I consider Cheltenham too. I go to Oxford much less socially now. I've given up going to plays in town. I tried going by train but they're too unreliable and I've ended up missing things. Buses take ages and are also unreliable. Parking is too restrictive. The whole hostility of parking in Oxford puts me off: the price, the fact that there's no spaces and also the congestion. I don't even consider Oxford if I need something. I always think where else can I get it." (Female resident aged 45, mother of 3 children)

> "There is a perception that it is more difficult to park in Oxford than elsewhere. A lot of people wouldn't drive into Oxford if they didn't have the resources to solve the parking problem. For the 'nice' people of Charlbury, they've got connections – an estate agency, a college – that provides a parking space. The cost factor does make people think about it. Also people consider the risk of the fine that they get from the wardens." (Middle aged male)

As the above quote states, for the 'connected', parking policies in Oxford are a non-issue:

> "I've got a parking space in Oxford that I can use where I used to work, so I can chose to come into Oxford by car if I want to." (Retired academic)

For some of the other interviewees, the restrictions associated with parking in Oxford have meant that they evaluate the need for parking against the activity they plan to undertake in Oxford and then make a decision as to which mode choice would most suit their needs.

The following quote shows that the respondent chooses to use the park and ride for activities such as going to a movie which could take longer than the two hour maximum parking at St Giles where she would normally park to go into central Oxford. She presents shopping as an activity which she does not enjoy but sometimes must tolerate, giving it a time limitation that relates to the maximum parking interval allowed at St. Giles in Oxford:

"I'm not too good at shopping and can only manage a couple of hours at the most, so I tend to just drive in to Oxford and pay for parking at St Giles which covers the couple of hours. It is expensive but if I have to go to the east side of town I go to the car park at St Clements where you only pay 50p for an hour. That's much better. If I'm going to the cinema at Magdalen St, I use the park and ride. The experience of shopping in Oxford isn't good so I can understand why people say they go to other places like Cheltenham." (Female resident aged 44)

Sometimes, however, the choice becomes not so much one of mode as destination with an alternative location, where parking is perceived to be easier, being substituted for Oxford. A 36 year old father who works in Oxford stated that "parking in Oxford puts you off". He has a parking space at work in West Oxford but, for leisure trips, he suggested that the family would tend to go to Kidlington, Banbury or Witney rather than Oxford because of the deterrent effects related to finding parking in the city. He did not think parking was expensive but that the congestion and having to search for spaces was most off-putting. However, it was not only those with access to a car who expressed a preference for going to other destinations:

"If we want to go for big shopping, more expensive things, say to John Lewis, we go by train to Reading." (Female 30 year old without access to car)

This quote takes us back to the views expressed on the internet forum about the unattractiveness of Oxford as a shopping destination. From the statements made by participants, it appears that there are fundamental perceptions amongst the public that Oxford is not a particularly desirable location to visit for shopping trips. This view is exacerbated for car users who conflate congestion, parking search time and costs with the unattractiveness of the destination and suggest that they find alternative locations more desirable as a result. For some, there is a willingness to use the Park and Ride system but this appears to be very closely associated with the activity that they intend to participate in while in the city.

Thus, the ways in which parking policy can affect rural residents with access to a car can result in a variety of responses. What is clear from the empirical research is that parking policy can result in space and time exclusion as city centres become "no-go" areas for those whose only suitable mode of access to the centre is the car.

In June 2005, following the Conservative party's win in the local County Council elections in May, some liberalization of the restrictions on on-street parking in Oxford were announced. These changes would allow motorists free on-street parking in the evenings and on Sundays, as well as a introducing a waiver of the 60p parking charge at the Water Eaton and Thornhill park and ride sites (which are operated by the County Council) (Ffrench, 2005). Making the announcement of the Conservatives intention to adhere to their election pledge to introduce free on-street parking, the County Council's executive member for transport suggested that the authority was aware of the need to encourage people to travel into Oxford in order to protect its vitality:

Oxford is not just a historic monument – I want it to be a thriving, interesting place with a real buzz and that is why we are bringing in these changes. On-street parking charges were designed to deter commuters, and this isn't necessary in the evening and on Sundays. (Ffrench, 2005:11)

This implies cognizance of the detrimental impacts prevailing parking policy may be having on the city. By extension, any negative effects on the city centre will affect not only the local urban residents but, also, the people who live in rural areas which, through geographically proximity, would tend to be dependent on the near urban centre.

The role of community voices in shaping transport interventions

As indicated earlier, there are inherent dangers in only listening to the more vocal residents of a study area. An absence of contributions from the less-connected to research, planning and scheme/policy discourses may result in promotion of proposals which augment the 'hidden' residents' isolation from local decision-making, thereby intensifying their feelings of powerlessness on a number of fronts. This relational lack of power may operate with respect to their more financially-privileged neighbours, the local political authorities and the wider national system of governance. This underlines the importance of seeking out and hearing the hidden community voices. People whose voices may not be generally heard may not be as organized as the more vocal interest groups. Nevertheless, it is important that their views are heard and that inclusive approaches are used to engage with members of different groups. Such approaches build on local knowledge and allow residents to be involved in practical, local solutions. This is a key Government policy objective:

> Planning shapes the places where people live and work. So it is right that people should be enabled and empowered to take an active part in the process. Community involvement is vitally important to planning.
>
> The planning system already provides many opportunities for local people to participate in key decisions about their areas. The Government wants to build on these strong foundations. An accessible and transparent planning system, which provides continuing opportunities for local people to participate, is essential to deliver our objective of creating inclusive, accessible, safe and sustainable communities. (ODPM, 2004a:2)

However, while public involvement in planning is necessary, it is important that a balance is struck to avoid consultation fatigue amongst the potentially-affected public. For example, while carrying out this study it became apparent that in the Cowley Road area of Oxford an exemplary consultation exercise had been undertaken about proposed accident reduction and environmental improvement proposals[4]. One of the consequences of the success of this consultation was that when local people were approached for this study to talk about their views on transport, they appeared slightly apathetic about the subject and expressed the view that, generally, they did not feel that they had any transport or travel problems that they wished to discuss.

---

4   The Cowley Road consultation is discussed in greater detail in Chapter 4.

Returning to the issue of involvement of members of different social groups in planning, the Scottish Executive (2004) recently reported on research conducted to explore the extent to which planning decisions in Scotland are based on an accurate assessment of the views of the affected local people. Of particular relevance to this research was the report's consideration of whether those that are involved in the planning process represent the broader population. The Scottish Executive research found that:

> (T)hose who volunteered views to the local authority came from a particular cross section of the community dominated by the middle aged and the elderly. People under 35 are largely absent from the process. Retired people dominate the responses. White Caucasians dominated the responses to all three planning applications…Women are slightly more likely than men to become involved in the planning process… (Scottish Executive, 2004: executive summary)

Identifying dynamics and projecting forward: the baseline scenario, policy changes and transport interventions

Introduction

In this section, the findings related to the proposed home zone are discussed.

How planned home zone may affect local residents

A home zone[5] has been proposed for the Hughes Close/Sturt Close of Charlbury. This is a typical post-war rural council house development located in an enclosed

---

5   Home Zones are an attempt to strike a balance between vehicular traffic and everyone else who uses the street, the pedestrians, cyclists, business people and residents. Some see Home Zones as a way of "reclaiming" local streets from a traditional domination by cars. Others see it more modestly as a way of trying to restore the safety and peace in neighbourhoods that are becoming overwhelmed with speeding traffic. Home Zones work through the physical alteration of streets and roads in an area. These alterations force motorists to drive with greater care and at lower speeds. Many countries support this with legislation allowing the Home Zones to enforce a reduced speed limit of 10 miles an hour. The benches, flower beds, play areas, lamp posts, fences and trees used to alter the streets and roads offer many additional community benefits to the Home Zones and are considered to enhance the beauty of an area and increase the housing prices.

Home Zones, while on the surface offer substantial benefits to and area, are the source of some controversy. It has been reported that such schemes have delayed the response rates of the emergency services to the streets within the Zone. Other reports describe local authorities being inundated with complaints from residents demanding that the road humps and chicanes be removed as they are causing huge tailbacks through the streets. People have shown concern that encouraging children to play in roads, even specially adapted roads such as Home Zones, has introduced a danger which was not previously there. It has also been reported that the residents of a home zone in America are actively campaigning to have the road alterations removed as they can no longer park near their houses. (http://www.homezones.org/concept.html)

residential area immediately off Sturt Road. The plan at Figure 5.2 shows the layout of the streets and the proposed home zone. The County Council reports that there are 93 houses in the two streets.

Consultants MVA and Building Design Partnership (BDP) have been appointed to design the Charlbury home zone. They have underlined the importance of consideration of social impacts when designing a home zone:

> When developing a Home Zone, it is important to understand not only the observed needs of a community, such as traffic flows and reduced accident rates, but also the longer term social impact achieved by making structural changes in the area," says MVA Deputy Director, Tim Cuthbert. "We will be encouraging residents to share ideas and collaborate on street design to improve the quality of their outdoor living space. (MVA Press Release Ref: 33497/525, 2 February 2004) @ http://www.mva-group.com/news/2004/ mvahomezoneoxfordshire.htm accessed 100405

Mr. Cuthbert's assertion of the importance of the needs of the community when developing a home zone raises a vital point about the proposals for Sturt and Hughes Closes. Dialogue with residents of these two streets suggests that there is some cynicism amongst the community about the benefits of the scheme.

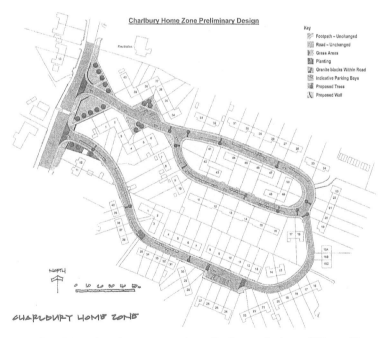

Figure 5.2   Plan showing proposed preliminary design of Home Zone

A number of residents expressed concerns that any trees or benches that may be introduced as part of the project would be likely to be vandalized. In addition, they conveyed an impression that the community had not asked for any traffic engineering intervention in the area. Rather, they implied that, although consultation had taken place on the scheme, their views would not be considered to be important in the scheme design and that their input would be of little value in the local authority's decision-making process:

> "We've had a lot of papers round about the plans but it'll not make any difference. Anyway, the Council will do what it wants." (Elderly female resident, Hughes Close)

Other interviewees were rather apathetic about the proposals. One retired male suggested that he could not envisage how the home zone would make any difference for him or his wife. Another man of 95 living on Hughes Close said 'the Council don't get round to doing things, so I don't expect changes to happen.' This view was shared by a 70 year old female resident of Sturt Close who felt that as she had lived there for 48 years, nothing would change for her. A 74 year old female resident of Sturt Close, when asked about her views on the planned Home Zone, stated:

> "They are going to do it anyway. We've had loads of forms to fill but they'll do it anyway. There's loads of vandalism. They're all on drugs round there (indicating towards the playground area)… They say they are going to put in trees and things but I'm not sure how it'll work for us."

However, while several respondents appeared to be indifferent to the proposals, the strength with which some others viewed the plans as detrimental is captured by one of the participant's words in Box 5.5.

Box 5.5 Taking account of an affected resident's views

Winnie's words: the voice of an 81 year old resident of Hughes Close

"I've lived here 26 years and we bought our bungalow 20 years ago. The council are planning to put 5 trees in by the pathway in front of my house as part of this home zone. I wrote to them when they asked for comments saying I didn't want the trees because they will block the window. I'm 81 and sitting at my window and looking over Wychwood Park is what I enjoy now that I can't get out much. I told them they were going to obscure my window on the world. Also, my husband used to win prizes for the garden and I still have a vegetable patch. Those trees will obscure the vegetables…. I've got heart trouble, so I can't walk to the shops. I drove until I was 76 but there's a time when you have to be sensible. With this home zone, I feel they've walked right over me. I've had a lovely view and it'll take the sun off my bungalow. 5 trees is far too many. Then there's the wall too. That may not be too bad, depends how the youth use it. There have been accidents here. It is a bad spot but on the main road not these side streets. They widened the road after I came here now they want to narrow it. Can't see the reason. Things are bad enough here with kids

---

breaking things. If they put those trees in, they'll vandalize them too. We don't want this zone, we don't want more vandalism. I feel I'm being treated like I don't matter. I mean I hear they are deciduous trees. Well, who's going to clean up the leaves? I sweep up the ones from the tree that's there now and in the cold, more leaves will just be unsafe. Other people round here have told me they don't want this either and people say they'll put down poison to kill the trees... Also, in the dark with trees it will be dangerous for people especially women to walk. My neighbour works at Co-op and has a shift at 6 in the morning. I don't think she'll feel safe walking amongst the trees. People have been attacked in Charlbury – it's not like people think it is here.

It is a waste of time (the home zone). On the options sheet they sent us, there was no option to say we didn't want it. So now they say people in Sturt and Hughes wanted it but we just had to choose the least bad of the options. It is unfair that I've said 4 times I don't want it and they just won't listen."

If it is indeed the case that the home zone is not being provided as a result of an expressed community need, and efforts to investigate the origins of the scheme through examination of Oxfordshire County Council Transportation Committee reports have not helped clarify its genesis, then the criteria upon which strategic decision-making on schemes of the order of £250,000 within the local authority may need to be revisited to determine whether there is any value in investment of considerable sums in schemes that have not been developed in response to accurate problem definition. As the interviewees in this research have implied, there is a danger that people feel apathy towards interventions that they feel are being imposed upon them and this, in turn, undermines not only the scheme's success but also the local authority's credibility.

Consultation that is perceived by local people to be 'token' in nature may mean that they feel that they are being subjected to a form of participatory exclusion. The table below was included in the Oxfordshire County Council Transportation implementation Committee Report which put forward the preliminary design for the home zone in October 2004. The table is provided in an Annex to the report and summarizes stakeholder comments on the design:

It can be seen that consultation was not particularly extensive. For example, when interviewed for this research, the owner of the only shop near to Sturt and Hughes Closes (immediately across the main road from these streets) had not heard about the planned scheme. Moreover, he felt that there was a much greater need for traffic on the main road outside the shop, where pedestrians cross, to be slowed down rather than on Sturt and Hughes Close. The consultation findings also show an absence of comments made by the most important stakeholders, the affected residents. This is of particular concern given that it appears to conflict with the County Council's

Table 5.4   Summary of Consultation Responses provided in report to Committee, Oxfordshire County Council – Charlbury Home Zone Stakeholder Consultation Responses

Stakeholder	Response
Police	Disappointed no proposals for play area Suggest walls are designed to prevent use by youths for seating Suggest trees are not placed in such a way as to provide hiding places for those committing car crime
Fire and Rescue Service	No concerns about scheme – happy to accept 3.5m pinch-points at junctions.
Charlbury Town Council	Support the scheme and the views of residents Request that memorial tree at entrance to Hughes Close be retained Suggest walls are topped to avoid people sitting on them Space for 2 notice boards must be retained

*Source: http://www2.oxfordshire.gov.uk/hlpdownloads/TI281004-10.htm_*

own reiteration, in its latest draft local transport plan (Oxfordshire County Council, 2005b: ch1), of its intention to carry out effective consultation:

The County Council seeks to:

- Ensure the purpose of the consultation is fully understood from the outset;

- Ensure the consultation process is conducted openly and honestly;

- Keep an open mind by making sure consultation is genuine;

- Ensure all consultation is fully inclusive and that the different groups consulted are as representative as possible;

- Ensure that all views expressed are taken into account when decisions are made;

- Communicate these decisions and feedback widely to the public and those who took part in the process;

- Understand the viewpoints of different groups/organisations;

- Understand what has gone on before, what local people want now and what they want in the future;

- Use consultation and public involvement, where possible, to raise people's awareness and understanding of the issues.

The neighbourhood renewal website, renewal.net, provides a report on Home Zones which looks at the evaluation of pilot home zones in the UK (renewal.net, 2005b). The report makes clear that the evidence from the pilot projects highlights that the success of a home zone is dependent on local resident interest. Several of the pilots were resident-led. This underlines the potential for failure of the Charlbury scheme. This potential is intensified by the evaluation report's findings that a Home Zone with the best chance of success usually features a champion within the local authority, a strong external facilitator and a strong residents' or tenants' group. None of these appear to be features of the Charlbury project. If a need perceived by the planning community is not being expressed by people in the neighbourhood, the implementation of what they feel is an unnecessary scheme may be interpreted as another way in which they have little or no control on their own circumstances. Rendering people voiceless in terms of their local area reiterates that they are powerless against a powerful local governance structure. Participation of subjects enhances democratic dialogue.

O'Dowd (no date) points out that lack of involvement of the public in decision-making may result in major community resistance once a scheme is implemented. Discussing public involvement in transport decision-making in the US, O'Dowd suggests that a "road map" is a critical tool for guiding citizens and officials through a public decision-making process. Adoption of a similar technique may be appropriate as an adjunct to a participatory decision-making process in the UK. The road map creates a vision of the process which O'Dowd contends "reduces frustration" (O'Dowd, no date:3). The other attributes of the approach are summarized by the author in the following quote:

> A road map that provides a clear understanding of the process provides participants with a vision of how to get where they have agreed to go. The road map does not have to outline the outcome; it needs to outline the process. When the process is done well, participants will defend the results even when they disagree with the outcome. Following a specific agreed upon road map can avoid frustrations on a decision-making journey. A public involvement road map should outline:

- existing conditions

- who should be involved

- destinations and stops to be made (O'Dowd, no date:3)

Concentrating on one of these issues, "who should be involved", it seems that some time should be spent in obtaining the views of groups who are often hidden from the consultation process. Given that home zones are designed to give priority to pedestrians and cyclists, they are likely to impact on the way in which children use their neighbourhood quite significantly. Yet, children are often not seen during consultation exercises. Writing in *The Guardian*, Rawles (2005) reports on the benefits of involving children in planning local communities. He quotes Ben Koralek, director of Shape, a Cambridge-based architecture and built environment centre, which is running a series of workshops in local schools as stating that:

On one level, our work with Making Neighbourhoods is essentially about social inclusion. Children of all ages are receptive to our work, and it can create opportunities for the so-called hoodie generation to develop a sense of ownership and play an active role in decision making in the future of their built environment. (Rawles, 2005)

By engaging children in decision making about their communities, they are being made more aware of the environment they live in and the way the planning process works. At the same time, their creativity and innovation can be harnessed to provide solutions which may challenge orthodox design, resulting in more appropriate measures to meet local needs and improve quality of life.

Conclusion: rural stories, rural lessons

This chapter has described the findings of the empirical work carried out in the rural field site of Charlbury in West Oxfordshire. The study shows that poor access to transport may be due to poor network coverage as well as infrequent and unreliable public transport. For some transport deficiencies, simple solutions such as lift-sharing already operate informally. These would benefit from formalization and could be usefully supplemented by interventions such as a rural car club.

The investigation indicates that there is potential to better meet the needs of local people by adopting inclusive and participatory approaches to needs assessment and scheme design. In addition, the research has revealed that policies beyond the immediate study area can be influential on people's transport decision-making and choices.

In the following chapter, the findings of the exploratory Q methodology study are described.

Chapter 6

Revealed Perspectives: Common Themes and Disparate Discourses

Introduction: transport and social inclusion through an alternative lens

In the previous two chapters, the findings of the main empirical work were described. This chapter provides an examination of the perceptions held by some of the research participants of how transport impacts on their lives. In contrast to the previous two chapters which examined the observable direct impacts of particular policies and interventions in terms of the pattern of outcomes, this chapter makes use of a new exploratory tool which better reveals the more basic ways in which transport may affect day-to-day living as seen through the eyes of each participant within a wider social and neighbourhood context. Thus, while the last two chapters concentrate on the information gathered through semi-structured interviews, focus groups and analysis of web-based conversation, this chapter describes an experimental demonstration study of the use of Q methodology to investigate perceptions of transport's impacts on an individual's life.

The Q study results suggest an innovative way of defining discourses which frame the more detailed qualitative research findings in the preceding chapters. The purpose of suggesting a framing discourse is two-fold: to provide a context for the qualitative research findings and to investigate the structure and patterning of opinion about transport across members of different social groups participating in this research.

Q methodology: a response to the need for more perceptive insights

The experimental study described in this chapter looks at transport as a component of a life which is social from the lens of individuals who live in neighbourhoods and communities. It attempts to unravel the range of perspectives that participants have on transport. It is anticipated that insights obtained by such an approach may help provide an understanding of how people's transport priorities are coloured by their experience, social connections and level of participation in their neighbourhood. At the same time, the study also seeks to investigate whether a particular perspective may be held across a number of social groups. This latter aim is directed at determining whether the traditional, 'pigeon-hole' type approach of placing people in social groups for ease of study with respect to transport issues may indeed be resulting in researchers and policy makers missing valuable insights into common experiences and perspectives of people from across a range of heterogeneous social groupings.

While this research looks at the impacts of transport on members of different social groups, building on work that has been done in other studies (see, for example, Hamilton et al., 1999 on women; Rajé et al., 2003a on gender, ethnicity and age), it also looks at the impacts of transport across various social groups. This wider approach takes account of the views of Church et al. (2000) who state that the individual group or category approach has limitations for the understandings arising from such studies. Anable (2005) underlines the tendency in travel research methodology and policy interventions to base segmentation of populations on a priori socio-demographic classifications. Anable suggests further that, by adopting a post hoc approach, whereby population segments are defined from the findings of the empirical investigation and participants are grouped according to their motivations, psychological make-up or world-views, more meaningful insights may be obtained.

By looking both at the social group level and at the cross-social group level, this study looks at the experiences of people from different social and geographical groups in order to explore the common perspectives and disparate views they may have. It proposes that across society there will be common discourses and different themes that will be revealed by individuals regardless of their membership of a particular social or spatial group. By this approach which sets out to reveal the views held across a variety of social groups, the research presents a new way of looking at transport needs which could facilitate the tailoring of policies and proposals towards identified needs. When a similar exercise was carried out by Barry and Proops (1999) on environmental discourses, the authors concluded that the methodology provided a useful tool for facilitating the development of policies that were more likely to target individual needs and thus more likely to be adhered to. Barry and Proops' research was based on Q methodology – the technique that has been adopted for carrying out the study described in this chapter.

As described in Chapter 3, the Q methodology study arose out of a desire to develop closer understandings of how research participants perceived transport's role in their lives. The importance of perceptions became evident as the research progressed and the need for an evolving methodology in response to the research's dynamics is also explained in Chapter 3. While the methodology chapter (3) introduced the Q methodology study, in order to describe the way in which the method operates with clarity, the ensuing sections of this chapter concentrate on the details of the development, administration and findings of the Q methodology study.

Detailed research design: the Q methodology study

Stages of study

The Q study was comprized of a number of stages:

1. Development of research instrument or set of opinion statements called the Q-sample. This sample was taken from a collection of items called a concourse which, in the case of this research, were statements selected from focus groups, interviews, secondary materials from relevant research, academic

papers, policy documents etc.

2. Administration of the Q methodology study, requiring participants to sort the statements along a continuum of preference according to a condition of instruction.

3. Interviews with participants after completion of the Q sort. To investigate their reasons for sorting that way and any other opinions on transport and its impacts

4. Analysis and interpretation of data obtained from Q sorts and interviews.

These stages are described in further detail in the following sections.

Selection of a concourse and Q-sample

A range of materials were used as sources of statements to be included in the Q concourse. Such an approach is described as quasi-naturalistic inquiry as it draws on a set of interrelated claims from a range of sources. Source materials made up an eclectic assortment including academic papers, newspaper articles, research reports, policy documents, journal articles and research participant statements: all were chosen to cover the wide variety of views available on the theme.

In order to make the statements presented to participants as clear, concise and comprehensible as possible, some quotations were refined and rephrased in order to retain their essence but make them at the same time more readily-understandable to research participants. Corr (2001:294) reports on a similar approach to Q sort development from the pool of generated statements:

> The statements were initially checked for duplication…The categorisation process involved grouping statements of similar content together…Under each theme, the statements were combined and, if necessary, rephrased to ensure that they were clear and easy to read while still relevant to the study. Care was taken at this reduction phase to ensure that the final statements were appropriate and applicable to the study, and comprehensive enough to include all the relevant aspects of the study.

The 180 statements that formed the concourse were categorized by issue. The thematic categories were access; impacts of transport; mode choice; barriers to travel; "forced" car[1]; public transport; trust, neighbourliness and community; the role of the social network; social isolation; the positive impact of travel and transport and, finally, policy suggestions and approaches. From this categorized concourse, 60 statements were chosen for the Q sample after a process which involved:

---

1   Peter Jones introduced the concept of the "forced" car suggesting that, as a result of deficiencies in the public transport system, people on low incomes may be forced to own and run a car causing a strain on limited household budgets. [See, for example, Jones (1998)]. Lucas et al. (2001) provide empirical evidence from focus groups that suggests that, as long as there is a shortfall in the availability of adequate and affordable public transport, even those on constrained incomes will seek to own cars. The authors describe this as "forcing" car ownership on low-income households.

1. removal of duplicates
2. rephrasing, where necessary
3. breadth of theme coverage
4. selection of clearest and most comprehensive statements.

Administration of Q study

Q-methodology does not require a large number of participants in order to generate a diversity of accounts:

> It is imperative to understand that in the application of Q-methodology, the domain is subjectivity and research is performed on small samples. The methodology is a combination of qualitative and quantitative research techniques that reveals dimensions of subjective phenomena from a perspective intrinsic to the individual to determine what is statistically different about the dimensions and to identify characteristics of individuals who share common viewpoints. Low response rates do not bias Q-methodology because the primary purpose is to identify a typology, not to test the typology's proportional distribution within the larger population. (Valenta and Wigger, 1997:501)

Watts and Stenner (2004:20) amplify the benefits of working with smaller groups of people when using Q:

> Yet the employment of *very* large numbers of participants in a Q methodological context can itself be problematic. Indeed, such an approach can easily negate many of the subtle nuances, complexities, and hence many of the essential *qualities* contained in the data. This is obviously counterproductive in the context of a qualitative technique…In keeping to smaller numbers, therefore, an emphasis on quality is maintained, pattern and consistency can still be detected within the data…

Barry and Proops (1999:339) provide insight into the concept of "finite diversity" which strengthens the view that larger sample sizes would not be of benefit in a Q study:

> It is not generally the case that there are as many discourses as there are participants; Q operates on the assumption of 'finite diversity'. Q allows the researcher to see if there are any patterns shared across individuals, and what are the diversity of accounts, without this resulting in chaotic multiplication. There are a limited number of ordered patternings within a particular discourse domain, and Q works on this assumption and attempts to reveal those ordered patternings (factors or discourses) in a structured and interpretable manner. It is, therefore, particularly suited to studying those social phenomena around which there is much debate, conflict and contestation, such as the environment, for its express aim is to elicit a range of voices, accounts and understandings.

Nevertheless, it is also important to point out that as a result of the relatively small size and non-random nature of selection of Q study participants, any accounts revealed by the method should be seen as representative of discourses that could be found amongst this research's participants and not as generalizable to a wider public:

> …Q method identifies how individuals with like views perceive an issue. Likewise it reveals how individuals with different views see the issue. Q is less concerned with the

ability to generalize the findings from the analysis and uses smaller, well-selected samples to analyze variability within cases (Rohrbaugh 1997). Q analysis does not yield statistically generalizable results. Instead, the results produce an in-depth portrait of the typologies of perspectives that prevail in a given situation. (Steelman and Maguire (1999:3)

The participant structure or P set is not random: "it is a structured sample of respondents who are theoretically relevant to the problem under consideration" (Van Exel, 2003:8). The P set is usually smaller than the Q set (Brouwer, 1999) and, "…because it is intensive, Q typically works with small numbers of subjects (10-40)" (Dryzek, 2004:10). Participants making up the P set in this study were recruited from interviewees who took part in the qualitative research as well as a mixed group of other residents of Oxfordshire chosen to reflect a range of socio-demographic features to test the diversity of accounts revealed by different groups of participants. The Q study adopted the following participant structure or P set:

Table 6.1   P Set structure

Target group	Young adults	Elderly	Car available	No car available	Total
Barton	3	2			5
Charlbury			4	3	7
Mixed group					6
Total					18

Participants were asked to rank-order the 60 opinion statements about transport and their neighbourhood within the context of impacts of transport and personal connections. The Q-methodology research technique was employed to structure an opinion typology from their rank-ordered statements. Each participant was provided with a set of cards, each with one uniquely-numbered statement printed on it. They were then asked to read all the statements and, while doing so, place them into three piles: those they most agreed with, those they most disagreed with and those that they had no opinion on or were neutral about. After they had completed this exercise, they were asked to decide where they felt each statement should be placed along a continuum moving from most disagree through neutral to most agree, using the following quasi-normal distribution:

Table 6.2   Quasi-normal distribution

	Most disagree							Most agree	
Value	-4	-3	-2	-1	0	+1	+2	+3	+4
Number of statements (n=60)	3	5	7	9	12	9	7	5	3

Given that the definition of social exclusion that has been adopted for this research is "Social exclusion is a process which causes individuals or groups not to participate in the normal activities of the society in which they are residents and has spatial manifestations", and that "inadequate transportation can deny individuals and communities the accessibility, social, health, symbolic and economic benefits that are enjoyed by included individuals and communities" (Miller, 2003), the Q study sought to examine the domain of opinion surrounding transport's role as a facilitator of inclusion which has the potential to enable access to social and economic resources, opportunities and activities.

Throughout the research, transport is seen not as an isolated entity but as a dynamic and integral component of a person's lived social experience. As such, issues of social connectedness, community and neighbourhood were considered to be of importance in the exploration of the symbiotic relationship between the shaping of our transport needs by our lives and the shaping of our lives by our transport needs. As a result, the condition of instruction to participants sorting statements was: "I would like you to think about the neighbourhood you live in, the places you need to go to and your use of the transport system while looking at these statements. Given your needs and experiences, I would like you to look at each of these statements and decide whether you agree with it, disagree with it or feel the statement does not apply to you, you are neutral about it or simply do not have an opinion on it or don't know".

In this study, consideration was given to both free and forced Q sorting methods. The two approaches are described in the following quote:

> (The) sorting or ranking procedure can be administered in two main ways. One method of sorting is known as the forced sorting procedure. The forced sort involves participants allocating a limited number of statements to each rank position on the continuum (ranging from statements that most represent a particular understanding of an issue to those statements that least represent the perspective). The forced sorting procedure ends when each rank position contains the specified number of statements, and participants are reasonably happy that the overall positioning of the statements on the continuum represents a particular understanding of the issue. An alternative to the forced sorting procedure is the free sorting procedure. The free sort does not specify the number of statements that should be placed on each rank position on the continuum. In other words, participants are free to place as many or as few statements on any one rank position. As with the forced sort, the procedure ends when the participant is reasonably happy that the overall rank positioning of statements represents a perspective or understanding of the topic (see Brown 1980, Senn 1996). (Lazard, 2003:2)

For this work, a forced distribution was adopted in order to facilitate ease of input to bespoke software for analysis of the Q sorts. Two of the participants in this study stated that they found having to adopt a forced distribution of statements difficult. This is a criticism of the methodology which has been made elsewhere in the literature. Some critics have suggested that the forced choice procedure is unnatural because it requires the subject to conform to what they may see as an unreasonable requirement. For example, Chinnis et al. (2001) highlight the difficulties associated with forcing a participant to adhere to a bell-shaped distribution and concede that it is possible to allow those who find it difficult to adopt their own free distribution.

Other researchers have investigated the value of forced versus free distributions and concluded that there is little variation in the overall result whichever sorting pattern is adopted:

> An examination of free and forced sorting procedures was undertaken by Block (1956). He compared these two procedures by firstly asking participants to sort a Q set using a free procedure and then sort these statements again using a forced approach. He claimed that this comparison shown (sic) no appreciable differences in the sorting patterns that emerged. In other words, sorting patterns converged to the shape of a quasi normal distribution when the free sort procedure was used. (Lazard, 2003:4)

Once the sorting task was completed, the researcher recorded the pattern of distribution of the numbers of each participant's statements onto a grid on an A4 sheet of paper as a record of their Q sort. The researcher then interviewed the respondent about the Q sort and asked him/her questions about his/her neighbourhood and experience of transport. As the process was heavily dependent upon the willingness of respondents to participate in the research, all participants were offered the incentive of being entered into a prize draw at the end of the study for £100 worth of Marks and Spencers' vouchers[2].

Data analysis

Participant profile   The 18 person P set was made up of a range of respondents from different socio-demographic and geographic backgrounds as shown below:

Table 6.3   Participant profile

Code	Age	Gender	Car	Ethnicity	Income	Employment	Location
Ot01	38	M	Y	W	G	Y	E Oxford
Ot02	26	F	N	B	A	S	E Oxford
Ot03	28	F	Y	W	G	Y	Kidlington
Ot04	68	M	Y	I	E	R	W Oxford
Ot05	38	F	Y	M	E	S	W Oxford
Ot06	66	F	Y	W	E	R	W Oxford
Ch01	63	M	Y	W	G	R	Charlbury
Ch02	30	M	N	W	G	Y	Charlbury
Ch03	30	F	N	W	G	Y	Charlbury
Ch04	59	F	Y	W	E	Y	Charlbury

---

2   This incentive was chosen because discussions held with residents and local authority officers in Barton suggested that most local people would not be happy to have to sign to receive individual payment for participation in the research. There was a feeling that any payment may affect a person's benefit and would therefore dissuade people from being involved in the study. In addition, there was an expressed distrust of signing for money as some people were said to be more comfortable to operate outside the gaze of officialdom.

Ch05	45	F	Y	W	G	Y	Charlbury
Ch06	36	M	Y	W	G	Y	Charlbury
Ch07	81	F	N	W	A	R	Charlbury
Ba01	66	M	Y	W	E	Y	Barton
Ba02	38	F	Y	W	B	Y	Barton
Ba03	27	F	Y	W	B	N	Barton
Ba04	70	F	N	W	A	R	Barton
Ba05	36	F	N	W	A	N	Barton

Key

Car	Access to car?	Yes or No	
Ethnicity	White	Bangladeshi	Indian
	Mixed race		
Income (household)	A <£5000	B £5000-9999	C £10000-14999
	D £15000-19999	E £20000-24999	F £25000-29999
	G >£30000		
Employment	Y Employed	S Student	R Retired
	N Unemployed		

Procedure The Q-sorts obtained from the participants were correlated in 18 by 18 matrices using PQMethod[3] software and then factor-analysed using Principal Components Analysis to find associations among the different Q sorts. The results of this analysis are shown in Table 6.4

Principal Components Analysis generated eight factors (Table 6.3). Addams (in Addams and Proops, 2000:27) advises that "by convention, only (unrotated) factors with eigenvalues[4] greater than or equal to one are considered significant and retained". Based on this guidance, the five factors with eigenvalues above 1 were selected for further analysis.

These five factors were subjected to Varimax rotation to identify significant, orthogonal (uncorrelated) factors. The standard error (SE) for a factor loading is calculated by the expression $1/\sqrt{N}$ where N equals the number of statements. In this case, with 60 statements, the SE = $1/\sqrt{60}$ = 0.13. Persons with loadings in excess of 2.58(SE) are considered statistically significant at the 0.01 level (Dayton in Addams and Proops, 2000:77) and thus 'indicative of a meaningful relationship between the

---

3 Freeware statistical programme tailored to the requirements of Q studies available at www.rz.unibw-muenchen.de/~p41bsmk/qmethod/pqmanual.htm.

4 An eigenvalue is a measure that reflects the amount of variation accounted for by the corresponding factor. In essence, the relative magnitude of the eigenvalues can be used to order the importance of the factors. By convention, only (unrotated) factors with eigenvalues greater than or equal to one are considered significant and retained, those with lower eigenvalues are considered too weak to warrant serious attention. Although a variety of statistical criteria may be used in Q "to decide which factors are to be retained as 'real' and significant (since some of the factors may result largely from chance and should be discarded)... One of the most widely used rules is the eigenvalue criterion, whereby a factor's significance is estimated by the sum of the squared factor loadings of all variables (Q sorts) for each factor." (Addams, 2000:27).

Table 6.4   Unrotated factor matrix

Factors / Sorts	1	2	3	4	5	6	7	8
1 Ot01	0.7282	-0.0223	0.2570	0.0338	0.3680	-0.0601	0.0228	-0.3063
2 Ot02	0.5611	-0.1895	-0.2684	-0.4564	-0.0598	-0.2102	0.1769	0.3321
3 Ot03	0.6993	0.0898	-0.3448	0.0772	-0.1438	-0.1920	0.1352	0.0302
4 Ot04	0.4547	0.4010	-0.1279	0.1221	0.3152	-0.5405	-0.0320	0.0870
5 Ot05	0.4683	0.5786	-0.1419	0.3977	-0.0520	0.0555	-0.0295	-0.0163
6 Ot06	0.2751	0.6757	-0.1975	-0.1319	-0.1475	-0.1410	0.1824	-0.2611
7 Ch01	0.6029	-0.2404	-0.2962	0.1800	0.1602	0.3305	-0.1469	0.3709
8 Ch02	0.6705	-0.2871	0.2257	-0.1901	-0.0345	0.0057	0.1533	-0.2816
9 Ch03	0.6271	-0.4091	-0.2668	0.0447	-0.0957	0.2288	-0.1575	-0.1280
10 Ch04	0.5733	-0.4590	0.0703	-0.0860	-0.3309	0.1805	0.2071	-0.0532
11 Ch05	0.6963	-0.1122	-0.0156	0.1858	-0.2259	-0.0289	0.4004	0.0318
12 Ch06	0.7645	-0.1736	0.1365	-0.0952	0.0171	-0.1041	-0.3957	-0.1065
13 Ch07	0.0483	0.4822	-0.1717	-0.0535	0.4831	0.5153	0.3703	-0.0630
14 Ba01	0.7593	0.2165	0.0476	0.3133	0.0489	0.0811	-0.2446	0.0770
15 Ba02	0.6488	0.1320	0.3599	-0.3974	0.2189	0.1290	-0.1391	0.0664
16 Ba03	0.1385	0.6699	0.1881	0.1144	-0.5288	0.2041	-0.1629	-0.0306
17 Ba04	0.0603	-0.3638	0.5490	0.5716	0.0802	-0.1159	0.2832	0.1574
18 Ba05	0.2483	0.5818	0.4985	-0.2906	-0.1042	0.0520	0.0842	0.3501
Eigenvalues	5.5244	2.7741	1.3126	1.2107	1.0610	0.9522	0.8451	0.6921
% expl.Var	31	15	7	7	6	5	5	4

participant's Q sort and the factor type' (Addams in Addams and Proops, 2000:25). Thus, in this study, loadings in excess of 2.58(0.13) or 0.34 are significant at the 0.01 level.

With significant loadings deemed to be equal to or greater than 0.34, four of the participants were purely loaded on Factor 1. Six participants' sorts were mixed with significant loadings on more than one factor including Factor 1. Only one participant was purely loaded on Factor 2, however, four others were significantly loaded on Factor 2 and one or more other factors. Five sorts were significantly loaded on Factor 3, of these, only one was purely loaded. Factor 4 had one purely loaded sort and two mixed sorts with significant negative loadings. Two participants were purely loaded on Factor 5 while five were significantly loaded on Factor 5 as well as one or more other factors. Taking all of these together, nine of the participants were purely loaded on one factor and nine were mixed, that is, significantly loaded on more than one factor. Any sorts with significant loadings on more than one factor are designated as "confounded" and eliminated from subsequent analysis. Factors with both positive and negative sorts, such as Factor 4, are designated as "bipolar."

Watts and Stenner (2005:31) have recognized that the rejection of confounding Q sorts from the final analysis can result in the loss of valuable perspectives. To counter this, they have employed a strategy which

…minimises confounding and which duly maximises the number of significantly loading participants in a particular study. Let's suppose you…have calculated that a significant loading in your study (at p<0.01) must reach ±0.34 or above. You then find that (in using this significance level) 35 of 50 participant Q sorts load on a single factor, 4 have no significant loading and the remaining 11 are confounded. This means that 15 participant Q sorts (30% of the data) are not being used to construct the various factor exemplifying item configurations. In such circumstances, it may be sensible to consider *raising* the level at which a loading is said to be significant (which will only make your criterion *more* stringent from a statistical viewpoint). In the example, we might look again at the solution with a significance level of ±0.35 or above, then ±0.36 or above, and so on. At ±0.40 we find that 42 of the 50 participants load significantly on a single factor, 5 now have no significant loading and only 3 are confounded. In other words, only 8 participants (16% of the data) are now not being used. We also find that raising the level still further (to ±0.41 or above) only serves to increase the number of Q sorts with no significant loading and hence to *reduce* the overall numbers of participants with significant (and usable) loadings. At ±0.40, therefore we have *maximised* the number of participants with significant loadings and have duly achieved our most satisfactory solution.

As we have seen in this study, when significant loadings are considered to be equal to or greater than ± 0.34, 9 Q sorts purely loaded on a single factor and 9 sorts were confounded, that is 50% of the data would not be available to the ensuing analysis. However, the technique adopted by Watts and Stenner described above enables the inclusion of a larger proportion of the empirical data. The deployment of this procedure was considered to be particularly appropriate with a small, yet heterogeneous P set where the availability of a larger number of perspectives to the analysis could lend a depth and richness that a smaller and truncated data set may not capture. Thus, a process of iteratively adopting a higher level at which a loading was considered to be significant was employed (see Table 6.5).

Table 6.5   Illustration of iteration towards maximized number of participants with significant loadings

Designed statistically significant loading	Loaded significantly on single factor	Number of participants	
		With no significant loading	With confounded sorts
± 0.34	9	0	9
± 0.40	11	0	7
± 0.45	13	0	5
± 0.50	14	0	4
± 0.55	15	0	3
± 0.56	15	2	1

It was found that when significant loadings were considered to be equal to or greater than ± 0.55, 15 of the 18 Q sorts loaded significantly on a single factor and only 3 were now confounded. Raising the level to ± 0.56 did not result in an increase in the number of sorts loaded significantly on one factor but did introduce 2 sorts with no significant loading, thus reducing the number of significant and usable loadings. Therefore, ± 0.55 maximized the number of significant and usable Q sorts. Table 6.6 shows the results of Varimax rotation on the 5 factors with significant purely loaded sorts at the ± 0.55 significance designation.

Table 6.6   Factor matrix

Loadings Q SORT	1	2	3	4	5
1 Ot01	0.4351	-0.0498	0.5872X	0.2417	0.3720
2 Ot02	0.5523X	-0.1136	0.3191	-0.4618	-0.0412
3 Ot03	0.6999X	0.2392	0.0395	-0.1725	0.2533
4 Ot04	0.2140	0.1773	0.1687	0.0278	0.6259X
5 Ot05	0.2965	0.5779	-0.0676	0.0890	0.5484
6 Ot06	0.0511	0.5727X	0.0714	-0.3836	0.3571
7 Ch01	0.6758X	-0.1799	0.0301	0.0442	0.2741
8 Ch02	0.5501	-0.0437	0.5460	0.0627	-0.1174
9 Ch03	0.7831X	-0.1542	0.0609	-0.0336	-0.0334
10 Ch04	0.6739X	-0.0138	0.2600	0.0501	-0.3698
11 Ch05	0.6981X	0.2227	0.1599	0.1420	0.0210
12 Ch06	0.6197X	0.0231	0.5008	0.0639	0.0557
13 Ch07	-0.2013	0.0156	0.0876	-0.1924	0.6443X
14 Ba01	0.5652X	0.3330	0.2470	0.2371	0.4227
15 Ba02	0.2366	0.0867	0.8183X	-0.0788	0.1856
16 Ba03	-0.0588	0.8899X	0.0229	-0.0136	0.0085
17 Ba04	0.0790	-0.1050	0.0744	0.8550X	-0.1290
18 Ba05	-0.2109	0.5755	0.5973	-0.0627	0.0874
% expl Var	24	12	12	7	11

(X indicates a defining sort or exemplar)

In Q studies, it is generally considered that a factor may be accepted if there are two or more Q sorts loaded significantly on it. By this principle, factor 4 was eliminated from further consideration. Eight of the participants or variables are purely loaded on Factor 1, two on Factor 2, two on Factor 3 and two on Factor 5. Three of the sorts are confounded. In the discussion that ensues, these factors have been termed Discourse A (Factor 1), Discourse B (Factor 2), Discourse C (Factor 3) and Discourse D (Factor 5) respectively.

In summary then, this Q study investigated the subjective landscape of 18 participants on the domain of transport. Eighteen separate perspectives on transport have been rendered, based on statements drawn from a number of sources, yet these 18 have been shown to condense around 4 operant types (Discourses A, B, C and D)[5]. The intellectual structure of these discourses is examined in the next section.

---

5   Given the small number of participants in comparison to conventional survey methods, it is important to underline that, while Q does not require a large number of participants to provide useful results, this study is exploratory and the results can only be seen to reflect viewpoints from within the small study population.

New insights: themes, discourses and perspectives

For each of the discourses found, a factor array or composite Q sort has been produced by calculating factor scores. Addams (in Addams and Proops, 2000:29) describes a factor score as:

> ...the score gained by each item or statement of the Q set as a kind of weighted average of the scores...In other words, the factor score shows how each item or statement would have rated on a factor had it been measured directly. This creates idealised Q sorts representing distinct attitudes. This factor array will, of course, be most like the array of a participant who has a very high loading on the factor.

The four "ideal type" Q sorts (Barry and Proops, 1999:341) representing the distinct attitudes of each of the discourses in this study are shown in a table of factor scores (Table 6.6). This table enables comparison of the factors on the ranking of a statement or item (Addams in Addams and Proops, 2000:32), for example, the first extracted or idealized Q sort (for Discourse A) has statement 1 at -1 (slightly disagree), while this Q sort has statement 5 at 4 (strongly agree) and so on.

Table 6.7   Statements and scores on four extracted discourses

No	Statement	Statement score by discourse			
		A	B	C	D
1	Without a car, it is difficult to see friends and family because of transport problems.	-1	3	-1	0
2	It is now necessary to travel ever-increasing distances to access almost everything (shopping, work, education, leisure, health etc).	-1	1	1	3
3	Transport is one of several barriers inhibiting access to employment.	0	0	1	-1
4	I end up going to the expensive shops because I can't get to the supermarket.	-2	-3	-3	-1
5	I enjoy living in this area because there are good facilities nearby like doctors, dentists, the library and buses.	4	-4	-2	0
6	Sometimes people drive too fast round here.	2	3	4	-2
7	The car seems to be taking over from walking and public transport. Sometimes there are no dropped kerbs and walking and crossing is difficult because all junctions are busy.	1	-1	2	0
8	Britain's roads are among the safest in the world.	2	-3	-1	0
9	My house is very noisy because of all the traffic on the road.	-4	0	0	-1
10	Transport is not a major concern to me.	-3	1	-3	-2
11	Travelling by car has an impact on others. While we have some of the safest roads in the world, cars are still a more dangerous way to travel than public transport. They also have an impact on the environment and congestion.	3	-2	3	1

12	Many times I've been late for appointments because of traffic.	-2	2	0	1
13	There are parking problems everywhere, especially in the city centre.	2	3	-1	3
14	The only casualties of car-mad Britain are the environment and the quality of life of local communities on roads carrying too much traffic.	0	-1	2	0
15	Most of the time, I depend on walking to get around.	0	-2	0	-4
16	I rely on taxis because I don't have a car.	-2	-4	-3	-4
17	Owning and driving a car is a symbol of wealth, status and power.	-1	0	-3	-3
18	I can do anything I want to do and go anywhere I want because I have access to a car.	0	4	-1	-1
19	I always drive because there is no bus service where I live.	-3	-2	-2	-2
20	People choose the car for many journeys because it allows them to travel direct from one place to another in comfort.	3	4	1	-1
21	Walking and cycling offer a healthy and enjoyable alternative, particularly for short trips.	4	0	2	1
22	I find the costs of travelling, whether by car, taxi or bus, are very high or unaffordable.	-3	2	1	2
23	I am not willing to travel long distances or spend a long time travelling.	-1	-4	-1	-1
24	People don't have pride in the area. Walking is horrible because of things like chips and papers on the road.	-3	2	-3	0
25	I cannot afford a car really but I have to have it. I have to do without certain things to pay for it. The car has become a necessity for me now.	0	3	-2	-1
26	I have a car but, if there was good public transport available, I would not need a car.	0	1	-2	-4
27	We should have a transport system which dissuades people from using cars but the present system doesn't.	0	-1	3	0
28	Public transport should be made more affordable.	2	0	0	2
29	When the buses are on time and they run as they should, they're good.	3	-1	0	-2
30	There are often too many rough people on the buses.	-1	-2	-4	1
31	I think the biggest problem is a lack of public transport information.	1	-2	-2	1
32	Buses need to be attractive enough for motorists to choose them over the car for some trips.	1	0	1	-3
33	I think if you live somewhere near people with similar backgrounds, a similar social group, you feel comfortable with them.	-2	-1	2	-1
34	I can trust people I've known a while but you just can't trust everyone.	1	2	0	4
35	I feel comfortable in this area.	4	-1	0	-1
36	I like the community spirit here – people always meet on the street.	2	-2	2	-3

37	It's changed around here. It's the social scene, you know, now no one mixes. People used to play on the streets and Mums chatted over the fence. There was no traffic and neighbours looked out for each other.	-2	0	1	3
38	As long as you have a neighbour you can rely on and they can rely on you, it's great.	0	1	0	1
39	Communities need better local transport and safer streets – not more cars.	1	-2	4	-2
40	At the local shop(s) you are paying for convenience because it is (they are) open longer hours and easy to get to but there is a smaller range and it is expensive.	-1	4	-1	2
41	I am frightened to go out at night in this area.	-4	1	-4	1
42	People don't care about others anymore.	-2	2	0	2
43	Better transport, commuters working away from home and better shopping opportunities outside the area mean that local people have fewer opportunities to get to know one other.	0	1	1	0
44	No one else is involved in the decisions I make when planning a journey.	0	3	0	-2
45	Friends, neighbours or family help me by getting shopping or doing errands for me, so that I don't have to travel to do those things.	-2	-3	0	1
46	I live far away from my relatives and so there is no one to rely on.	-3	2	0	0
47	I can always rely on my relatives to help me make a journey but I tend to try to be independent.	-1	-1	-1	-3
48	I just stay home and lead a very lonely life.	-4	-3	-4	0
49	I haven't got a car and it's hard to be independent if you haven't got one.	-1	-3	0	2
50	I feel awkward asking others to do things, like taking me places such as the shops.	-1	0	-2	3
51	Transport performs an important role in determining a person's life style.	0	1	-1	-2
52	Transport should not be considered on its own but as the link between the home and the activity.	1	-1	2	0
53	Good transport is essential for a successful economy and society. It provides access to jobs, services and schools, gets goods to the shops and allows us to make the most of our free time.	2	0	1	4
54	The car provides many benefits, but the challenge is to ensure that people have other options, including good quality public transport and the opportunity to walk or cycle.	3	0	4	2
55	For most people, most of the time, the road network functions well.	2	-1	-1	-1
56	Transport provides important access to social support networks through links with family and friends.	1	2	2	2

57	When decisions are being made about transport, the people who use the transport system should be involved in the decision-making process.	3	1	2	4
58	Making it more difficult and more expensive to park the car is the most likely way to encourage infrequent or non-users of buses to use them more.	0	0	-2	-3
59	Pedestrians are treated as second class citizens in many high streets, yet they are vital to their success. Too many main roads are just rivers of traffic. We're not talking about banning cars but we need to civilize our main roads by resetting the balance.	1	0	3	1
60	If more people took up walking and cycling, the Government might not have to worry so much about the problem of obesity, which is costing the NHS millions.	1	0	2	0

In the following sections, the four distinct discourses revealed by this group of respondents are discussed both in light of the ideal type Q sorts detailed in Table 6.7 and within the context of comments made by participants during post-Q sort interviews.

Discourse A

The contented resident

Discourse A was shared by the largest number of respondents (44% of the P set). This discourse identified strongly (4) with the following statements:

5.   I enjoy living in this area because there are good facilities nearby like doctors, dentists, the library and buses.

21.   Walking and cycling offer a healthy and enjoyable alternative, particularly for short trips.

35.   I feel comfortable in this area.

The discourse agreed, but to a lesser extent (3), with these statements:

11   Travelling by car has an impact on others. While we have some of the safest roads in the world, cars are still a more dangerous way to travel than public transport. They also have an impact on the environment and congestion.

20.   People choose the car for many journeys because it allows them to travel direct from one place to another in comfort.

29   When the buses are on time and they run as they should, they're good.

54.   The car provides many benefits, but the challenge is to ensure that people have other options, including good quality public transport and the opportunity to walk or cycle.

57.   When decisions are being made about transport, the people who use the transport system should be involved in the decision-making process.

At the other end of the continuum of agreement, this discourse disagreed most strongly (-4) with the following:

9.   My house is very noisy because of all the traffic on the road.

41.   I am frightened to go out at night in this area.

48.   I just stay home and lead a very lonely life.

Meanwhile, the discourse disagreed to a lesser extent (-3) with these statements:

10.   Transport is not a major concern to me.

19.   I always drive because there is no bus service where I live.

22.   I find the costs of travelling, whether by car, taxi or bus, are very high or unaffordable.

24.   People don't have pride in the area. Walking is horrible because of things like chips and papers on the road.

46.   I live far away from my relatives and so there is no one to rely on.

In analysing any viewpoint, it is also instructive to take account of the statements which participants designated as falling in the middle of the scale at '0'. Such statements were deemed to be unimportant, irrelevant or ones for which they had no view:

3.   Transport is one of several barriers inhibiting access to employment.

14.   The only casualties of car-mad Britain are the environment and the quality of life of local communities on roads carrying too much traffic.

15.   Most of the time, I depend on walking to get around.

18.   I can do anything I want to do and go anywhere I want because I have access to a car.

25.   I cannot afford a car really but I have to have it. I have to do without certain things to pay for it. The car has become a necessity for me now.

26.   I have a car but, if there was good public transport available, I would not need a car.

27.   We should have a transport system which dissuades people from using cars but the present system doesn't.

38.   As long as you have a neighbour you can rely on and they can rely on you, it's great.

43.   Better transport, commuters working away from home and better shopping opportunities outside the area mean that local people have fewer opportunities to get to know one other.

44.   No one else is involved in the decisions I make when planning a journey.

51.   Transport performs an important role in determining a person's life style.

58.   Making it more difficult and more expensive to park the car is the most likely way to encourage infrequent or non-users of buses to use them more.

This discourse has been labelled "The contented resident" to reflect the positive views expressed about neighbourhood, transport and social life.

The discourse emphasizes contentment on a number of levels: with the local neighbourhood's facilities [Statement 5 (+4)], the availability of social connections and support, if needed [Statement 46 (-3)], and residential ambience [Statement 9 (-4), Statement 24 (-3)]. Satisfaction with the texture of local life may also explain why this discourse appears not to be concerned about increasing the social viability of the local neighbourhood [Statement 38 (0), Statement 43 (0)]. This perspective sees transport as an important factor in a respondent's life [Statement 10 (-3)] and views it as an affordable [Statement 22 (-3)] good. It views the car as a facilitator of direct and comfortable travel [Statement 20 (3)], while recognising the role of an efficient bus service [Statement 29 (3)]. The narrative expresses feelings of security about the local area [Statement 35 (4), Statement 41 (-4)]. The discourse shows an awareness of healthier transport options [Statement 21 (4)] and recognizes the impacts of transport on other people and the environment [Statement 11 (3), Statement 54 (3)].

Eight participants loaded significantly on this factor. None of these were negative loadings. Five of the seven participants from Charlbury loaded significantly on this factor, one of whom did not have access to a car. The one Barton resident who loaded significantly on this factor was the highest income earner amongst participants from that area, employed and a car owner. He was also actively involved in the local community, for example, he served as the chairman of a resident's project. Amongst the non-field site specific participants, one respondent living in East Oxford and one from Kidlington, where local facilities are readily accessible, loaded significantly on this factor. This narrative was shared by persons ranging from age 26 to 66. Both male and female respondents reflected this viewpoint. In addition, people from various income levels loaded significantly on this factor, from one whose household income is under £5,000 per annum to five with incomes of over £30,000. The sort with the highest significant pure loading (0.783) on this discourse, that is the main exemplar or person whose array most closely matched this factor's, was a newly-married 30 year old white female resident of Charlbury who commutes to Oxford by train to work at the University and does not have access to a car.

Discourse B

The car as escape from local deficiencies

This discourse characterizes the views of 11% of the P set. It identifies strongly (4) with the following statements:

18.   I can do anything I want to do and go anywhere I want because I have access to a car.

20.   People choose the car for many journeys because it allows them to travel direct from one place to another in comfort.

40.   At the local shop(s) you are paying for convenience because it is (they are) open longer hours and easy to get to but there is a smaller range and it is expensive.

This narrative also agrees, but to a lesser extent (3), with these statements:

1.   Without a car, it is difficult to see friends and family because of transport problems.

6.   Sometimes people drive too fast round here.

13.   There are parking problems everywhere, especially in the city centre.

25.   I cannot afford a car really but I have to have it. I have to do without certain things to pay for it. The car has become a necessity for me now.

44.   No one else is involved in the decisions I make when planning a journey.

In contrast, the discourse strongly disagrees with the following:

5.   I enjoy living in this area because there are good facilities nearby like doctors, dentists, the library and buses.

16.   I rely on taxis because I don't have a car.

23.   I am not willing to travel long distances or spend a long time travelling.

The discourse disagrees to a lesser extent (-3) with these statements;

4.   I end up going to the expensive shops because I can't get to the supermarket.

8.   Britain's roads are among the safest in the world.

45.   Friends, neighbours or family help me by getting shopping or doing errands for me, so that I don't have to travel to do those things.

48. I just stay home and lead a very lonely life.

49. I haven't got a car and it's hard to be independent if you haven't got one.

In addition, this discourse considers the following statements to be irrelevant or unimportant (0):

3. Transport is one of several barriers inhibiting access to employment.

9. My house is very noisy because of all the traffic on the road

17. Owning and driving a car is a symbol of wealth, status and power.

21. Walking and cycling offer a healthy and enjoyable alternative, particularly for short trips.

28. Public transport should be made more affordable.

32. Buses need to be attractive enough for motorists to choose them over the car for some trips.

37. It's changed around here. It's the social scene, you know, now no one mixes. People used to play on the streets and Mums chatted over the fence. There was no traffic and neighbours looked out for each other.

50. I feel awkward asking others to do things, like taking me places such as the shops.

53. Good transport is essential for a successful economy and society. It provides access to jobs, services and schools, gets goods to the shops and allows us to make the most of our free time.

54. The car provides many benefits, but the challenge is to ensure that people have other options, including good quality public transport and the opportunity to walk or cycle.

58. Making it more difficult and more expensive to park the car is the most likely way to encourage infrequent or non-users of buses to use them more.

59. Pedestrians are treated as second class citizens in many high streets, yet they are vital to their success. Too many main roads are just rivers of traffic. We're not talking about banning cars but we need to civilize our main roads by resetting the balance.

60. If more people took up walking and cycling, the Government might not have to worry so much about the problem of obesity, which is costing the NHS millions.

This discourse has been called "The car as escape from local deficiencies" to capture the pervasive indication of the need for a car to navigate around the inadequacies perceived in the local neighbourhood.

This narrative is dominated by issues related to the car. The car is seen as the facilitator of access to all services and goods [Statement 18 (4)] and as an important tool in the maintenance of social connectivity [Statement 1 (3)]. It allows the user to travel in comfort directly to their destination [Statement 20 (4)] and enables access to a wider range of goods at reasonable prices [Statement 40 (4), Statement 4 (-3)]. This is particularly important since this discourse portrays local facilities as unsatisfactory [Statement 5(-4)]. While the discourse views the car positively, it recognizes that having a car involves some financial hardship [Statement 25 (3)]. This narrative expresses a high degree of independence [Statement 44 (3), Statement 45 (-3)], as well as a lack of loneliness [Statement 48 (-3)]. While there is an expressed willingness to travel long distances [Statement 23 (-4)], there are some concerns about car-based travel such as parking problems in the city centre [Statement 13 (3)] and road safety locally [Statement 6 (3)] and nationally [Statement 7 (-3)].

Two white female car owners were significantly loaded on this factor. One lived in Barton and one in West Oxford. One was retired while the other was a single mother. The Barton resident's household income was between £5,000 and £9,999 and the retiree's income fell in the bracket £20,000 to £24,999. Post-Q sort discussions with both indicated that they perceived that there was a need to travel in order to access services such as a supermarket and that the car allowed them to do this conveniently and with minimal effort.

Discourse C

The multi-mode advocate

Eleven per cent of participants share Discourse C. This narrative most strongly agrees (4) with these statements:

6.   Sometimes people drive too fast round here.

39.   Communities need better local transport and safer streets – not more cars.

54.   The car provides many benefits, but the challenge is to ensure that people have other options, including good quality public transport and the opportunity to walk or cycle.

Meanwhile, there is agreement, but to a lesser extent (3) with the following:

11.   Travelling by car has an impact on others. While we have some of the safest roads in the world, cars are still a more dangerous way to travel than public transport. They also have an impact on the environment and congestion.

27.   We should have a transport system which dissuades people from using cars but the present system doesn't.

59.   Pedestrians are treated as second class citizens in many high streets, yet they are vital to their success. Too many main roads are just rivers of traffic. We're not talking about banning cars but we need to civilize our main roads by resetting the balance.

At the other pole, this discourse most strongly disagrees (-4) with these statements:

30.   There are often too many rough people on the buses.

41.   I am frightened to go out at night in this area.

48.   I just stay home and lead a very lonely life.

There is slightly less disagreement (-3) with the following:

4.   I end up going to the expensive shops because I can't get to the supermarket.

10.   Transport is not a major concern to me.

16.   I rely on taxis because I don't have a car.

17.   Owning and driving a car is a symbol of wealth, status and power.

24.   People don't have pride in the area. Walking is horrible because of things like chips and papers on the road.

Discourse C allocates the following as unimportant, irrelevant or statements for which the respondent holds no opinion (0):

9.   My house is very noisy because of all the traffic on the road.

12.   Many times I've been late for appointments because of traffic.

15.   Most of the time, I depend on walking to get around.

28.   Public transport should be made more affordable.

29.   When the buses are on time and they run as they should, they're good.

34.   I can trust people I've known a while but you just can't trust everyone.

35.   I feel comfortable in this area.

38.   As long as you have a neighbour you can rely on and they can rely on you, it's great.

42.   People don't care about others anymore.

44.   No one else is involved in the decisions I make when planning a journey.

45.   Friends, neighbours or family help me by getting shopping or doing errands for me, so that I don't have to travel to do those things.

46.   I live far away from my relatives and so there is no one to rely on.

49.   I haven't got a car and it's hard to be independent if you haven't got one.

The label "The multi-mode advocate" has been chosen to reflect that, despite the availability of a car, there is an expressed willingness in this discourse to choosing from a number of modes the most suitable for a journey.

This discourse is the least car-dominated of the four factors identified, with the car being seen as one of several transport options. It recognizes that there is a need for viable alternatives to the car [Statement 54(4) and Statement 27(3)]. In addition, it calls for a re-balancing of the streetscape away from car priority to accommodate softer modes such as walking [Statement 59 (3), Statement 39(4) and Statement 11(3)]. Transport is characterized as important in this narrative [Statement 10(-3)]. Participants expressing this viewpoint feel safe at night in their local area [Statement 41(-4)] and think that local people have pride in their environment [Statement 24(3)]. The discourse describes an active and fulfilling social life [Statement 48(-4)] and does not regard ownership of a car as a status symbol [Statement 17 (-3)].

Two 38 year old camper van owners loaded significantly on this factor: a male from East Oxford and a female from Barton. The female respondent was on a low income with household earnings of between £5000 and £9999 per annum. Both had chosen to run old vans which offered the utility of being used for accommodation on holidays as well as being suitable for use for day-to-day or regular trip-making when required. Discussions with both suggested that they often walk in their local area, for example, the female respondent walks to work each day on the Barton estate, although this is clearly not the only mode of transport they consider, or use, regularly. For example, the male participant is also a regular cyclist. This points to an openness to choice of mode to suit activity that this discourse appears to characterize. The need for non-car modes to be given increased preference in the road environment is summed up by the male participant, commenting on Statement 59 (Pedestrians are treated as second class citizens...):

> "As a model, we need a change of culture. Pedestrians and cyclists should have priority... Cyclists feel less important than pedestrians – like third class citizens."

Discourse D

The disaffected theorist

This final discourse is, once again, shared by 11% of the P set. It identifies strongly (4) with the following statements:

> 34.   I can trust people I've known a while but you just can't trust everyone.

> 53.   Good transport is essential for a successful economy and society. It provides access to jobs, services and schools, gets goods to the shops and allows us to make the most of our free time.

> 57.   When decisions are being made about transport, the people who use the transport system should be involved in the decision-making process.

The narrative also agrees with these statements, but to a lesser extent (3):

> 2.   It is now necessary to travel ever-increasing distances to access almost everything (shopping, work, education, leisure, health etc).

13. There are parking problems everywhere, especially in the city centre.

37. It's changed around here. It's the social scene, you know, now no one mixes. People used to play on the streets and Mums chatted over the fence. There was no traffic and neighbours looked out for each other.

50. I feel awkward asking others to do things, like taking me places such as the shops.

In contrast, this discourse strongly disagrees (-4) with the following statements:

15. Most of the time, I depend on walking to get around.

16. I rely on taxis because I don't have a car.

26. I have a car but, if there was good public transport available, I would not need a car.

Meanwhile, it disagrees to a lesser extent (-3) with the following:

17. Owning and driving a car is a symbol of wealth, status and power.

32. Buses need to be attractive enough for motorists to choose them over the car for some trips.

36. I like the community spirit here – people always meet on the street.

47. I can always rely on my relatives to help me make a journey but I tend to try to be independent.

58. Making it more difficult and more expensive to park the car is the most likely way to encourage infrequent or non-users of buses to use them more.

This discourse places the following statements in the middle of the continuum, deeming them to be irrelevant, unimportant or ones for which there is no view (0):

1. Without a car, it is difficult to see friends and family because of transport problems.

5. I enjoy living in this area because there are good facilities nearby like doctors, dentists, the library and buses.

7. The car seems to be taking over from walking and public transport. Sometimes there are no dropped kerbs and walking and crossing is difficult because all junctions are busy.

8. Britain's roads are among the safest in the world.

14. The only casualties of car-mad Britain are the environment and the quality of life of local communities on roads carrying too much traffic.

24.   People don't have pride in the area. Walking is horrible because of things like chips and papers on the road.

27.   We should have a transport system which dissuades people from using cars but the present system doesn't.

43.   Better transport, commuters working away from home and better shopping opportunities outside the area mean that local people have fewer opportunities to get to know one other.

46.   I live far away from my relatives and so there is no one to rely on.

48.   I just stay home and lead a very lonely life.

52.   Transport should not be considered on its own but as the link between the home and the activity.

60.   If more people took up walking and cycling, the Government might not have to worry so much about the problem of obesity, which is costing the NHS millions.

The term "disaffected theorist" has been chosen to capture two essential aspects of this viewpoint: a) the expression of discontent with a number of transport-related issues and changes in society over time and b) the recognition that, in theory, people should be involved in decisions about transport and that transport is important to society.

This narrative recognizes that transport is essential to national economic and social success [Statement 53(4)], while pointing out that people now have to travel longer distances to meet their daily needs than they did in the past [Statement 2(3)]. It calls for involvement of local people in transport decision-making [Statement 57(4)]. The discourse describes a heavy reliance on car-based travel and indicates that, even if there were good public transport available, it would not encourage modal shift by participants expressing this perspective [Statement 26(-4) and Statement 32(-3)]. Indeed, even increases in car parking charges would not persuade these participants to use buses [Statement 58(-3)]. This narrative suggests that people are living increasingly isolated lives [Statement 37 (3)] and a discomfort with relying on others [Statement 50 (3)]. It implies that this atomistic social structure may have affected community spirit in local neighbourhoods [Statement 36 (-3)].

Two retired participants loaded significantly on this factor, an 81 year old white female from Charlbury and a 68 year old Indian male from West Oxford. The female respondent lives alone on a low income of under £5,000 per year. Their ages may help explain why their statement sort appears to express some dissatisfaction with changes that have occurred over time. The elderly female referred in interview to her physical mobility difficulties which prevented her walking in her neighbourhood and rendered her dependent on friends from outside her town for lifts. She also looked back favourably at a time when she could drive and therefore go everywhere she wished to. The male respondent had very little experience of using the bus system, although he did use rail for inter-urban trips. He had always had a car and felt that, as local services in his neighbourhood were extremely poor, his car allowed him to travel out of Oxford for trips such as food shopping. He characterized walking into central Oxford (where, for example, his nearest supermarket and post office are located) as difficult because of the lack of continuous pavements through the railway station junction area and, a more direct walking route as undesirable, requiring the use of a steep pedestrian footbridge over the railway which has uneven, loose stairs and is often used as a trading point by drug dealers.

The four factors or discourses that have emerged indicate that there are differences between the ways in which different individuals view transport, their neighbourhood and social connections. However, in this study group, these differences fall into four main viewpoints. The predominance of Discourse A amongst residents of Charlbury may be indicative that spatial issues such as rurality or perceived local availability of key services and goods may be important factors in determining common ways of defining perspectives on transport. Similarly, the discovery that two retired people share Discourse D may point to age as a defining factor for this narrative. However, to assume that these particular socio-demographic characteristics are defining factors would be to ignore the fact that, for example, there are other retired people in the sample who do not share Discourse D, so being elderly cannot be the only reason for defining this discourse. Similarly, while rural dwelling may mean some residents of Charlbury emphasize Discourse A, this is not generalizable since there are other residents of the town in the sample who do not adhere to this narrative and, at the same time, there are residents of urban areas who share the viewpoint. It is more important to note what can be inferred from this Q study and that is that people across different social groups can share common perspectives and that within a particular social group there can be a number of perspectives.

Work by Anable (2005) and Dudleston et al. (2005) using conventional survey techniques and cluster analysis found that, as in the current work, socio-demographic factors had little bearing on the travel profiles of the segments derived from empirical study, suggesting that attitudes and experiences can cut across personal characteristics. Anable (2005:65) highlights the benefits of post hoc definition of segments in the study group and indicates that this is "a way of extracting naturally occurring, relatively homogenous and meaningful groups to be used in designing targeted hard and 'soft' transport policies".

Reflecting on the results of this exploratory Q study in the context of the implications for targeting of policies and resources, it appears that of the four discourses, Discourse D 'The disaffected theorist' may potentially be the most vulnerable to social exclusion. The level of dissatisfaction expressed about the local area and the transport system points to a possible frustration about not being able to participate fully in desired activities or access services with ease. Targeting this segment of the population with transport interventions that help overcome some of the concerns expressed in the discourse, through interventions such as demand responsive transport, improved pedestrian routes and lift-sharing, may have the greatest propensity to increase social inclusion.

The Q study has provided new insights into the ways in which participants' subjectivity is structured with regard to transport and its wider social dimensions. This exercise has indicated that a social category approach to understanding transport impacts may not always be the most appropriate model for revealing the nature of peoples' constructions of their experience. Indeed, each of the four discourses exhibited by this heterogeneous study group do not appear to align uniquely with any one definitive social group or category. Becker (1998:44) provides a useful means for describing the pitfalls of the category approach when he states that "looking at people and objects as fixed entities with an inherent character makes them analytically immune to context – if not in theory, certainly in practice". Transport is highly contextualized, highlighting the importance that prevailing circumstances and conditions may have to the perceptions and experiences of any one individual. Becker suggests further that it may be beneficial to forget "…about types of people as analytic categories and (look) instead for types of activities people now and then engage in." (Becker, 1998:44). By doing so, Becker (1998:43) asserts that this would allow us to "…make room in our analysis for the independent variation of whole subsystems of phenomena that are neither totally unrelated nor related in any profoundly deterministic way".

Similarly, in a paper on accessibility, social exclusion and social justice, Farrington and Farrington (2005) highlight the range of definitions of the "accessibility unit". They suggest that "it may be the individual, the household or 'groups' defined on the basis of different parameters such as location, personal characteristic, time of day, or stage of life cycle. Definitions might also distinguish between urban and rural contexts" (Farrington and Farrington, 2005:3). The authors caution that such categorisation imports a set of value judgements and that there is a need to be aware in analysis and policy-making that such an approach "describes the 'experience' of 'greater or lesser accessibility' in defined frameworks which impose their own values and constraints" (Farrington and Farrington, 2005:3).

The value of Q

This section describes how Q methodology has contributed towards a more incisive appreciation of the position that transport plays in people's daily lives. The intention here is to provide an account of how Q added value to the empirical insights by complementing the information gained through other methods of primary data collection, interviews and focus groups, and the secondary data which had been obtained via a combined methodology using focus group, travel diary and interview techniques. The section begins with a discussion of the benefits of Q. This is followed by a comparison of the method with other data collection techniques. Throughout the narrative, attention is also drawn to any limitations of the method which have been revealed during the course of this work.

Steven Brown writes (Brown, 2005:summary cited in contribution by Brown to Q-Method ListServ Q-METHOD@LISTSERV.KENT.EDU, 06 May 2005) that

> There is a disconnect in the study of empowerment between the concept of empowerment on the one hand and its measurement on the other. The concept includes the idea of examining the world "through the eyes and spirit of the poor," but measurements often focus on objective features of poverty, such as available services, potentially empowering incentive structures, access to justice, pro-poor markets, and similar empowering

opportunities; i.e., the focus has been mainly on the potential realities of the poor; however, empowerment will not take place if opportunities do not enter into the actual realities of the poor. Q methodology is introduced as a conceptual framework and set of technical procedures that are capable of illuminating the perspectives of all participants, including the poor...

While Brown writes in the context of the developing world, the opinion he expresses about the gap between the concept of empowerment and its measurement is equally relevant to the disconnect that exists in the UK between the concept of transport and social inclusion on the one hand and the measurement of the extent of the interplay between these two themes. Drawing on Brown's discourse, the concept of transport and social inclusion includes the idea of examining the transport needs of social groups who are considered by researchers to be vulnerable to exclusion, but measurements often focus on location of services and employment opportunities, existence of public transport links without regard to the timings of such services and use of sophisticated mapping tools. As Brown states with respect to empowerment, the focus has been mainly on the potential realities of those vulnerable to social exclusion; however, transport will not contribute to social inclusion if opportunities to overcome existent transport deficits do not enter the actual realities of those who are vulnerable to social exclusion.

Q methodology "is a conceptual framework and set of technical procedures that are capable of illuminating the perspectives of all participants" (Brown, 2005) and thereby provides a method for measurement, from each participant's perspective, of how they perceive that transport affects their life. Such viewpoints are valuable in their propensity to point towards how solutions may be tailored to specifically address needs that may not be easily revealed by other methods. In addition, the method forces the participant to evaluate between attributes to present a pattern that reflects their opinion most closely: this is a particular strength of the technique since it assists the researcher in discerning the relative importance a respondent attaches to a variety of issues that he may be experiencing and thus helps in prioritizing needs amongst a group of participants.

One of Q methodology's main advantages over other research techniques is its ability to tap into a diversity of opinion amongst a study group (Lazard, 2003). It is particularly useful in an experimental situation where a researcher may have a notion about the structure of opinion but may wish to investigate whether the study group in question reflects these viewpoints:

> When the researcher is armed only with a suspicion and a few observations that a social entity exists, and when faced with the complication that, even if it were established, it could be described in a variety of ways, the technique required is one that captures subjectivity. These are the circumstances that can benefit from Q-Methodology. (Ekinci and Riley, 2001:205)

Alternatively, Q may also reveal new ways of constructing social realities that the researcher had not predicted and, moreover, may indicate that perspectives may be far more nuanced than the traditional literature may suggest:

Researching diversity requires an approach that forces variability rather than one that attempts to control or reduce it. A study of individuals or even a descriptive statistical study focussing on samples of individuals would be inadequate…Q methodology generates the expression of understandings through the structuring of a large number of culturally derived statements. The statements represent a "…thought maze through which the subject's attitude wanders, attaching itself to this idea, rejecting that one and ignoring others" (Brown, 1980:31). This approach has the added benefit of allowing the unexpected to emerge; ideas that are culturally opaque to the researcher or which are obscured from view can gain prominence, sometimes challenging the researchers' own assumptions… (Aldrich and Eccleston, 2000:1632)

With one of its main attributes being that it gives meaning to findings even from small numbers of participants, Q is extremely useful in exploratory research for developing insights without the need for large scale participant sampling. Large numbers of subjects are typically of little concern in Q since the categories (i.e. factors) that it produces are qualitative in nature, hence independent of quantity. What Q demonstrates is the existence of certain ways of thought (the factors). Adding more persons simply fills up factor space but has little impact on a factor and what it is that distinguishes it from another factor. Purposive sampling is merely designed to provide sufficient diversity so that those factors inherent in the situation have a good chance of being revealed. We cannot guarantee that all of the factors have been revealed, but then neither could a random sample of participants guarantee this.

As a result of its basis on a purely operant, subjective approach to analysis, Q goes beyond traditional questionnaire-based approaches by enabling systematic investigation that minimizes researcher influence, providing a subjective view of the world from the perspective of the respondent, that is, the person's preference structure is revealed. As in a questionnaire-based survey, people react to statements. However, they have greater flexibility to express beliefs than they would in a survey. It is the analysis of the different ways in which participants respond to statements they are given which reveals the discourses amongst a study population in greater depth than could be achieved through survey methods:

Q analysis addresses the covariances of respondents across variables by transposing the data matrix. Factor analysis, or some other clustering technique, is then used to discover groups or categories of *respondents* that have given similar patterns of responses to the variables. Thus, the Q method is very helpful in the development of typologies or in the discovery of discourses, and within the diversity of the sample of respondents used, it can identify differing attitude structures. The theoretical basis of the Q method is the examination of reality constructions of different individuals, without imposing the researcher's own construction of reality (Kitzinger, 1986), to 'examine the world from the *internal* standpoint of the individual being studied' (Brown, 1980). The units of analysis in a Q study are discourses instead of individuals (Dryzek and Berejikian, 1993). Rather than assuming common meaning, Q looks for clusters or 'species' of meaning within a population. (Kalof in Addams and Proops, 2000:179)

When a participant performs a Q sort, the basic task in a Q methodology experiment, he immerses himself for a period of time in evaluating the fundamental building blocks of the ensuing discourses (the statements) against each other. For this process to be successful, the participant needs to concentrate and immerse themselves in the research. This is rather distinct from some participant's approaches to questionnaire completion where the quickest technique may be sought, such as randomly ticking boxes, to complete the task. During the Q methodology study described in this book, it was easily discernible from their enthusiasm that although subjects found the process challenging, they appeared to enjoy getting involved in the experiment. This is believed to be beneficial to the soundness of ensuing results of the experiment.

Brown, as the current leading proponent of the method, suggests that Q's advantage lies in its ability to reveal functional categories beneath the structural categories that are necessarily imposed by any approach that is in the tradition of content analysis, i.e. in Q, the categories that emerge are functionally tied to the ways in which people think, from their own vantage point whereas in content analysis (say of focus group or interview transcripts) at some point the observer must organize all of the material into (what to him are) meaningful categories. (Brown, 2005: contribution to Q-Method ListServ Q-METHOD@LISTSERV.KENT.EDU, 07 April, 2005)

Conclusion: reflecting on the Q study findings

By detecting "patterns and connections that otherwise might be passed over by nonstatistical methods" (Valenta and Wigger, 1997:501), the analysis sought to achieve two main objectives:

1. reveal the different discourses or points of view (factors) on transport, neighbourhood and social connectedness amongst the study group and
2. investigate patterns of relationships among individual responses within the context of the characteristics of respondents that define each discourse[6].

Through this approach, it was anticipated that it may be possible to determine whether people within a particular social group share a similar point of view with respect to transport, as well as exploring the homogeneity (and heterogeneity) of views that may be revealed across different social groups. These insights sought to reveal whether the more traditional, category-type approach to understanding the social aspects of transport is the most appropriate approach or whether a less group-specific approach provides more useful ways of seeing peoples' views and needs.

The findings of this innovative Q methodology study suggest that the category approach may not always be beneficial to our understandings of people and transport and that it may be more appropriate not to try to place people in such social groupings. Instead it may be pertinent to adopt a more disaggregated approach to understanding how people use the transport system and their environment. Such approaches can be beneficial in conferring recognition, dignity and respect to affected individuals. One way in which this can be achieved is by re-orienting approaches to transport

---

6   Kalof (in Addams and Proops, 2000) uses a similar approach for examining discourses of animal concern.

understandings to concentrate on the activities an individual wishes to participate in and the location of this activity: making the connection between individual and activity is the role of the transport system. This has implications for policy-making, apposite investment in transport and the development of appropriate transport interventions which are targeted at the needs of local people and communities.

By complementing the findings of the in-depth interviews and analysis of web-based talk described in Chapters 4 and 5 with the perspectives revealed by this Q methodology study, this study provides a close examination of the discourses and ideologies on transport and social inclusion that are prevalent amongst the communities studied in this research. It is important to note that although these discourses should not be seen as representative of all possible discourses amongst the wider transport system-using British public, they represent a valuable insight into the types of ideological positions held by members of a study population on the specific theme of transport and connectedness.

This type of intensive research approach, using a combination of the techniques of in-depth interviews with Q methodology, is useful as a means of investigating ideologies and discourses which methods such as travel diaries and focus groups would not be as effective in revealing. An additional benefit of the intensive research approach is that it facilitates the researcher's own re-evaluation throughout the empirical research period of their positionality and the nature of their relationship with both the research subjects and the research itself. Hoggart et al. (2002:249) provide a succinct insight into this aspect of intensive research when they write:

> In essence, intensive research is a human construction that is conducted in a social context. The recognition of researcher positionality and constantly renegotiated researcher-researched dynamics means intensive research products are framed by discourses and ideologies.

In this chapter, the social impacts of transport have been explored using a technique that has not been applied to this issue in the past. We have seen that Q methodology offers new and interesting insights into individual perspectives on transport within the context of social connectedness and neighbourhood. The discovery of these understandings provides an opportunity for reflection upon the fundamental factors that influence people's perceptions of the impact of a rather prosaic, and often taken for granted, aspect of daily living. By according real status to the social practices and cultural values around transport through such techniques, policy frameworks and project proposals may in future more closely match people's actions, needs and understandings of travel.

In the final chapter, the implications of the empirical research findings for the wider UK transport context are discussed.

Chapter 7

Contemporary Transport Issues and Contexts: Theoretical, Methodological and Policy and Planning Implications

Introduction: key findings, contexts and implications

On the basis of the evidence presented in this research, even though transport does not appear as a dominant concern on initial interview, it does appear as an important social exclusion issue when people are probed about their daily lives. This study began with the aim of investigating how transport impacts on the lives of people from different social groups. Throughout the book, the voices of research participants have been used to provide their comments, thoughts and stories as a means of contextualizing day-to-day experience of the transport system. By bringing the voices of those involved to the fore, the preceding chapters have highlighted the importance of micro-level individual experiences and contexts to the macro-level development of transport policies and interventions that meet the needs of local people.

In concluding, this research has arrived at five key findings:

- It is necessary, and important, to probe to obtain a true reflection of transport's role in people's lives.
- There is an "experience" gap between the experiences of transport system users and the understandings of users' experiences amongst planners and policy makers.
- There is a "consultation" gap, characterized by planning which is inconsistent and often perfunctory rather than planning which is truly participatory.
- There is a "communication" gap, whereby a lack of awareness amongst the planning and policy-making community of local needs leads to interventions which are unnecessary or exacerbate existing problems.
- It is important to look at the heterogeneity of experience of the transport system and beyond the limits of socio-demographic categories when investigating transport-related social exclusion.

This chapter will explore these findings in more detail. The interpretation of findings is set within a framework which addresses a) the theoretical, b) the methodological and c) the policy and planning implications in turn. The chapter begins with a discussion of the theoretical issues arising from the research. The subsequent section highlights methodological issues around the investigation of the social aspects of transport which have been revealed through the study. The chapter then goes on to examine the implications of the findings for transport policy-making and planning. This is followed by suggestions for further research. The chapter closes by reflecting on the need for greater transparency with respect to transport planning and policy making and by drawing attention to the fact that transport-related social exclusion has been neglected in the policy environment.

Theoretical implications of the research

Introduction

In this section, the theoretical conclusions which can be drawn from the research findings are described. In the first sub-section, the indication from participants that they do not place as great an importance on transport as had been expected at the start of this study is discussed against the research findings on the links between transport and social networks. This is followed by a discussion of the connections between the macro policy environment and micro level atomistic data analysis.

The prevalence of the autonomous traveller?

One of the main findings of this research is that people report a high degree of autonomy in the decision-making that surrounds their travel. This requires contextualisation. While it had been anticipated that participants would report that they negotiate, for example, around the schedules of other members of their household or with others in other households (as other researchers have found, see for example, Jones et al., 1983, Pickup, 1988 and Grieco et al., 1989), almost all participants reported that they are the only ones involved in the decisions they make about travel[1]. As a result of the new household forms discussed in Chapter 2, this may have been anticipated in single member households, and also amongst people who always have a car available to them or those who do not have childcare responsibilities, but was unexpected amongst those participants who use the public transport system, do not have access to a car and may have childcare needs.

The purportedly high levels of autonomy may reflect wider social phenomena such as a rise in the individual as central in our society (Etzioni, 1993). It may be

---

1   Two interviewees overall (out of 39 in both case studies) referred to the need to consider arrangements with other people before they could travel. One was an elderly woman with a disabled husband: she had to arrange for someone to care for him if she was leaving the home. The other was a young single mother of 2 who described her reliance on baby-sitters (her mother and sister) to look after the children when she went to the gym (located towards Oxford about 2 kms from her home). Despite having to negotiate around their arrangements, both interviewees still described themselves as the primary decision-makers with respect to their travel. However, when the wider context of people's trip-making was examined, dependence on others to access goods, services and facilities was much more evident than the participants' perceptions of the independence of their decisions with respect to travel would suggest.

the case that in an increasingly mobile society, individuals have grown accustomed to seeing themselves as isolates and have become conditioned into independent decision-making when it comes to travel. Steg and Tertoolen (1999), writing about determinants of car use, associate use of a car with habit and lifestyle and indicate that individual choice and behaviour are determining factors in car dependence. The importance of the individual and the link to travel behaviour suggests that, in an increasingly mobile society, even those without access to a car have habit-forming and lifestyle factors which centre on the autonomous individual as the key travel decision maker. As we have come to expect mobility as a way of life, our desire to travel whenever and however we need to has become almost hard-wired into our psyche.

In addition, the research findings indicate that there is a possibility that the autonomous choice phenomenon which seems to be prevalent in our travel decision-making transcends traditional social categories and has become a part of an atomistic, 21st century culture. This research could not distinguish a particular social group, defined by say ethnicity, age or gender, which was most characterized by independence of decision-making. Rather, it was commonplace for most participants to report that they did not refer to anyone else when making their decisions around travel.

However, when the wider context of people's travel needs and trip-making patterns was examined, dependence on others to access goods, services and facilities was much more evident than the participants' perceptions of the independence of their decisions would suggest. Notwithstanding the first responses from participants that solitary journeys and solitary transport decision-making were taking place, the research revealed that there are help structures which are concealed yet play an essential part in accomplishing travel. When asked directly about the decisions they make about travel, participants were quick to point out that such decisions were individually determined. However, in depth discussion with the same individuals revealed a different patterning to the ways in which journeys were made: lift-giving, exchange of favours and reliance on others were all described in the context of travel. The following sub-section describes the reliance on social networks to achieve travel objectives, while we reflect here on the possible reasons for the apparent conflict between stated and actual actions with regard to transport and travel.

While people's perception is as functioning individuals, in fact, further exploration reveals that there is a pattern of exchange. The discordance between statement and action has methodological implications for the researcher since it is necessary to explore in greater depth the ways in which people travel if the true nature of decisions and exchange are to be revealed and understood. For example, the opinion polls described in Chapter 4 suggested, based on two general questions, that transport was not a dominant concern amongst people in the UK and initial responses in this research appeared to substantiate this claim. However, further reflection on the overall findings indicates that transport is indeed an important concern and points to the need to ask the right questions and to probe for clearer insights. While the work of TRaC (2000) and Lucas et al. (2001), referred to in Chapter 4, also appeared to confirm the unimportance of transport amongst people who are socially excluded, taken as a whole, this research's findings suggest that this may be a myth generated by a combination of simplistic questioning, a lack of probing for understandings and a moral pressure amongst participants to conceal the help structures upon which they depend.

The latter may be a cognitive trick to preserve dignity and exude self-sufficiency to the researcher who may be viewed by the participant as threatening or successful, rather than reveal acceptance of informal support which the participant associates negatively with dependence and coping strategies. As a consequence of the potential inaccuracies in insights obtained without probing, it is likely that there has been an under-recording of the true nature of transport problems in the UK. This has implications for the literature around transport and social exclusion which is largely reliant upon perfunctory rather than in-depth understandings and thus liable to perpetuation of ambiguous conceptions of transport needs in society.

The linkage between transport networks and social networks

This study has examined both the impact of the spatial structure of the social network on an individual's demand for travel and how the nature of, and the extent to which, social networks supply or facilitate travel. This builds on a concept that Altschuler et al. (2004) raise when examining the findings of their qualitative investigation of local services and amenities, neighbourhood social capital and health. Altschuler et al. found that, in lower income neighbourhoods, there was evidence of residents utilizing social capital in an effort to procure that which they were not able to purchase with financial capital, namely, a neighbourhood whose amenities far outweigh its liabilities.

The idea that social capital or social networks can be used to facilitate the acquisition of something that is unattainable through other means is equally applicable to transport. As Payne (2000:5) reminds us, our lives are primarily based on sociality:

> …our day-to-day life is a social one. Our very survival depends on a complex, largely invisible, taken-for-granted web of group activities that produce, deliver and regulate the production and consumption of goods and services. We cannot exist in isolation from one another…

Banister (1980:4), describing latent demand for travel as "an extension of the concept of mobility", alludes to the importance of social networks in substituting travel by another on behalf of an individual who has a latent demand for travel:

> …should one or more of the demand or supply assumptions be relaxed; this would usually result in an increase in demand, but there is no reason why movement should not be degenerated (e.g. through the introduction of mobile services or a neighbour doing a shopping trip for a group of old people rather than they themselves doing it.)

In this case, neighbourhood social capital is facilitating the satisfaction of the elderly peoples' need to access goods which they would have had to travel to obtain if their personal network could not make the supply of goods possible by alternative means. The findings of this research highlight the practice amongst participants of the satisfaction of travel demand through social network substitution that Banister portrays in the quote above. Specifically, for the less mobile, social networks can provide an alternative to public transport.

While this study was not conceived as being comparative, the ways in which different people transact their daily activities of life can help illustrate how they negotiate around the transport system they have available to them. For the less mobile, connectivity to satisfy their day-to-day needs can be supplied through a "vector": someone else accessing the goods or service on their behalf, that is, this other person may carry out an errand on behalf of the less mobile. For others, there is a reliance on "lift-giving" and combining of trips with others. In contrast, for those who are not presented with mobility difficulties, access to goods and services can be extremely selective. For these people, spatial and time-based challenges may be largely overcome by the propensity for a car to allow them to travel where they want to when they want to[2].

Connecting the macro policy environment and micro level atomistic data analysis

This research has examined local and individual experience of the transport system. It deliberately looks at micro-level data centred on individual citizens to provide understandings of day-to-day needs which can then inform macro-level policy-making and planning.

---

2   The use of support networks can be very important in accomplishing travel where public transport does not provide adequate services. These support networks can be the lifeline to essential goods which may not be available locally or which may be too expensive at the local shop for someone on a low income. During an interview with an elderly participant in Barton, her retired friend delivered her bread and milk which he buys for her regularly at the Somerfield supermarket in Headington. He travels by bus to the supermarket to shop because both he and his friend find the general store on the Barton estate too expensive and the range of goods poor or "not fresh". In contrast, the availability of one's own car and provision of accessible private non-residential car parking in the urban centre allows one retired study participant from Charlbury the luxury of making choices of quality goods on a much wider spatial scale. He described his choices thus:

"I've got a parking space in Oxford (at my old department) so I can chose to come into Oxford by car if I want to…I go to Witney to shop at Waitrose but always buy my bread in Oxford (at Maison Blanc). I buy certain things in certain places."

These simple examples illustrate that the car bestows a power to transact business and access goods over far wider horizons. The car-owning retiree travels between relatively distant locations on his own in pursuit of the goods he chooses to obtain to suit the flexibility his disposable income confers. In contrast, the public transport dependent retiree does not have the financial resources (or, possibly, the desire) to travel longer distances to obtain the goods to satisfy his needs. Instead, his resources are used to travel a relatively short distance and to use the regular trip to provide a service for a friend. In this way, the social connection between the two elderly residents of Barton means that one can rely upon the other to source better quality goods beyond the local area and thereby circumvent her lack of access to transport.

Micro-level analysis helps those involved in the macro-level policy environment understand the problems and contexts in which policies and interventions have to work. In addition, micro level investigation facilitates the operation of policy to be displayed from the point of view of the system user. In this way, micro level atomistic data builds evidence which can be fed into macro-scale policy and intervention development. This represents a re-ordering of policy-making from a top-down to a bottom-up approach.

Transport planning has, traditionally, emphasized strategic needs. For example, the Headington roundabout changes discussed in the urban case study in Chapter 4 have been designed with the perspective that the roundabout is a node on the strategic inter-urban road network and with little regard being given to the mix of uses it is put to on a daily basis in its role as a facilitator of local access to a wider urban network. A re-focusing of orientation to take account of local, and arguably, atomistic needs can mean that policies and interventions make better use of available, limited resources as they take account of local communities' as well as more dispersed needs.

In Chapter 1, it was reported that the Government's 10 Year Plan for Transport had been criticized for being too focused on infrastructure and large scale projects. From the micro level analysis carried out for this study, it does indeed appear to be the case that local needs are not being met by current policies and interventions in the two case studies. Instead, for people in these two areas, transport planning has tended to be top-down with little regard being given to local contexts.

The UK Government's Modernising Government White Paper published in 1999 defined policy making as "the process by which governments translate their political vision into programmes and actions to deliver 'outcomes' – desired changes in the real world" (The Stationery Office, 1999:12). In other words, policy making is about achieving real changes in people's lives and all policy decisions should be demonstrably rooted in knowledge and research which reflects local experience and practice. Top-down policy making and analysis often ignores the realities of how policies affect people. But, at the same time, bottom-up approaches can be accused of generating information that is too locally-specific. However, with transport being organized at a macro level but implemented locally, it is essential that the 'local' is central to transport policy-making and analysis.

In order to illustrate the importance of micro-level understandings to macro-scale policy making, the findings of this study in relation to car availability are discussed here. These findings suggest that, in analysing the social impacts of transport, the most useful categorisation may be car availability versus non-car availability. In a mobile society where car travel is dominant and much of transport planning such as road building and service location decisions have strengthened its dominance, access to a car can affect the choices an individual is able to make and thus affect his quality of life. Looking at social groups delineated by indicators such as gender, age, ethnicity, the ultimate difference in experience of the transport system is determined by whether the individual member of each of these social groups has access to a car or not. Notwithstanding cultural differences between these different social groups which may influence their travel needs, it is car availability (or lack thereof) which operationalizes how the different needs can be satisfied. Other authors have drawn attention to the centrality of car availability to an individual's ability to satisfy their social needs and gain access to the facilities and services they need in a mobile society. Banister (2002) describes the lack of access to a car for some as being a problem with a car-based society. Lucas et al. (2001) suggest that the Labour Government's agenda for transport notes differential access to cars in a car-dominant society as potentially contributing to the social exclusion of some. Similarly, households without a car, in a society in which household car ownership is the norm, are described as "socially excluded" in the report by TRaC (2000) on social exclusion and the availability of public transport, since "they cannot fully participate i.e. behave as the vast majority of society behaves" (TRaC, 2000:76).

While this study corroborates the link between car access and an ability to participate in society, an important caveat must be attached to this assertion and this is what makes this a valuable illustration of the way in which micro-scale understandings can inform macro-scale policy-making. As this study has shown, in general, car availability facilitates flexibility over time and space constraints enabling access to services, facilities and social activities. However, the study provided cautionary evidence that, for some individuals, the car can act as an unwelcome social isolator[3]: in Chapter 4, a young female participant described living in relative isolation from others in her neighbourhood, as her regular activities involved travelling a distance in her old car to care for her infirm mother. The argument against macro-level approaches works in two ways in relation to this finding: firstly, aggregate, social category approaches to investigating transport-related social exclusion may not have revealed this highly-individual experience and, secondly, macro-level policy-making generally assumes that access to a car facilitates social participation.

Instead, the unwanted social isolation of the individual with a car underlines the importance of looking at individual needs with respect to transport issues and the need to move away from the conventional category approaches that have pervaded the transport and social inclusion literature thus far. Church et al. (2000:195) also provide an instructive statement on the use of a category approach which accords with, and intensifies, the views expressed here:

> Firstly, particular social groups may not be homogeneous in terms of their material affluence, or activity patterns, which will affect transport needs and accessibility preferences. Secondly, the reasons why individuals may be disadvantaged in relation to transport are often multi-dimensional whereas this approach often encourages a focus on a particular dimension of the problem, such as age, which may not fully acknowledge the interaction with other social and economic factors. Thirdly, these studies rarely consider detailed geographical factors, such as the relations between residential location, where the activities that they want to participate in are located, and their need and ability to move between the two.

The views about the inappropriateness of social category approaches expressed by Church et al. above with respect to transport and social exclusion can also be found amongst authors writing about social exclusion from other perspectives. Commins

---

3   It is recognized that, for some, the time they spend alone in their car provides a desirable break from other distractions and responsibilities. It is not those who see the car as a 'welcome' social isolator who are of concern here.

(2004:60), writing about what he perceives as a lack of concern for examining the issue of rural social exclusion in European Union member countries, states that there has been "a heavy emphasis on the problems of certain social categories (e.g. the unemployed, older people) or on the problems of urban communities". In his criticism of such social category approaches, Commins writes that:

> ...in policy discussions which focus on social categories (e.g. the unemployed, youth, women) there is an implied view that the nature of their problems (and the solutions thereto) can be the same for the members of any category, irrespective of whether they live in rural or urban areas. (Commins, 2004:61)

The findings of the experimental Q methodology study described in Chapter 6 suggest that it may be more appropriate not to try to place people in social groupings that may create false boundaries around their experiences and perspectives. Instead, the research suggests it may be more pertinent to adopt more disaggregated or micro-scale approaches to analysing people's interaction with the transport system, if macro-level policy making and planning is to attend more effectively to prevailing accessibility difficulties amongst the affected public.

Methodological implications of the research

Introduction

In this section, issues arising from the methodological approach adopted are discussed. We start by looking at the potential for placing subjectivity at the centre of the study of transport and social exclusion. Then the following two sub-sections discuss the value added to this type of study by the use of analysis of web-based talk and Q methodology respectively.

Investigating subjectivity in transport: towards a quality of life perspective

While traditional approaches to researching the social aspects of transport have largely concentrated on measurement of indicators such as distance travelled, fare paid and number of trips made, there is an argument for placing individual perspectives at the centre of such analysis. This type of approach gives due regard to quality of life issues related to transport. Fares, distance travelled and number of trips made all affect quality of life and the aggregate term appeals as a more appropriate indicator because it takes account of qualitative issues such as the planning a traveller must undertake in order to make a trip, their feelings about the environment in which they travel and the emotive issues and impacts that influence their overall experience of using the transport system.

Banister (2002) suggests that social welfare and an inclusive society have tended to be of secondary importance in the policy rhetoric around sustainable development and that the use of headline indicators[4] in the UK sustainable development strategy should only be seen as a way to identify "where quality of life is improving or getting worse" (Banister 2002:115). Instead, there has been a tendency to use indicators to monitor trends

> …that we already know about, rather than actually tackling the problems at source. …The indicators do not say anything about why change has taken place, as they cannot be linked to causal factors. There is a real danger that 'indicator watching' is merely observing the symptoms rather than the underlying causes of changes in the quality of life. (Banister, 2002:115)

Banister goes on to suggest that quality of life is a much more fundamental concept than that suggested by these indicators. The author relates quality of life to various attributes at the individual, community and national level which cannot be rendered into a tangible series of indicators. While arguably much more difficult to determine than quantifiable factors such as those described by Banister, quality of life is central to an individual's experience of day-to-day living. By understanding the texture and differentiation in people's perception of how they relate to the transport system and, by extension, to the wider community they live in, transport planning which places people at the centre of policy-making will result. This can be achieved through a re-orientation of focus away from the dominance of quantitative approaches towards qualitative and participatory planning that seeks understandings as much about causation as it does about the role of individual perspectives in creating a transport system that improves quality of life for all. Such less prescriptive approaches can open up new, more empowering ecological ways of including local people in local decisions.

The value of web-based talk

This research reveals that internet forums and electronic talk can yield useful insights into local concerns and are a valuable, though under-utilized, resource for the transport researcher. Using electronic media cuts down on the transaction costs of communication and enables dialogue over barriers of time and geography. Analysis of data from internet forums can be likened to listening to conversations at local coffee mornings where valuable understandings of a community's concerns can be obtained. In this research, the overall methodology was greatly complemented by the use of internet forums which helped structure the fieldwork focus. The benefits

---

4   In Banister's example, the headline indicators for "social progress which recognizes the needs of everyone" in the UK sustainable development strategy are listed as a) tackling poverty and social exclusion: measured by numbers of children in low-income households, adults without qualifications and in workless households, elderly in fuel poverty; b) equip people with the skills to fulfil their potential: measures by qualifications at age 19; c) improve health of the population overall: measured by expected years of healthy life; d) reduce the proportion of unfit (housing) stock: measured by number of homes judged to be unfit to live in; and e) reduce both crime and people's fear of crime: measured by level of crime (Banister, 2002:116)

of the approach in exposing current concerns are likely to be equally helpful in other research on the social aspects of transport.

The web-based forums were very useful in transcending the initial statements by potential participants that transport was not an issue for them. The internet conversations provided an alternative view, indicating that there were local concerns about transport issues (for example, valuable insights obtained about Charlbury are described in Chapter 5) , thus serving as a measure of prevailing transport issues through what could be described as "virtual probing" – discovering the real concerns in a community rather than accepting the cursory indication from potential participants that they did not experience any difficulties using the transport system or were entirely self-reliant with regard to the their travel decisions.

Q as a tool for new insights

The exploratory study suggests that Q methodology can facilitate the development of more nuanced understandings about transport's impacts on people's lives. The technique provides a conceptual framework which helps illuminate participant perspectives. In the case of this study, Q helped reveal four distinct attitudes towards transport amongst participants. Each of these discourses can be characterized by a unique descriptive label which helps convey the essence of the particular viewpoint. These labels are respectively: Discourse A: The contented resident; Discourse B: The car as escape from local deficiencies; Discourse C: The multi-mode advocate and Discourse D: The disaffected theorist.

Using Q methodology in transport research is new. The results of the analysis add a new dimension to the findings of more traditional approaches such as focus groups and travel diaries: a representation of a participant's operant values at the time of the empirical research. In other words, an insight into what motivates the participant and how this colours his/her interaction with the transport system as he/she goes about the daily activities of life.

One of the main findings of this research has been to reveal that the concerns, challenges and issues of any one social group may not be very different from those of other social groups. Within this context, the Q methodology study has helped to clarify that there are common perspectives across people participating in this research which do not appear to be related to the traditional social groupings, defined by factors such as gender, ethnicity and age, that transport research has tended to investigate. Instead, it may be the case that assumptions that membership of a particular social group mean that all members have similar and generalizable experiences and views may be distracting policy-makers and academics from the true nature of the variability of individual experience. It may indeed be more appropriate for future research into the social aspects of transport to look for common perspectives amongst a population and then develop and tailor solutions that are suitable to meet the key concerns that constitute the viewpoint. Such approaches can avoid the "ghettoisation" (Brook Lyndhurst, 2004:84) that sees particular groups as problematic and having particular problems. Although Brook Lyndhurst (2004) focused on the ageing population, their comments on the dangers of ghettoisation are equally relevant to the other social groups that have been investigated in this research. Brook Lyndhurst (2004:84) describe the risks of a ghettoized approach thus: "It prevents clear thinking by policy makers: it blocks effective delivery of services; and it marginalizes older people, both practically and psychologically".

Thus we can conclude that micro-scale analysis such as that provided by Q is useful in enabling the researcher to see beyond conventional categorisation. For the policy maker and planning practitioner, the central message of this finding is that the local context is nuanced and efforts should be made to capture the range of community and individual perspectives which should inform policy and intervention development.

Policy and planning implications of the research

Introduction

In the following sub-sections, the policy and planning implications of the findings are put into a wider context. The first sub-section deals with the institutional issues raised in the research in relation to transport policy and planning. This is followed by a discussion of the findings about consultation and communication with the public who are affected by policy and planning decisions.

Institutional implications

The 'experience' gap: disengagement and dissatisfaction amongst UK transport system users   It is apparent from the microcosms of experience described in this volume that, in terms of transport, there is some dissatisfaction amongst users and disengagement amongst institutional actors with the public realm. Skidmore and Craig (2004:12-13) have drawn attention to the requirement for public involvement and participation in the shaping of public services generally:

> (P)eople will not be satisfied by what the public realm has to offer unless and until they become more active participants in shaping it. Improving the quality of the goods and services the public realm provides, like health and education, and reaffirming the values that underpin it, like trust, openness, solidarity and legitimacy, depends on finding ways to mobilize new forms of participation by citizens.

Practical and active participation in transport decision-making should place people at the centre of the process. Skidmore and Craig (2004:13) suggest that in order to start with people, there must be an understanding of "the lives they lead, the values they hold, the relationships they care about and the interests that motivate them". These are the fundamental insights that would help give transport planning and policy-making a much more people-focused orientation. From the empirical evidence in this research, it appears that, in order to achieve this focus and better fulfil individual and community needs, there should be a reconnecting of people with the institutions which make transport policy and develop interventions.

This reconnection can be facilitated through the development of improved understandings of user needs. Bentley (2005) suggests that the rhetoric around public services reform has tended to start from the abstract rather than the real experience of users and this is explicitly the case for transport amongst this study's participants. It is probable that this apparent gap between real user experience and the shapers of policies is not unique to the cases studied in this research. For example, while much policy attention and consultancy monies have been invested in the creation of accessibility planning tools in the UK, there is little evidence of how the products of this investment have changed people's experience of the transport system.

One way in which real user experience could be better revealed, and thus any changes after intervention for the user be more usefully gauged and measured from a baseline position, is through the enhancement of an approach called HATS[5]. HATS was developed at the Transport Studies Unit at Oxford University in the 1980s. In this technologically-advancing era, an electronic form of HATS would have the potential to reveal time and space patterning of activity and travel needs and thus provide a solid basis for policy and intervention planning which enables repeated measuring of such patterning after the introduction of interventions/policies over a future timeline. Such an approach would facilitate the re-shaping of transport planning to place the user at the centre, thereby helping overcome a criticism which has been levelled at the public realm that is encapsulated in the following quote from Leadbetter (2004:28): "...the asymmetry at the heart of public services: professionals and providers have the budgets, power and information; users do not". Electronic HATS has the potential to rebalance the power relationship inherent in transport planning towards the system user and his needs: such approaches can break down the institutional barriers between planners and users.

Inconsistency between policies of different local authority departments   The research revealed that there are inconsistencies across local authority departments and that these impact on the community they serve. For example, despite Oxfordshire County Council stating that they have a commitment to weaving social inclusion issues through all Council policy and activity, the planning decisions around the gated community in Barton, described in Chapter 4, do not appear to reflect that doctrine. In addition, in terms of transport, the Authority states that it promotes public transport usage and the lessening of dependence on car travel. However, the development in question is not well-located for access to non-car transport networks and its marketing clearly indicates that one of its main attributes is its proximity to the inter-urban road network. The granting of permission to build a gated community in a deprived neighbourhood may be interpreted as a form of complicity between institutional actors (e.g. housebuilder and local planning authority) in perpetuating and extending socially divisive and exclusionary features in the built environment.

---

5   HATS – Household Activity Travel Simulator comprises of a set of display equipment that forms part of a household in-depth interview which has some of the features of unstructured or semi-structured techniques, but in other respects is highly structured. The simulator seeks to depict the household's pattern of activities in time and space and enable an exploration of hypothetical questions through the consideration of possible responses amongst the household group. Further information on the HATS technique can be found in Jones et al. (1983).

Although these findings are unlikely to be unique to the case study described in this study, they do help to elucidate the "silo-esque" nature of current local government institutions and provide a concrete example of the way discrepancies across policy areas can be manifest in local communities.

Consultation and participative planning: gaps in practice and understanding

The 'consultation' gap: consultation for consultation's sake?   Returning to the issues around consultation and participation raised in Chapters 4 and 5, there is evidence (Rajé, 2003; Rajé et al., 2004a; Rajé et al., 2004b) to suggest that, despite the assertion by the then Department of Environment, Transport and the Regions that public participation is a key element in effective transport planning, involvement of local people in the process does not appear to have been a priority in all scheme design projects. Some of the participants in this research suggested that they felt that although public exhibitions about the roundabout proposals had been held, they were not optimistic that their views would be taken into account or needs met by the redesign.

Similarly, research carried out in Bristol and Nottingham on behalf of the Department for Transport on congestion charging (Rajé, 2003; Rajé et al., 2004a) indicated that levels of awareness of proposals for charging schemes in the two study cities were different: awareness was low in Bristol and high in Nottingham. It was apparent that there must have been different local authority strategies for public education campaigns though the extent of the differences was difficult to determine. Public acceptability requires that residents feel that they are involved in the process of policy-making and introduction. Given that there would be impacts of road user charging on all Bristol residents to some degree, it was clear that there needed to be public involvement in the policy's evolution. A campaign that includes mechanisms for involving everyone in a decision that affects them in their communities can make a major contribution to the policy's outcome as the decision-making structure is more inclusive and democratic. Such an approach encourages widespread ownership and helps ensure that a scheme is designed to reflect the needs and aspirations of the people it will affect.

Entering into discourse with local communities can enable planners to develop greater insights into people's day-to-day experience of transport. Without such dialogue, community consultation that is merely token in its purpose results. Respondents in the Bristol and Nottingham research (Rajé, 2003) reported that often they were uncertain about the nature and the detail of consultation which had happened between public authorities and the community even within the community centre where the consultation had taken place. Ensuring that communities are effectively consulted is very different from what appears to have been token consultation.

The importance of effective consultation is heightened when one considers hard-to-reach groups such as people from ethnic minority backgrounds, the elderly and the young. Innovative approaches are needed to overcome current barriers to consultation with harder to reach groups. Indeed, as the work of Needham (2002:711) indicates, transport itself can be a barrier to participation in consultation. Needham, reporting on consultation in Oxford, not only highlights problems councils face in expanding consultation 'but also shows how it can be used to entrench existing power relations':

> This demand problem (i.e. lack of willingness to participate in consultation) is likely to be particularly intense among the 'hard to reach' groups that Oxford has sought to target. Officers' efforts to increase participation among young people, ethnic minorities and poorer communities have had only limited success. In part, this reflects an assumption that lack of participation indicates lack of interest, with officer efforts directed at mobilizing interest in consultation rather than tackling entrenched problems that limit participation. Childcare and transportation needs, for example, were not mentioned. The council publishes some public documents in languages other than English, but the selection of languages reflects earlier waves of immigration into the area rather than the current situation. Translation facilities are not offered at area committee meetings, perhaps recognizing that invitation letters sent out in English are unlikely to encourage attendance by non-English speakers.

The importance of public consultation becomes increasingly clear as the detail of travel and transport experiences, such as those revealed in this research, is reviewed. Effective consultation requires that schemes pay attention to public suggestions for improvement and that consultation not simply be used as a one way street of providing information on that which has already been decided:

> It is quite clear that some organisations are simply going through the motions of public participation in response to the exhortations and veiled threats of various government pronouncements on the topic. It is equally clear, however, that many organisations see recent innovations as an opportunity to address some of the shortcomings of existing democratic practice. These organisations are actively seeking to renew democracy through the imaginative use of various techniques, at the heart of which is a simple belief that more participation must be better for democracy than less. (Pratchett, 1999:632)

The 'communication' gap: towards more aware planning   It would be erroneous to suggest that there is a total absence of awareness amongst planning and policy-making practitioners of the needs of local residents and the importance of seeking to address issues that communities face on a daily basis. After all, these practitioners are themselves residents of communities and may share some of the concerns of people affected by their decisions. Increasingly, more sophisticated tools are being developed to help planners make decisions that are more finely-tuned to local needs. As Chapter 2 indicates, one of these tools which became available in 2005, is Accession, a bespoke accessibility planning software tool developed by transport consultants MVA on behalf of the DfT to assist local authorities in England in preparing accessibility strategies in second Local Transport Plans (LTPs). However, it should be noted that the DfT does not require local authorities to use the software (Titheridge, 2005). It has also been suggested (Titheridge, 2005:8) that the software may only help local authorities perform one part of the task of accessibility modelling:

> Accession seems to provide all the tools necessary for local authorities to be able to carry out the mapping audits required as part of the accessibility planning process. However, it does not seem as if it is particularly geared towards helping local authorities with the third

stage of the process – option appraisal. An accessibility analysis tool could be developed which helped local authorities to:

 a) Identify the full range of potential solutions available for tackling a particular problem;

 b) Model the positive and negative and wider impacts of each option;

 c) Help identify potential barriers to implementation of each option; and

 d) Assess the value for money of each option.

Given apparent doubts about the robustness of tools such as Accession, the importance of participatory consultation to conception and construction of socially-focused transport schemes is heightened. There is a potential in over-reliance upon new and untested tools for the needs of local people and communities to be lost in the design of interventions and policies.

Future research and policy recommendations: eliminating transport based exclusion

The research has revealed some insights which would benefit from greater investigation. In terms of methods, the experimental Q study has helped uncover individual participant motivations and attitudes towards transport and its role in a person's life. The deployment of this technique on a wider scale would be beneficial to investigate more closely the prevailing range of perceptions about transport. Such an exercise could inform policy-making. For example, understanding that the disaffected theorist typology described in Chapter 6 is fully cognisant of the negative effects of transport on the environment but still does not alter his car-based behaviour may make the policy-maker aware that education and information campaigns on environmental impacts are unlikely to influence people with such opinions and therefore time and finance may be more usefully invested in trying to initiate change amongst more amenable sections of the population.

The study has also indicated that the use of electronic sources can assist in forming frameworks for research. The role of transport forums in revealing local concerns appears to be largely untapped in the literature. Further study of forums discussing transport issues may help align research and consultancy funding to more appropriately investigate and meet expressed needs of the community.

The car has been seen in the social exclusion literature as a source of environmental and road safety concerns. This research indicates that it can also act, rather paradoxically, as a social isolator. More research on car use, particularly amongst single member households, may help to reveal whether the cocooning effect that the car has in cutting people off from others and facilitating travel to destinations beyond the local neighbourhood, is contributing to social exclusion for some.

The research has highlighted the potential contribution junction delay can make to the decisions people make about travel. It would be useful to investigate further the phenomenon of turning delays at main junctions linking low income estates to the road network to see whether there is a link between junction delay and activity participation amongst those in a marginal socio-economic position.

Conclusion: creating transport transparencies

Transport policy has been characterized as having no coherence in its discourse and no consistent storyline (Vigar, 2002) and as lacking in any clear direction (Banister, 2002). There is also a perception of a divergence between professional transport planning and public discourses which this research evokes. This has also been discussed by Whittles (2003) in his work on urban road pricing. Whittles (2003) argues that the divergence urgently needs to be resolved. He suggests that sociological techniques can be the bridge between the two opposing perspectives. This volume contributes to a literature which seeks to bridge this gap in the field of transport and social exclusion.

In this research, it is suggested that by adopting more sensitive and people-focused communication and treating citizens with appropriate respect, the professional transport planning sphere would greatly benefit from the insights obtained and be in a better position to deploy limited financial resources to meet real local needs. By bridging the perceptible discourse gap, quality of services could be improved and public bodies become more accountable and responsive to community need. Such an approach can empower citizens and lead to a rebalancing of public infrastructure to meet the common good of all residents.

Transaction of daily activities requires negotiation around the transport system. This research has shown that, for the less mobile, social networks can provide an alternative to public transport. For the more mobile, the availability of a car to one person can result in hidden displacement effects for another. Women who are largely dependent on walking can become "tired". However, for these women, walking stretches limited household budgets that may be even more constrained if they had to cover the costs of public transport fares also.

This study contributes to the on-going discussion of transport's role in preventing people participating in activities. The research indicates that transport can act as a barrier to access to activity participation on a number of levels. The transport barrier can be spatial, when a service or activity is only available to a potential participant at a distance and therefore requires travel. If a viable means of transport to the activity location is not available, then transport becomes a factor in limiting activity participation. The barrier can be temporal, when a transport service is available to link potential participant with activity location but not at a time that allows the trips to and from the activity to be made. The barrier can be informational, when someone wishes to take part in an activity but cannot find out how to travel there, cannot understand the available travel information or does not realize that an available transport service operates within an accessible corridor of the origin and/or destination.

The research has also revealed a much more insidious way in which transport may limit activity participation: through the development of transport policies and solutions without due consideration of local needs. Lack of participation, whether intentional or involuntary, by the affected public in need definition, comparative proposal evaluation, scheme design and subsequent evaluation, means that citizens may be rendered impotent in their control of interventions that will ultimately impinge upon their ability to participate in activities. Disregard for local needs results in transport investments and policies which are inappropriate, do not alleviate prevailing barriers to activity participation and, therefore, work against the objectives of social inclusion. Interventions should give due regard to the resolution of challenges that are currently experienced in a community rather than being developed in the absence of local perspectives. Meaningful community engagement with stakeholders from across the spectrum of activity needs and life styles is an important aspect of inclusive planning.

The research indicates that it is necessary for transport investment to be appropriate and responsive to locally-identified need for it to be successful in increasing activity participation. In the absence of apposite local focus and tuning to specific needs, any transport investment may be in danger of introducing additional barriers to accessibility for some more vulnerable people in an affected community. It is also clear that for some, a high level of investment is not the requirement. Instead, they need tailored solutions which make obstacles to participation surmountable. These obstacles may be in many forms, for example, for the information-deprived, personalized travel planning may be a key solution.

This research has shown that there is a need for transport policy and practice to be informed by local experience. An appreciation of the plurality of individual lived experience of transport, both poor transport and good transport, can engender amongst the planning and policy-making practitioners an empathy for how people's lives are affected by the systems they design. It is only through sustained interaction with people in local communities that real needs and experiences can be revealed. There is little benefit in involvement of local people if such involvement is only perfunctory in nature. The local transport plan process requires that consultation takes place with the local public. However, within the process there is an opportunity for obfuscation of the detail of such consultation: an authority could consult with business leaders, active community groups and motivated members of the community, yet, some people from the affected public may never hear about the authority's plans or even that consultation may be taking place because appropriate channels of communication, for example, with ethnic community members may not have been adopted. Despite its inadequacies, such consultation could legitimately be reported by the local authority to have taken place, although the character of the exercise would not be reported.

A more transparent and inclusive approach to service planning and policy making can be mutually-beneficial to the transport system user and the practitioner. Leadbetter (2004:19) suggests that "a new organising logic for public provision" that places the user at the centre of service design and delivery could be beneficial in the development of high quality services. We have seen, in the case of Cowley Road reported on in Chapter 4, how participatory planning can work towards meeting the individual needs of various members of the community. This was achieved largely by an approach that facilitated participation through what Leadbetter has termed "personalisation". Much of the success of this person-focused approach is attributable to the transparency with which planners and consultants involved the affected public in an interactive process of consultation, design, feedback and adaptation. As McCarthy et al. (2004:15) indicate "the right kinds of transparency" can help to rebuild public trust in institutions and also "improve organisational performance itself". It is hoped that in the future such inclusive approaches do not need to be showcased as the exception but, instead, that they should be accepted, and expected, as the norm.

The research has provided a number of examples of ways in which transport can negatively impact on people's lives and has warned of the dangers of investing in measures which do not assuage these negative impacts. In terms of the two transport interventions examined closely in this study, the roundabout improvement and home zone, there appears to be little expressed desire in the two case study communities to see the schemes implemented. In both areas, there is some doubt as to the need for the interventions and the consultation process has not helped to engender local support. Instead, the consultation exercises for both interventions may have been counter-productive resulting in research participants expressing some doubt with respect to the credibility of the planning institutions involved.

In terms of social inclusion, the research gave little evidence that either intervention would actively promote a resident's participation in activities or ability to access services. The findings suggest that other forms of transport intervention such as personalized travel marketing schemes, lift-sharing and individualized solutions (e.g. car clubs, demand responsive transport) would be more appropriate for increasing activity participation and meeting social inclusion objectives.

Over the past few years, the UK transport and social inclusion/exclusion literature has focused largely on the findings of the Social Exclusion Unit's report "Making the Connections" published in 2003. While the report helpfully collates information on how social exclusion may be exacerbated by transport, it can only be seen as a basis for subsequent policy development. For example, it promotes the concept of accessibility planning but it is not clear on how such techniques may assist the systematic appraisal of relative effectiveness of proposed transport schemes, interventions and policies in terms of social inclusion and exclusion.

There is also some concern, at a more global level, about the commitment of government to incorporation of social inclusion objectives across all policy domains. One year after the publication of "Making the Connections", the Office of the Deputy Prime Minister (ODPM) published a discussion paper entitled 'Tackling Social Exclusion' (ODPM, 2004b) which includes very little reference to transport. Given that the Social Exclusion Unit which published "Making the Connections" sits within the ODPM, it is difficult to be convinced that there is indeed commitment within government to overcoming some of the obstacles to greater social inclusion if joined-up thinking is not even demonstrated within this one department tasked with moving social exclusion issues up the political agenda.

Similarly, the Department for Transport's draft Evidence and Research Strategy (DfT, 2006) evokes comparable concerns about the Department's commitment to lessening transport-related social exclusion given the scant references to the subject within the document. While government makes pronouncements about its commitment to promoting social inclusion, the policy environment is characterized by its inattention to the detail of reducing social exclusion. Until the policy environment fully embraces social inclusion, there will be little progress in moving beyond the transport system users' vocabulary of autonomy, which conceals real experience, towards understandings of the observation of dependence associated with travel which are necessary if transport-related social exclusion is to be addressed effectively.

Appendices

Appendix 1

Interview Guide

Name…………………………………………………………………………............

Address………………………………………………………………………............

Age………………………….. Ethnicity…………………………………….........

Gender………………….… Access to internet…… Mobile…………..........

Car owner………………… Household Income………………...........(code)

Local Newspaper……..……… Local radio/TV…………………………..........

How many people live in your household?...

I am carrying out research into people's views about transport and their local area. I will start by asking you some questions about your local area and then I'll move on to asking about your experience of transport.

SECTION A

1. **How long have you lived in the area?**…………………………...............

2. **I would like to ask you about your local area. Would you say this area** (note any additional comments on back of page)

   a. is a place you enjoy living in or not?   Yes   No
   b. is a place where neighbours look after each other or not? Yes   No
   c. has good local transport or not?   Yes   No

3. **Could you tell me please which, if any, of these you have done in the past fortnight?**

   Went to visit relatives   ☐
   Had relatives visit you   ☐
   Went out with relatives   ☐

Spoke to relatives on the phone   ☐
Went to visit friends   ☐
Had friends visit you   ☐
Went out with friends   ☐
Spoke to friends on the phone   ☐
Spoke to neighbours   ☐
None of these   ☐
Anything else....................................

4. **Do you join in the activities of any of the following organisations on a regular basis?**

Political parties   ☐
Trade unions (including student unions)   ☐
Environmental group   ☐
Parents'/School Association   ☐
Tenants'/ Residents' group or Neighbourhood watch   ☐
Education, arts or music group/evening class   ☐
Religious group or church organization   ☐
Group for elderly people (eg lunch clubs)   ☐
Youth group (eg scouts, guides, youth clubs etc)   ☐
Women's Institute/Townswomen's Guild   ☐
Women's Group   ☐
Social club/working men's club   ☐
Sports club   ☐
Other group or organization...
None   ☐

5. **Do you think that people can generally be trusted?**

Yes........... No.......... Not sure..........

SECTION B

1) What are the main transport issues in Barton/Cowley Road/Oxford/Charlbury? What are the good things, what are the bad things?

2) Can you describe what kinds of things you do on a day-to-day basis? What are the main activities you are normally involved in?

3) What activities would you like to do/what journeys would you like to make but can't and to what extent is this due to transport factors? For example, have you missed a hospital appointment, missed a class, or visit to friends and relations because of transport difficulties?

4) Do you rely on friends or relatives to help you to get about or to do trips for you, such as shopping, returning library books, picking up prescriptions etc?

5) How often do you visit relatives when they are healthy/when they are sick?

6) Has there been an occasion in the past year when you haven't been able to travel on your own? If so, what did you do, who did you ask to help you?

7) If you were temporarily housebound and needed somebody to bring medicines to you, how many people do you know who would be willing to do this service for you?

8) When you make a journey, how many other people are involved in the decision-making/ providing support to make the journey?

9) If someone helps you by giving you a lift or getting something from the shops for you, do you do anything for them in exchange? Do you exchange favours?

10) I would now like to ask you about where you go to to do different things.

Where do you go to shop for food? How do you get there? Do you find this easy or difficult?

Where do you go to get a newspaper? How do you get there? Easy/difficult

Where do you go to the post office? How do you get there? Easy/difficult

Where do you go to see the doctor? How do you get there? Easy/difficult

Can you give me the names and contact details of the 3 main people you rely on to help you do things/to help you travel? For example, the person you ask to give you a lift, the person you negotiate with to use the car, the person who gets the shopping for you, the person who you go shopping with…

I would like to send them a copy of the diary to be completed and then ask them the questions I have asked you today.

Appendix 2

Principal participants in study

Barton

Alias	Some descriptive notes
Walter	elderly employed male with car
Mary	36 year old unemployed single mother of 3 on low income
Tracey	21 year old single mother of 2 mixed race children, volunteer on low income
Jean	70 year old female full-time volunteer on low income
Gwen	38 year old mother of 3, employed on low income, with car
Jan	22 year old single female, unemployed on low income, carer, with car
Kerry	27 year old single mother of 2, unemployed, with car
Evelyn	elderly female with disabled husband, on low income
Alice	36 year old mother of 2 with disabled husband in hospital long-term, low income, with car
Sue	27 year old mother of 3, low income, husband works away from home
George	elderly male, low income
Mike	30 year old male with 2 children, low income, cyclist
Sandy	28 year old mother of 2, part-time worker, low income, deaf

Charlbury

Alias	Some descriptive notes
Christina	55 year old married female, low income, works locally, non-driver, husband drives
Robert	62 year old single male retired academic, car-owner
Adam	30 year old married male, works from home, no car access
Laura	30 year old married female, commutes by train to Oxford, no car access
Liz	45 year old married mother of 3, commutes to part-time work in Reading by train, car owner
Eve	48 year old single female, low income, car owner, works locally
Neil	36 year old married father of 3, commutes to Oxford by car
Kate	Retired married female, low income, non-driver, husband drives
Jim	Retired married male, low income, car owner
Phil	90 year old married male, low income, disabled, no car access
Vera	74 year old female, low income, no car access
Elizabeth	69 year old female, low income, non-driver, children provide lifts
Winnie	82 year old widow, low income, no car access
Donna	42 year old single mother of 2, car-owner

Other Oxfordshire residents

Alias	Some descriptive notes
Rahul	68 year old retired male car driver, lives in West Oxford
Pauline	66 year old retired female car driver, lives in West Oxford
Rose	38 year old single female car driver, lives in West Oxford
Juliet	28 year old married female, lives in Kidlington, commutes to Wallingford by car
Greg	38 year old male with 2 children, lives in East Oxford, car driver, cyclist
Maya	26 year old single female, lives in East Oxford, no car access

Consolidated Bibliography

Acheson, D. (1998). *Independent inquiry into inequalities in health report*. London, The Stationery Office.

Adams, J. (2001). *Hypermobility: too much of a good thing*. PIU Transport Seminar, London.

Adams, J. (2005). "Hypermobility: a challenge to governance". *New Modes of Governance: Developing an Integrated Policy Approach to Science, Technology, Risk and the Environment*. C. Lyall and J. Tait. Aldershot, Ashgate.

Addams, H. and J. Proops (2000). *Social discourse and environmental policy: an application of Q methodology*. Cheltenham, Edward Elgar.

Aldrich, S. and C. Eccleston (2000). "Making sense of everyday pain." *Social Science and Medicine* 50: 1631-1641.

Altschuler, A., C. Somkin and N. Adler (2004). "Local services and amenities, neighbourhood social capital and health." *Social Science and Medicine* 59(6): 1219-1230.

Anable, J. (2005). "'Complacent Car Addicts' or 'Aspiring Environmentalists'? Identifying travel behaviour segments using attitude theory." *Transport Policy* 12(1): 65-78.

Anonymous (1994). *Transportation: Environmental Justice and Social Equity*. *Transportation*: Environmental Justice and Social Equity Conference, Chicago, Illinois.

Arthurson, K. (2003). *A Critique of the Concept of Social Exclusion and its Utility for Australian Social Housing Policy*. UK Housing Studies Association Conference, Bristol.

Atkinson, R. and S. Davoudi (2000). "The Concept of Social Exclusion in the European Union: Context, Development and Possibilities." *Journal of Common Market Studies* 38(3): 427-448.

Atkinson, R. and J. Flint (2001). "Accessing Hidden and Hard-to-Reach Populations: Snowball Research Strategies." *Social Research Update* (33).

Atkinson, R. and J. Flint (2003). "Fortess UK? Gated communities, the spatial elites and the time-space trajectories of segregation." *Gated Communities: Building Social Division or Safer Communities?*, Department of Urban Studies, University of Glasgow, September 18-19.

Atkinson, R. and J. Flint (2004). "Fortress UK? Gated communities, the spatial revolt of the elites and time-space trajectories of segregation." *Housing Studies* 19(6): 875-892.

Axhausen, K. (2003). *Social networks and travel: some hypotheses*. Arbeitsbericht Verkehrs-und Raumplanung, Institut für Verkehrsplanung und Transportsysteme, ETH Zürich, Zürich.

Bailey, K. and T. Grossardt (2004). "Towards Structured Public Involvement: Enhancing Community Involvement in Transportation Decision Making."

WorldMinds: Geographical Perspectives on 100 Problems. D. G. Janelle, B. Warf and K. Hansen. Dordrecht, Kluwer Academic Publishers: 547-552.

Banister, D. (1980). T*ransport mobility and deprivation in inter-urban areas.* Farnborough, Eng, Saxon House.

Banister, D. (2002). *Transport Planning*. London, Spon.

Banister, D. (2005). *Unsustainable Transport: City transport in the new century.* London, Routledge.

Barry, J. and J. Proops (1999). "Seeking sustainability discourses with Q methodology." *Ecological Economics* 28: 337-345.

Becker, H. S. (1998). *Tricks of the trade: how to think about your research while you're doing it.* Chicago, University of Chicago Press.

Bentley, T. and J. Wilsdon (2003). *The Adaptive State: Strategies for personalising the public realm*. London, Demos.

Bentley, T. (2005). *Everyday democracy: why we get the politicians we deserve.* London, Demos.

Beuret, K., H. Aslam, S. Gross, A. Osman and F. Khan (2000). *Ethnic Minorities and Visible Religious Minorities: Their Transport Requirements and the Provision of Public Transport.* London, Department for Environment, Transport and the Regions.

Boardman, B. (1998). *Rural Transport Policy and Equity*, CPRE, Countryside Commission and Rural Development Commission.

Bonsall, P. and C. Kelly (2005). "Road user charging and social exclusion: The impact of congestion charging on at-risk groups." Traffic Demand Management Symposium, Napier University, Edinburgh.

Bostock, L. (1998). "Poor bodies: the body as resource when caring in disadvantaged circumstances." BSA Annual Conference, Edinburgh 6-9 April.

Bostock, L. (2001). "Pathways of disadvantage? Walking as a mode of transport among low-income mothers." *Health and Social care in the Community* 9(1): 11-18.

Bradshaw, J., Kemp, P., Baldwin, S. and A. Rowe. (2004). *The Drivers of Social Exclusion.* A review of the literature for the Social Exclusion Unit in the Breaking the Cycle series. ODPM. London.

Bridge, G. and S. Watson (2002). "Lest power be forgotten: networks, division and difference in the city." *The Sociological Review* 50(4): 505-524.

Brook Lyndhurst (2003). *Sustainable Cities and the Ageing Society: the role of older people in an urban renaissance*. London, ODPM.

Brouwer, M. (1999). "Q is accounting for tastes." *Journal of Advertising Research* 39(2): 35-39.

Brown, S. R. (1980). *Political subjectivity: Applications of Q methodology in political science.* New Haven, CT, Yale University Press.

Brown, S. R. (1996). "Q Methodology and Qualitative Research." *Qualitative Health Research* 6(4): 561-567.

Brown, S. R. (2005). *Applying Q methodology to empowerment. Measuring empowerment: Cross-disciplinary perspectives.* D. Narayan. Washington D.C,

The World Bank.: 197-215.

Cabinet Office (1999). *Rural Economies*. London, Cabinet Office.

Campbell, C. and P. Gillies (2001). "Conceptualizing `Social Capital' for Health Promotion in Small Local Communities: A Micro-qualitative Study." *Journal of Community and Applied Social Psychology* 11(5): 329-346.

Campbell-Jackson, M. (2002). *Public Involvement in Transportation: Collaborating with the customers. Transportation Research News*. Washington D.C., National Academies. May-June 2002.

Cancian, F. (1992). "Feminist Science: Methodologies that Challenge Inequality." *Gender and Society* 6(4): 623-642.

Carter, J. (2003). *Small Area Surveys*: Barton. Oxford, Oxford City Council.

Cartmel, F. and A. Furlong (2000). *Youth unemployment in rural areas*. York, Joseph Rowntree Foundation.

Casas, I., K. Clifton, M. Litwin and M. Schlossberg (2003). *Expanding Frameworks and Finding Focus*. Montreal, STELLA/NextGen.

Castells, M (2001). *The Internet Galaxy: Reflections on the internet, business and society*. Oxford, Oxford University Press.

CBI (2005). *Transport policy and the needs of the UK economy*. Transport Brief. London, CBI.

Centre for Economic and Social Inclusion (2002). *Social Inclusion*, Centre for Economic and Social Inclusion. 2002.

CfIT (2001). *European Best Practice in delivering Integrated Transport: Key Findings*. London, Commission for Integrated Transport.

CfIT (2002a). *Obtaining Best Value for Public Subsidy for the Bus Industry: Appendix 7*. London, LEK.

CfIT (2002b). *CfIT's initial assessment report on the 10 Year Transport Plan*, CfIT. 2002.

CfIT (2003). *Local Authority Survey*, CfIT. 2003.

Chapman, R., E. Goldberg, G. Salmon and J. Sinner (2003). *Sustainable Development and Infrastructure: Report for the Ministry of Economic Development*. Wellington, New Zealand, New Zealand Ministry of Economic Development,.

Chinnis, A., D. Paulson and S. Davis (2001). "Using Q Methodology to assess the needs of emergency medicine support staff employees." *Adminsitration of Emergency Medicine* 20(2): 197-203.

Church, A., M. Frost and K. Sullivan (2000). "Transport and social exclusion in London." *Transport Policy* 7: 195-205.

Clark, A. (2004). "Station parking is club for elite." *The Guardian*. London.

Clifton, K. (2003). "Examining Travel Choices of Low-Income Populations: Issues, Methods, and New Approaches. Moving through nets: The physical and social dimensions of travel" *10th International Conference on Travel Behaviour Research*, Lucerne, 10-15. August 2003.

Cloke, P. J. (1984). *Wheels within Wales*. Lampeter, St. David's University College.

Cloke, P., P. Crang and M. Goodwin (1999). *Introducing Human Geographies*. London, Arnold.

Commins, P. (2004). "Poverty and Social Exclusion in Rural Areas: Characteristics,

Processes and Research Issues." *Sociologia Ruralis* 44(1): 60-75.

Corr, S. (2001). "An Introduction to Q Methodology, a Research Technique." *The British Journal of Occupational Therapy* 64(6): 293-297.

Countryside Agency (2004). *State of the Countryside Report 2004.* Countryside Agency. Wetherby, Countryside Agency.

Crossley, A. (1979). *A History of the County of Oxford - Vol. IV*: The city of Oxford.

Darling, A. (2004). *Renewal in Government: transport.* Neighbourhood Renewal Unit. London, ODPM. 2005.

Davey-Smith, G. and M. Egger (1992). "Socio-economic differences in mortality in Britain and the United States." *American Journal of Public Health* 82: 1079-1081.

Davis, A. (1998). "Submission to the Independent Inquiry into Inequalities in Health. London," Input paper: *Transport and pollution.*

DEFRA (2002a). *Foundations for our future - DEFRA's sustainable development strategy.* London, DEFRA.

DEFRA (2002b). *England Rural Development Programme: Access to Rural Services.* London, DEFRA.

Demos (2004). *Public spaces; shared places? Why?* London, Demos. 2005.

DETR (1998a). *A New Deal for Transport: Better for Everyone. The Government's White Paper on the Future of Transport.* London, DETR.

DETR (1998b). *Breaking the Logjam: The Government's Consultation Paper on fighting traffic congestion and pollution through road use and workplace parking charges.* London, HMSO.

DETR (2000a). *Transport 2010: The 10 Year Plan.* London, DETR.

DETR (2000b). *Guidance on Full Local Transport Plans.* London, DETR.

DETR (2002). *Relationship between transport and economic development.* Summary report by SACTRA, UK Government on behalf of the United Nations.

DfT (2001). *Road accident involvement of children from ethnic minorities.* London, DfT.

DfT (2002a). *Delivering Better Transport: Progress Report.* London, DfT.

DfT (2002b). *A review of personalised journey planning techniques.* London, DfT.

DfT (2003a). *Transport Trends, 2002.* London, DfT.

DfT (2003b). *Graffiti and vandalism on and around public transport.* London, Dept for Transport.

DfT (2004a). *The Future of Transport.* London, DfT.

DfT (2004b). *Full Guidance on Local Transport Plans* (Second Edition): Draft for consultation. London, DfT.

DfT (2004c). *Background on demonstration and partnership projects.* London, DfT.

DfT (2006). *Evidence and Research Strategy* (Draft). London, DfT.

Docherty, I. (2001). "Interrogating the 10 year transport plan." *Area* 33(3): 321-328.

Donaghy, K, Rudinger, G and S. Poppelreuter (2004) "Societal Trends, Mobility Behaviour and Sustainable Transport in Europe and North America". *Transport*

Reviews, Vol. 24, No. 6, 679–690

DPTAC (2002). *Attitudes of disabled people to public transport: research study.* London, DPTAC.

Dryzek, J. and Berejikian (1993). "Reconstructive democratic theory." *American Political Science Review* 87: 48-60.

Dryzek, J. (2004). *Handle with care: The deadly hermeneutics of deliberative instrumentation. Empirical approaches to deliberative politics*, Firenze, European University Institute.

Dudleston, A., S. Stradling and J. Anable (2005). *Public Perceptions of Travel Awareness - Phase 3. Development Department Research Programme.* Edinburgh, Scottish Executive.

ECMT (2000). *Transport and Ageing of the Population.* Paris, ECMT.

ECMT (2001). *Implementing Sustainable Urban Transport Policies: Key Messages for Governments.* Paris, ECMT.

Eisenstadt, N. and S. Witcher (1998). "Social Exclusion and Poverty." *Outlook: The Quarterly Journal of the National Council of Voluntary Child Care Organisations* (1): 6-7.

Ekinci, Y. and M. Riley (2001). "Validating quality dimensions." *Annals of Tourism Research* 28(1): 202-223.

Etzioni, A. (1993). *The spirit of community: the reinvention of American society.* New York, Simon and Schuster.

EUBusiness (2000). *Social Exclusion in EU Member States.* Brussels, European Union.

European Environment Agency (2001). *Access to Transport Services Indicator Fact Sheet TERM 2001* 16 EU.

Evans, J. H. (1997). "Worldviews or Social Groups as the Source of Moral Value Attitudes: Implications for the Culture Wars Thesis." *Sociological Forum* 12(3): 371-404.

Farrington, J. and C. Farrington (2005). "Rural accessibility, social inclusion and social justice: towards conceptualisation." *Journal of Transport Geography* 13: 1-12.

Fernandez, R. (1993). "Review of American Apartheid: Segregation and the Making of the Underclass." *Contemporary Sociology* 22(3 (May)): 365-366.

Few, R. (2002). "Researching actor power: analyzing mechanisms of interaction in negotiations over space." Area 34(1): 29-38.

Ffrench, A. (2003). "£2m 'hamburger' plan for Green Road roundabout." *This is Oxfordshire.* Oxford.

Ffrench, A. (2005). "Tories honour pledge on free parking in city." *The Oxford Times.* Oxford: 11.

Fischer, C. S. (1982). *To dwell among friends : personal networks in town and city.* Chicago/London, University of Chicago Press.

Fischhoff, B. (1991). "Value elicitation: Is there anything in there?" *American Psychologist* 46(8): 835-847.

Foley (2004). *The Problems of Success: Reconciling Economic Growth and Quality of Life in the South East.* London, ippr.

Foley, J., N. Sansom and T. Grayling (2005). *Keeping the South East Moving.*

London, ippr.

Foucault, M. (1986). *Disciplinary power and subjection in Power.* S. Lukes, ed. Oxford, Blackwell: 229-42.

Friends of the Earth (2001). *Environmental Justice: Mapping Transport and Social Exclusion in Bradford,* Friends of the Earth.

Gibbs, A. (1997). "Focus Groups." *Social Research Update* (19).

Gillies, P. (1997). "Social capital: recognising the value of society." *Healthlines* September: 15-17.

Giuliano, G. (1992). "Transportation Demand Management: Promise or Panacea?" *Journal of American Planning Association,* Vol. 58, No. 3, pp. 327- 435

Glaister, S. (2002). "UK Transport Policy 1997-2001." *Oxford Review of Economic Policy* 18(2): 154-186.

Glendinning, A., M. Nuttall, L. Hendry, M. Kloep and S. Wood (2003). "Rural communities and well-being: a good place to grow up?" *Sociological Review* 51(1): 129-156.

Goldblatt, P. (1990). "Mortality and alternative social classifications." *Longitudinal Study: Mortality and Social Organisation.* P. Goldblatt. London, HMSO: 164-192.

Graham, S. and S. Marvin (2001). *Splintering Urbanism: networked infrastructures, technological mobilities and the urban condition.* Abingdon, Routledge.

Graham, D., S. Glaister and R. Anderson (2002). *Child pedestrian casualties in England: the effect of area deprivation.* London, Centre for Transport Studies, Imperial College.

Gray, A. (2001). *Towards a Conceptual Framework for Studying Time and Social Capital.* Families and Social Capital ESRC Research Group Working Paper No. 3. London, South Bank University.

Grayling, T. (2002). "Transport and exclusion." *The Guardian.* London.

Grayling, T., K. Hallam, D. Graham, R. Anderson and S. Glaister (2002). *Streets Ahead: Safe and Liveable Streets for Children.* London, ippr.

Gregory, R., & Keeney, R. L. (1994). "Creating policy alternatives using stakeholdervalues." *Management Science* 40: 1035-1048.

Grieco, M., L. Pickup and R. Whipp (1989). *Gender, transport and employment : the impact of travel constraints.* Aldershot, Avebury.

Grieco, M., J. Turner and J. Hine (2000). "Transport, employment and social exclusion: changing the contours through information technology." *Local Work* 26.

Grieco, M. (2002). "Limitations of transport policy: a review." *Transport Reviews* 22(4): 509-511.

Grieco, M and Hine, J. (2002) "Transport, Information Communication Technology and Public Service Failure: Community Monitoring and Demand Responsive Transport." Paper presented to National Science Foundation under auspices of STELLA network, Arlington, Virginia, January 2002

Grieco, M. and F. Rajé (2004). "Stranded mobility and the marginalisation of low income communities: an analysis of public service failure in the British public transport sector." Paper presented at the conference on Urban Vulnerability and

Consolidated Bibliography 223

Network Failure, University of Salford.

Halden, D., D. McGuigan, A. Nisbet and A. McKinnon (2000). *Accessibility: Review of measuring techniques and their application.* Edinburgh, Scottish Executive Central Research Unit.

Hamilton, K., S. Ryley Hoyle and L. Jenkins (1999). *The Public Transport Gender Audit: the Research Report.* London, Transport Studies, University of East London.

Hampshire, A. and K. Healy (2000). *Social capital in practice.* Paddington, NSW, The Benevolent Society.

Hanson, Susan and I. Johnston (1985). "Gender Differences in Work Trip Lengths: Implications and Explanations." *Urban Geography*, Vol. 6, No. 3, pp. 193-219

Hardy, C. and S. Leiba-O'Sullivan (1998). "The power behind empowerment: implications for research and practice." *Human Relations* 51: 451-83.

Harper, S. (1987). "The rural-urban interface in England: a framework of analysis." *Transactions of the Institute of British Geographers* 12: 284-302.

Hay, A. M. (1995). "Concepts of equity, fairness and justice in geographical studies." *Transactions of the Institute of British Geographers* 20(4): 500-508.

Hay, A. (2005). "The transport implications of Planning Policy Guidance on the location of superstores in England and Wales: simulations and case study." *Journal of Transport Geography* 13: 13-22.

Help the Aged (2001). *Mobility and Transport for Senior Citizens: Are we getting there?* London, Help the Aged,.

Henderson, S. and B. Henderson (1999). *Transport provision for disabled people in Scotland.* Development Department Research programme. Edinburgh, Scottish Executive.

Hetherington, S. (2001). *Transport and Social Exclusion: A response by The Children's Society*, The Children's Society.

Hills, J., J. Le Grand and D. Piachaud (2001). *Understanding Social Exclusion.* Oxford, Oxford University Press.

Hine, J. and F. Mitchell (2001). *The Role of Transport in Social Exclusion in Urban Scotland.* Edinburgh, Scottish Office Central Research Unit.

Hine, J. and F. Mitchell (2003). *Transport Disadvantage and Social exclusion.* Aldershot, Ashgate.

Hine, J. and M. Grieco (2002). *Scatters and Clusters in Time and Space: Implications for Delivering Integrated and Inclusive Transport.* American Association of Geographers, Los Angeles.

Hine, J. (2002). "Comments on: Limitations of transport policy." *Transport Reviews* 22(4): 506-508.

Hirst, J. (1996). *The influence of rurality on the access to health services of women with young children in poverty.* Leeds, Leeds Metropolitan University.

Hiscock, R., A. Ellaway and S. Macintyre (2002). "Means of transport and ontological security: Do cars provide psycho-social benefits to their users?" *Transportation Research Part D: Transport and Environment* 7(2): 119-135.

Hodge, I. and S. Monk (2004). "The economic diversity of rural England: stylised fallacies and uncertain evidence." *Journal of Rural Studies* 20: 263-272.

Hodgson, F. C. and J. Turner (2003). "Participation not consumption: the need for new participatory practices to address transport and social exclusion." *Journal of Transport Policy* 10: 265-272.

Hoggart, K., L. Lees and A. Davies (2002). *Researching Human Geography.* London, Edward Arnold.

Horn (2002) "Fleet scheduling and dispatching for demand-responsive passenger services". *Transportation Research Part C: Emerging Technologies*, 10, 1, 35-63

House of Commons (2002). 10 Year Plan for Transport. Eighth Report of Session 2001-02. London, The Stationery Office.

Jenkins, S. (2001). *Barton Road in History of Headington.* Oxford.

Jones, P., M. Dix, M. Clarke and I. Heggie (1983). *Understanding Travel Behaviour.* Oxford, Gower.

Jones, P. (1998). *Urban road pricing: public acceptability and barriers to implementation. Road Pricing, Traffic Congestion and the Environment - Issues of Efficiency and Social Feasibility.* K. J. Button and E. Verhoef. Cheltenham, Edward Elgar.

Joseph Rowntree Foundation (2001). *Policies against car congestion 'hit low-income motorists hardest'.* York, Joseph Rowntree Foundation.

Jürgens, U. and M. Gnad (2002). "Gated communities in South Africa - experiences from Johannesburg." *Environment and Planning B: Planning and Design* 29(3): 337-353.

Keeney, R. L. and H. Raiffa (1976). *Decisions with Multiple Objectives.* New York, John Wiley and Sons.

Keeney, R. L., D. von Winterfelt and T. Eppel (1990). "Eliciting public values for complex policy decisions." *Management Science* 36(9): 1011-1030.

Kempson, E. (1996). *Life on low income.* London, Policy Studies Institute.

Kenyon, S. (2002). News Release. Southampton, University of Southampton @ www.externalrelations.soton.ac.uk/media/0247.htm accessed 300604.

Kenyon, S., G. Lyons and J. Rafferty (2002). "Transport and social exclusion: investigating the possibility of promoting inclusion through virtual mobility." *Journal of Transport Geography* 10(3): 207-219.

Hyun-Mi Kim (2005) *Gender and Individual Space-Time Accessibility: A GIS-based Geocomputational Approach.* PhD Thesis, Ohio State University

King, D. and S. Stedman (2000). *Analysis of Air Pollution and Social Deprivation.* National Environmental Technology Centre. Culham, Abingdon, Oxon.

Kintrea, K. and R. Atkinson (2001). *Neighbourhoods and social exclusion: the research and policy implications of neighbourhood effects.* Glasgow, Department of Urban Studies, University of Glasgow.

Kitzinger, C. (1986). *Introducing and developing Q as a feminist methodology: A study of accounts of lesbianism. Feminist social psychology.* S. Wilkinson. Milton Keynes, Open University Press: 151-172.

Klaeboe, R. (1992). "Measuring the environmental impact of road traffic in town areas" paper to Planning, Transport, Research and Computation Summer Annual Meeting. London, Planning, Transport, Research and Computation.

Knowles, P. (no date). *The Cost of Policing New Urbanism.* Bedford, Bedfordshire Police.

Kwan, M.-P. (2003) "New information technologies, human behavior in space–

time, and the urban economy." Paper presented at STELLA TRB Session 335, Washington, DC, USA.

Latham, A. (2003). "Research, performance, and doing human geography: some reflections on the diary-photograph, diary-interview method." *Environment and Planning A* 35: 1993-2017.

Law, J. (1991). *A sociology of monsters. Essays on power, technology and domination.* London, Routledge.

Lazard, L. (2003). "Whose story is it anyway? An examination of the advantages and disadvantages of using forced or free distributions in Q methodological research." *PsyPAG Quarterly* September.

Leadbetter, C. (2004). P*ersonalisation through participation: A new script for public services.* London, Demos.

Ledbury, M. (2004). *UK car clubs: an effective way of cutting vehicle usage and emissions?* Environmental Change Institute. Oxford, University of Oxford.

Litman, T. (2003). *Measuring Transport: Traffic, Mobility and Accessibility.* Victoria, VTPI.

Lloyd, B. (2003). "Joyriding surge triggers action." *Oxford Mail.* Oxford.

London Health Commission (no date). *Involving children and young people in transport planning.* London, London Health Commission. 2004.

Lucas, K., T. Grosvenor and R. Simpson (2001). *Transport, the environment and social exclusion.* York, Joseph Rowntree Foundation.

Luxton, M. (2002). *Feminist Perspectives on Social Inclusion and Children's Well Being.* Toronto, The Laidlaw Foundation.

Lyons, G. (2003). "The introduction of social exclusion into the field of travel behaviour." *Transport Policy* 10(4): 339-342.

MacLeod, G. (2004). "Privatizing the city? The tentative push towards edge urban developments and gated communities in the United Kingdom: Final Report for the Office of the Deputy Prime Minister." London, University of Durham.

Madanipour, A., G. Cars and J. Allen (1998). Social exclusion in European cities. England, Jessica Kingsley Publishers.

May, T., A. Bristow, P. Mackie, C. Nash and M. Tight (2002). "The Ten Year Plan." *Traffic Engineering and Control* 43(8): 294-300.

McCarthy, H. and G. Thomas (2004). *Home Alone: Combating isolation with older housebound people.* London, Demos.

McCluskey, A. (1997). *Belonging and Being Excluded, Connected.*

McCray, T. M., M. E. H. Lee-Gosselin and M.-P. Kwan (2003). "Netting action and activity space/time: are our methods keeping pace with evolving behaviour patterns? Moving through nets: The physical and social dimensions of travel" 10th International Conference on Travel Behaviour Research, Lucerne, 10-15. August 2003.

McDowell, L. (2001). *Father and Ford revisited: gender, class and employment change in the new millennium.* Transactions of the Institute of British Geographers 26:448-464

McDowell, L., Perrons, D., Fagan, C., Ray, K. and K. Ward (2005). "The contradictions and intersections of class and gender in a global city: placing working women's lives on the research agenda." *Environment and Planning A* 37:441-461.

McKeown, B. F. and D. B. Thomas (1988). *Q methodology.* Newbury Park, CA, Sage.

McRae, S. (1999). *Changing Britain : families and households in the 1990s.* Oxford, Oxford University Press.

McWhannell, F. and S. Braunholtz (2002). *Young people and transport.* Edinburgh, MORI Scotland for Scottish Executive.

Metz, D. (2002). "Limitations of transport policy." *Transport Reviews* 22(2): 134-146.

Middleton, S., K. Ashworth and I. Braithwaite (1997). *Small fortunes: spending on children. childhood poverty and parental sacrifice.* York, Joseph Rowntree Foundation.

Miller, H. (2003). *Travel Chances and Social Exclusion.* IATBR, Lucerne.

Ministry of Transport (1963). *Traffic in Towns.* London, HMSO.

MORI (2001). The CfIT Report 2001: *Public Attitudes to Transport in England.* London, Commission for Integrated Transport.

Murray, J. (1991). *Headington in 1991.* Headington History. Oxford.

National Centre for Social Research (2002). In-depth Interviews, NatCen. 2003.

Needham, C. (2002). "Consultation: A Cure for Local Government?" *Parliamentary Affairs* 55: 699-714.

New Zealand National Health Committee (2003). *Impacts of Transport on Health: An overview.* Auckland, New Zealand National Health Committee.

Newman, O. (2003). *Creating Defensible Spaces.* New York, US Dept of housing and urban development.

NHS (no date). *Measuring the Right Things.* London. 2004.

O'Dowd, C. (No date). *A public involvement road map.* Arvada, Colorado, Athena's Consulting Network, Inc.

ODPM (2004a). *Community Involvement in Planning. Creating sustainable communities.* London, Office of the Deputy Prime Minister.

ODPM (2004b). *Tackling Social Exclusion: Achievements, lessons learned and ways forward.* London, ODPM.

ONS (2000). *General Household Survey.* London, Office of National Statistics.

ONS (2002). *Access local services: Carless households -twice the difficulties*, Office of National Statistics. 2003.

ONS (2004). *Social Trends 34.* London, Office of National Statistics.

ONS (2005). *Social Trends 35.* London, Office of National Statistics

Owen, V. (2002). "Smashed lights put tenants in danger." www.thisisoxfordshire.co.uk. Oxford.

Owen, V. (2005). "Mini family planning clinics set to open." *Oxford Mail.* Oxford.

Owens, S. (2005). "Making a difference? Some perspectives on environmental research and policy". *Transactions of the Institute of British Geographers* 30:287-292

Oxford City Council (2003). *Report on Census 2001.* Oxford, Oxford City Council.

Oxfordshire County Council (2000). *Oxfordshire Local Transport Plan (2001-2006).* Oxford, Oxfordshire County Council.

Oxfordshire County Council (2004). *Are we included? Why not?: Social Inclusion*

Scrutiny Review. Oxford, Oxfordshire County Council.

Oxfordshire County Council (2005a). *An Economic Profile of Oxfordshire.* Oxford, Oxfordshire County Council.

Oxfordshire County Council (2005b). *Transaction: Local Transport Plan for Oxfordshire 2006-2011* (Draft 11/04/05). Oxford, Oxfordshire County Council.

Page, D. (2000). *Communities in the balance: the reality of social exclusion on housing estates.* York, Joseph Rowntree Foundation.

Payne, G. (2000). *Social divisions.* Basingstoke, Macmillan.

Pearce, N. (2001). *A critical analysis of the way that social exclusion is defined in theory and practice.* Lancaster, Lancaster University.

Pedestrians' Association (2001). *Streets are for Living: The Importance of Streets and Public Spaces for Community Life.* London, Pedestrians' Association.

Philip, L. J. and M. Shucksmith (1999). "Conceptualising social exclusion." European Society of Rural Sociologists XViii Congress, Lund, Sweden.

Philo, C. (2000). S*ocial Exclusion. The Dictionary of Human Geography.* R. Johnston. Oxford, Blackwell.

Pickup, L. (1989). "A study to examine the public transport needs of low income households, with reference to the impacts of the 1985 Transport Act on Merseyside." TSU Ref. 410. *Transport Studies Unit*, University of Oxford

Power, A. and W. J. Wilson (2000). "Social exclusion and the future of cities. "Centre for the Analysis of Social Exclusion Paper 35. London, CASE.

Pratchett, L. (1999). "New Fashions in Public Participation: Towards Greater Democracy?" *Parliamentary Affairs* 52(4): 616-633.

Preston, J., F. Rajé, J. Hine and M. Grieco (2003). "The Social Exclusion Impacts of Traffic Restraint Policies." 35th UTSG Annual Conference, Loughborough University.

Preston, J. and F. Rajé (2005). "Thinking Outside the Box? Accessibility, Mobility and Transport-related Social Exclusion." Paper presented to Transport Flows and Spaces Session, organised by Transport Geography Research Group (RGS-IBG), AK Verkehr (DGfG) and Transportation Speciality Group (AAG). London.

Putnam, R. (2000). *Bowling Alone: The Collapse and Revival of American Community.* New York, Simon & Schuster.

Quarmby, D. (2002). "Delivering the transport renaissance locally." *Public Money & Management* Jul-Sep: 55-59.

Rajé, F., M. Grieco, J. Hine and J. Preston (2002). *Impacts of Road User Charging/ Workplace Parking Levy on Social Inclusion/Exclusion: Gender, Ethnicity and Lifecycle Issues - Interim Report*: Focus Groups. DfT, London, Transport Studies Unit, University of Oxford.

Rajé, F. (2003). "The impact of transport on social exclusion processes with specific emphasis on road user charging." *Journal of Transport Policy* 10(4): 321-338.

Rajé, F., M. Grieco, J. Hine and J. Preston (2003a). *Impacts of Road User Charging/ Workplace Parking Levy on Social Inclusion/Exclusion: Gender, Ethnicity and Lifecycle Issues - Final Report.* DfT, London, Transport Studies Unit, University of Oxford.

Rajé, F., C. Brand, J. Preston and M. Grieco (2003b). *Transport and Access to Health Care: Report on Transport and Health Profiles.* DfT, London, Transport Studies

Unit, University of Oxford.

Rajé, F., C. Brand, J. Preston and M. Grieco (2003c). *Transport and Access to Health Care: The Potential of New Information Technology - Report on Literature Review.* DfT, London, Transport Studies Unit, University of Oxford.

Rajé, F., M. Grieco, J. Hine and J. Preston (2003d). *Impacts of Road User Charging/ Workplace Parking Levy on Social Inclusion/Exclusion: Gender, Ethnicity and Lifecycle Issues - Interim Report: Travel Diaries.* DfT, London, Transport Studies Unit, University of Oxford.

Rajé, F. (2004). "Engineering Social Exclusion? Poor transport links and severance." *Municipal Engineer* 157(ME4): 267-273.

Rajé, F., M. Grieco, J. Hine and J. Preston (2004a). *Transport, demand management and social inclusion: the need for ethnic perspectives.* Aldershot, Ashgate.

Rajé, F., M. Grieco and R. McQuaid (2004b). *Edinburgh, road pricing and the boundary problem: issues of equity and efficiency.* scotecon. Stirling, Scottish Economic Policy Network.

Rajé, F. and M. Grieco (2004a). *Road user charging, workplace parking levies and social inclusion: the importance of perceptions of accessibility.* Oxford, Transport Studies Unit.

Rajé, F. and M. Grieco (2004b). *Road user charging and equity issues: developing parking displacement audits.* Association of American Geographers, Philadelphia.

Rawles, S. (2005). "Prescott's little helpers." *The Guardian.* London.

renewal.net (2002). *Crime and transport.* London, renewal.net.

renewal.net (2005a). *Rural car clubs: Tackling social exclusion in rural areas.* London, renewal.net.

renewal.net (2005b). *Home Zones.* London, renewal.net.

Risdon, A., C. Eccleston, G. Crombez and L. McCracken (2003). "How can we learn to live with pain? A Q-methodological analysis of the diverse understandings of acceptance of chronic pain." *Social Science and Medicine* 56: 375-386.

Rohrbaugh, M. (1997). How crucial is Q-sorting to Q-methodology? A comparison of forced-sort, free-sort, and no-sort formats. *International Society for Political Psychology,* Krakow, Poland.

Root, A., B. Boardman and W. J. Fielding (1996). *The costs of rural travel: final report.* Oxford, Energy and Environment Programme Environmental Change Unit University of Oxford.

Root, A. (1998). *Reconciling Environmental and Social Concerns: Transport.* University of Oxford, Joseph Rowntree Foundation.

Rosenbloom, S. (1988). *The Mobility Needs of the Elderly. Transportation in an Aging Society: Special Report 218*, vol. 2. T. R. Board. Washington D.C, National Research Council.

Rosenbloom, S. and L. Hakamin-Blomqvist (2004). *"*Paper presented at the third meeting" STELLA Focus Group 3, Lisbon, May

Rosenbloom, S. and E. Burns (1992). "Gender Differences in Commuter Travel in Tucson: Implications for Travel Demand Management Programs." *Transportation Research Record* 1404. Transportation Research Board, National Research

Council, Washington, D.C., pp. 82-90

Royal Academy of Engineering (2005). *Transport 2050: the route to sustainable wealth creation.* London, Royal Academy of Engineering.

Samers, M. (1998). "Immigration, 'Ethnic Minorities', and 'Social Exclusion' in the European Union: a Critical Perspective." *Geoforum* 29(2): 123-144.

Sarmiento, S. (1996). "Household, Gender and Travel in "Women's Travel Issues," U.S. Department of Transportation, Proceedings from the Second National Conference, October 1996:37-52.

Schintler, L. (2002) "Society, behavior, and private/public transport: trends and prospects in North America." Paper presented at the first STELLA Focus Group 3 meeting, Bonn, Germany.

Schmink, M. and C. Wood (1992). *Contested frontiers in Amazonia.* New York, Columbia University Press.

Schwartz, S.(2000) *Demand Responsive Public Transport.* Smogbusters Brisbane

Scott, J. (1994). *Power: critical concepts.* London, Routledge.

Scottish Executive (2004). *Planning and Community Involvement in Scotland.* Edinburgh, Scottish Executive.

Scourfield, P. (No date). *Social Exclusion.* London, Social Issues.

Senn, C. Y. (1996). *Q-methodology as feminist methodology: Multiple views and experiences. Feminist Social Psychologies: International Perspectives.* S. Wilkinson. Milton Keynes, Open University Press: 201-217.

Sharp, J. S., P. Routledge, C. Philo and R. Paddison (2000). *Entanglements of power: geographies of domination/resistance.* London, Routledge.

Shucksmith, M. (2000). *Exclusive countryside? Social inclusion and regeneration in rural areas.* York, Joseph Rowntree Foundation.

Sim, J. (1998). "Collecting and analysing qualitative data: issues raised by the focus group." *Journal of Advanced Nursing* 28(2): 345-352.

Sinclair, F. (2001). *Assessment of the effects of road user charging and the transport investment package proposals on social inclusion – recommendations for consultation and appraisal.* Edinburgh, Napier University.

Skidmore, P. and J. Harkin (2003). *Grown-up trust.* London, Demos.

Skidmore, P. and J. Craig (2004). *The Art of Association: Community organisations and the public realm.* Demos. London, Demos.

Smith, M. G. (1986). *Pluralism, race and ethnicity in selected African countries. Theories of Race and Ethnic Relations.* J. Rex and D. Mason. Cambridge, Cambridge University Press.

Smyth, K., M. McDonald and R. Powell (2001). *ROSETTA: D5 Context Intermediate Report.* Southampton, University of Southampton.

Social Exclusion Unit (2000). *Minority Ethnic Issues in Social Exclusion and Neighbourhood Renewal.* London, Cabinet Office.

Social Exclusion Unit (2001). *Preventing Social Exclusion.* London, Cabinet Office.

Social Exclusion Unit (2003). *Making the Connections: Final report on Transport and Social Exclusion.* London, Office of the Deputy Prime Minister.

Speak, S. and S. Graham (2000). *Service Not Included: Social Implications of Private Sector Service Restructuring in Marginalised Neighbourhoods.* York,

Joseph Rowntree Foundation.

Stanbridge, K. (2002). *Residential Reloaction.* Bristol, University of West of England. 2005.

Standing Advisory Committee on Trunk Road Assessment (SACTRA) (1999). *Transport and the Economy.* London, TSO.

Steelman, T. and L. Maguire (1999). *Understanding participant perspectives: Q-Methodology in National Forest Management.* 2004.

Steg, L. and G. Tertoolen (1999). "Sustainable transport policy: the contribution from behavioural scientists." *Public Money & Management* Jan-Mar: 63-69.

Steg, L., C. Vlek and G. Slotegraaf (2001). "Instrumental-reasoned and symbolic-affective motives for using a motor car." *Transportation Research* Part F: 4: 151-169.

Stephenson, W. (1935). "Technique of factor analysis." *Nature* 136: 297.

Storey, P. and J. Brannen (2000). *Young people and transport in rural areas.* York, Joseph Rowntree Foundation.

Tempest, M. (2002). "Timeline: Labour's transport policy." *The Guardian.* London.

The Benevolent Society (2000). *Stronger communities and social connectedness: social capital in practice.* Paddington, NSW, Australia, The Benevolent Society.

The Prince's Trust (2001). Young People and Ethnicity. London, The Prince's Trust.

The Stationery Office (1999). *Modernising Government.* London, UK Government.

Thrift, N. (1995). A *hyperactive world. Geographies of Global change: Remapping the world in the late twentieth century.* R. J. Johnston, P. Taylor and M. Watts. Oxford, Blackwell.

Titheridge, H. (2005). *Accessibility planning and accessibility modelling: a review.* London, University College.

Townsend, P. (1979). *Poverty in the United Kingdom : a survey of household resources and standards of living.* Berkeley, University of California Press.

TRaC at the University of North London (2000). *Social Exclusion and the Provision and Availability of Public Transport.* London, Department of the Environment, Transport and the Regions.

University of Oxford (2004). *Indices of Deprivation 2004.* London, ODPM.

Urry, J. (2003). "Social networks, travel and talk." *British Journal of Sociology* 54(2): 155-176.

Valenta, A. L. and U. Wigger (1997). "Q-methodology: Definition and Application in Health Care Informatics." Journal of the American Medical Informatics Association 4(6): 501-510.

van Eeten, M. (2000). "Recasting environmental controversies: a Q study of the expansion of Amsterdam Airport." *Social Discourse and Environmental Policy.* H. Addams and J. Proops. Cheltenham, Edward Elgar: 41-70.

van Exel, J., G. de Graaf and P. Rietveld (2003). "Determinants of Travel Behaviour: Some Clusters." Abstract of paper presented at 19th Annual Q Methodology Conference, Kent State University, Ohio, October 2003.

van Exel, J. (2003). "Inert or reasoned? an investigation of medium-distance travel decision making strategies using Q methodology." 19th Annual Q Conference,

Kent State University, Ohio.

Vigar, G. (2002). *The politics of mobility : transport, the environment, and public policy.* London, Spon Press.

Wachs, Martin (1988). "Men, Women, and Wheels: The Historical Basis of Sex Differences in Travel Patterns." *Transportation Research Record* 1135, Transportation Research Board, National Research Council, Washington, D.C, pp. 10-16

Watts, S. and P. Stenner (2005). "Doing Q Methodology: Theory, Method & Interpretation." *Qualitative Research in Psychology* 2(1): 67-91.

Wellman, B. (1996). "Are personal communities local? A Dumptarian reconsideration." *Social Networks* 18(4): 347-354.

Whittles, M. J. (2003). *Urban road pricing : public and political acceptability.* Aldershot, Ashgate.

Williams, C. C. and J. Windebank (2000). "A Helping Hand: Harnessing Mutual Aid to Combat Social Exclusion in Deprived Urban Neighbourhoods." *Local Governance* 26(4): 237-246.

World Bank (2001). *Cities on the Move: A World Bank Strategy Review.* Washington, World Bank.

WS Atkins (2000). *Older people: their transport needs and requirements.* London, DETR.

Index

accessibility 2, 27-32, 39-42, 45-51, 55, 58, 60-1, 63-4, 89-90, 104, 186, 197-8, 204-7

Barton 7, 15-6, 58-65, 72, 79-124, 165-8, 177, 180, 182, 195, 202, 215
bus 8, 14, 20, 25-6, 30, 32, 50, 55-6, 60, 69, 88-9, 94-9, 102, 106, 109, 113-7, 126-7, 136-7, 139-41, 148-51, 177, 195

car 2, 5, 7-11, 19-22, 25, 28-9, 50-1, 59, 63-4, 82-6, 97, 99, 101-10, 120, 125-6, 129, 133-7, 141-2, 145-52, 163, 192-3, 196-7, 202, 205
Charlbury 7, 15, 58-65, 72, 125-60, 200
crime 9, 39, 94, 99, 107, 109-11, 158, 199

deprivation 31, 38-40, 42, 47, 81, 82, 127, 130,
disability 5, 24, 40, 63, 100, 107

employment 2, 4, 7, 11, 26-8, 39, 41, 46, 56, 63, 81, 103, 114-5, 119, 128, 149, 164, 187
equity 47, 49, 61, 103
ethnic 5, 7, 14, 15, 23-4, 29, 31, 42, 44, 47, 61, 65, 79, 81, 123, 128, 203, 204, 207

focus groups 14, 15, 53, 56, 59, 66-8, 70, 73-6, 87, 91, 161-3, 186, 190, 200

gender 5, 7, 14, 26, 27, 29, 43, 44, 62, 68, 162, 193, 196, 200

HATS (household activity models) 202

Local Transport Plans 4, 11, 12, 20, 22, 23, 43, 50, 54, 158, 204, 207

mobility 1, 2, 6-9, 25, 26, 28-33, 36, 39, 41, 43, 45, 47, 48, 63, 85, 87, 89, 90, 95-6, 103, 105, 108, 117, 124, 132, 184, 193-5

neighbourhood 4, 30, 33-5, 39, 40, 42, 44, 47, 49, 50, 53, 57, 59, 62, 66, 73, 76, 79, 80, 86-8, 91, 94, 96-7, 99, 101-3, 108, 110, 116, 121, 135, 145-6, 154, 159-60, 161, 165-7, 177, 179, 184-5, 189, 190, 194, 197, 202, 205

Oxfordshire 4, 7, 15, 16, 43, 58, 59-61, 64, 65, 67, 83, 85, 100-2, 106, 113, 117, 125-8, 132, 140, 147, 149, 157-8, 165, 202

parking 14, 48, 49, 79, 85, 95, 107, 109-10, 133, 136-8, 146, 149-53, 173, 184, 195
public consultation 23, 55, 122, 204
public transport 6, 7, 10, 14, 25, 30, 32, 33, 43, 44, 50, 55-7, 60, 63, 65, 89, 93-4, 101, 103, 106, 109, 112, 114-5, 125, 141, 142, 145, 147-9, 160, 163, 172, 174-6, 180, 184, 187, 192, 195, 197, 202, 206

social capital 32-6, 57, 91, 106-7, 112, 147-8, 194,
social exclusion 1, 2, 4, 6, 7, 10-14, 15, 17, 19-21, 23, 24, 26, 28-33, 37, 38-41, 44, 45, 48-50, 53, 54-7, 60, 61-3, 65, 94, 98, 100, 103, 105, 106, 124, 135-6, 148, 150, 166, 185-7, 191, 192, 194, 197-9, 205, 206, 208-9
social inclusion 1, 3, 4, 7, 10-1, 13-4, 16-7, 19, 20-3, 25, 37, 38, 41, 42-4, 46, 49, 51, 53, 54, 60, 73, 74, 77, 79, 98, 100, 101, 117, 121, 124, 125, 160, 161, 185, 187, 190, 197, 202, 207-9

travel diaries 56, 73-5, 190, 200
travel behaviour 2, 11, 28, 38, 54, 76, 112,
        142, 193
trip-making 55, 126, 136, 147, 149, 182,
        192, 193

unemployment 39, 63, 70, 81, 85, 132,

women 5, 6, 8, 23-9, 42, 43, 47, 57, 68-9,
        91, 105, 121, 154, 157, 162, 198,
        206

For Product Safety Concerns and Information please contact our EU
representative GPSR@taylorandfrancis.com
Taylor & Francis Verlag GmbH, Kaufingerstraße 24, 80331 München, Germany

www.ingramcontent.com/pod-product-compliance
Ingram Content Group UK Ltd.
Pitfield, Milton Keynes, MK11 3LW, UK
UKHW021119180425
457613UK00005B/148